Slowly I rolled over in the bed and surveyed the room. There were four beds, one in each corner, except mine, which sat out a bit to allow for the door. Next to each bed, was a tall table on rollers. Two commiserating women were sitting on the edges of the beds opposite each other. Across from me, a third sobbing woman sat in her bed like a small frail child, her arms wrapped around her knees. On one wall was a clock and on the opposite wall were two windows with bars on the outside.

Oh my God, I thought. It was a mental ward.

What happened?

SILENCING THE VOICES

"Fascinating as a story in its own right . . . *Silencing the Voices* is also a valuable addition to the literature on dissociative phenomena. With the skills of a master storyteller, Jean Cline has given us a book that will be of help to anyone . . . who wants to understand both the torment of multiple personality and the long but engaging journey back to wholeness."

—Bryan Van Dragt, Ph.D.

SILENCING THE VOICES

One Woman's Triumph
Over Multiple Personality Disorder

JEAN DARBY CLINE

Foreword and Afterword by
JACK M. REITER, M.D., P.S.

Abby,
Blessings!
Jean Darby Cline

B
BERKLEY BOOKS, NEW YORK

WWW.KENTIACAY.COM

This is a work of nonfiction based on the author's experiences with multiple personality disorder. The author has changed the names and identifying characteristics of all persons who are included in the work, except for Dr. Jack M. Reiter, to protect their privacy.
Any similarity between the fictitious names used and those of living persons is entirely coincidental.

SILENCING THE VOICES

A Berkley Book / published by arrangement with
the author

PRINTING HISTORY
Berkley edition / June 1997

The Putnam Berkley World Wide Web site address is
http://www.berkley.com

ISBN: 0-425-15693-1

BERKLEY®
Berkley Books are published by The Berkley Publishing Group,
200 Madison Avenue, New York, New York 10016.
BERKLEY and the "B" design are trademarks
belonging to Berkley Publishing Corporation.

PRINTED IN THE UNITED STATES OF AMERICA

10 9 8 7 6 5 4 3 2

To my beloved husband

ACKNOWLEDGMENTS

First and foremost I thank Dr. Jack Reiter, my psychiatrist, for his immeasurable help in my healing process and for his continued encouragement in the creation of this book. Many thanks to Dr. Bryan Van Dragt for being the catalyst for understanding the little ones in my life.

I offer my utmost gratitude to Peggy King Anderson, author and teacher, who was my critiquer, mentor, and friend throughout this entire process.

Thanks to my editor, Denise Silvestro, who offered numerous suggestions and questions that added so effectively to the clarity and depth of emotion throughout.

There are numerous others to whom I am grateful for their help in either the production or promotion, including my agent, Nat Sobel, and Dr. Melvin Morse, line editor Lee Emory, screenwriter Stewart Stern, my pastor, plus many more friends who offered their insights and support.

Thanks also to my sisters and older brother, my daughters, my son, and my husband for their advocacy and for their detailed review to ensure accuracy of the events and conversations depicted in this book. I especially appreciate my husband, who had faith in this project as well as in me.

Above all, I thank the Lord for His love and guidance.

FOREWORD

ALL PSYCHIATRISTS LEARN ABOUT BREUER'S AND FREUD'S dissociative patient, Anna O., early in their psychiatric training program. However, no matter how much we may read about dissociative disorder, including multiple personality disorder (MPD), nothing can prepare us for the first such person with whom we actually work. Initially, psychiatrists usually experience confusion because we don't understand what is going on with our patient. Things don't fit, don't seem to make sense. Then something clicks in and we recognize that the person, most often a woman, has multiple personality disorder. Therapeutic work with such an individual is fraught with all sorts of problems and tests the acumen of the most talented therapist. Multiples can provide us with our greatest frustrations as well as our greatest rewards.

Dissociation is a very common phenomenon that people employ to protect themselves from the overwhelming emotions that are beyond their ability to cope with accompanying trauma. We have recognized this phenomenon more in the past five to ten years than previously. With its recognition, however, came some problems. It has only been in the past few years that some people have come in, saying, "I'm multiple," as a result of watching popular television talk shows or prior therapy with either well-skilled or, on other occasions, overzealous therapists.

From a learning perspective, I have been fortunate always to have one or two multiples in my practice over the twenty-two years I have worked in the field of psychiatry. Although I do not have a psychoanalytic orientation in my work, I was fortunate to have a psychoanalytically trained supervisor during my first year of psychiatric residency who helped me understand and deal with my first patient with MPD. Most of my cases have resolved or appear to be in the process of resolving successfully, but some have not. I recognize the trials and tribulations of the latter group, and further realize that there are many undiagnosed people with MPD who are coping with life and unresolved early childhood traumas with varying degrees of success.

The individuals I have worked with have generally been quite intelligent and have had a wide range of talents. I recognize that this may be an artifact of my practice, because an individual would have to be able to afford private therapy for me to work with him or her on a long-term basis. I have also observed a wide range of dissociative disorders, including MPD, when I have evaluated people in the forensic part of my practice. Their single common denominator was a childhood history of rather severe sexual and/or physical abuse.

Children who are severely abused cannot fully understand what is happening to them; they feel powerless and helpless. Ironically, they also come to believe that they're abused because something is intrinsically wrong with them; and they blame themselves. Such children experience a great deal of physical and emotional pain, sadness, fear, and anger. Sometimes, it is safer *not* to feel, and these children push almost all of their feelings away. They build a wall around themselves to protect them. They make use of the normal human ability to "dissociate," or to separate the awareness of some feelings or thoughts from the remainder of their experience. This defense allows the trapped child who is being hurt at least to escape mentally. In some cases, his or her body and mind appear to separate; the body is being hurt but the person no longer feels it, because the mind manages to escape to a safer place.

Dissociation works to channel the hurt so the person can function and survive, but dissociation has built-in problems. As one part of the person's mind emerges to awareness, it may not know where it is or how it got there. No part has the whole picture and some have "specialized" in one type of difficult situation or another. Parts may struggle with each other for control, and the team may not have much idea of how to function cooperatively. Dissociation can become such a habit that parts of the mind literally take off at the slightest sign of trouble. Another identity steps in, without advance warning, and has to deal with the situation. That someone is called an "alter," which is a term we use to describe a personality or a part.

Most people who become multiples do so when they are very young. Alters often have just one particular way of being. They don't change much over time the way a young child's imaginary friends change. When one alter comes out, others often go away. Alters can be babies, children, teenagers, adults, or elders; male or female; shy or outgoing; any combination of traits. The more the alters feel separate from each other and clearly defined, the less they are aware of each other's existence. As each begins to have memories and understand themselves to be part of a multiple, they each become better acquainted with each other, and this is usually helpful in therapy.

There continues to be a great deal of conflict in the mental health field regarding MPD. Some professionals still don't believe it exists, even though the American Psychiatric

Association lists MPD in its official diagnostic manual. Other people believe that therapists are inducing such states through suggestion. Most data indicates that MPD indeed is a very real disorder, and that it is greatly underdiagnosed. The vast majority of individuals who have MPD were severely abused as children and have utilized dissociation as a primary defense in dealing and coping with abuse. On other continents, children also develop MPD as a result of wartime atrocities, famines, or other overwhelming traumas.

A diagnosis of MPD is often dependent on the therapist's willingness to consider MPD as a valid entity, and to have an index of suspicion in appropriate situations. While patients may originally present saying "I'm depressed . . . I'm anxious . . . etc.," they don't often come in the door saying "I'm multiple." Making the diagnosis involves having an awareness of how dissociation presents. The therapist must allow things to progress, build confidence over an extended time period, and take the responsibility not to introduce material that the patient might incorporate. This is because the individual with MPD or any dissociative disorder is highly suggestible, and introduced material might be accidentally picked up and mixed in with the client, resulting in confusion for both the patient and the therapist.

Being a multiple does not make someone crazy, but being a multiple can lead to someone feeling as if they're crazy. The only time alters tend to present themselves is when they feel safe and they trust the therapist on some level. This, then, is one of the first goals in therapy, to earn the trust of the client and have the alters present themselves in therapy. Many alters are "parts" or "fragments," rather than more completely formed "beings," but multiples and their alters are unique, and predictions of how things will progress vary from one situation to another.

The usual goals of therapy are to help build teamwork among the individual parts, to help them learn to communicate feelings, share secrets, and work through upsetting memories. This results in a sense of cooperation, mutual support, trust, respect, and harmony.

We help clients to recognize the alters as allies who have come to their rescue, protected them, endured pain for them, and have hidden many of the person's feelings when it wasn't safe to have such feelings. As adults, the person doesn't need the protection that was once needed and used. Ideally, if the patient is not in an abusive or other denial-requiring situation, the bad things have stopped happening, and he/she is no longer in physical danger. At this time we can begin to address the issue of integrating the separate personalities.

The so-called "integration" or "fusion" of the parts is one goal of therapy, allowing a person to feel more whole, intact, in control, and to live without the symptoms that occasioned therapy in the first place. Before fusion, alters often question, "Do I have to be gone? I don't want to go away." I try to explain that a person is like an orchestra. When things are going well, the orchestra (integrated individual) plays in a synchronized manner and the sound (how that individual deals with life) is harmonious. We can still hear individual instruments (or parts), but they are well blended into the orchestral music. People with MPD are often impatient. However, they need to realize that they have most often been fragmented for a long time, and it usually takes a long time to come together.

Working with Jean has been rewarding and instructive for me. Every patient teaches me something new, without exception. People with multiple personality disorder reinforce my wonder about the resiliency of the individual—how a young child can suffer such terrible abuse, find ways to defend against its full impact, grow into an adult who, while having problems, is functional, and can actually reverse the problems. I have seen people who in their adult life were as afraid to deal with the affect that emerged with their childhood memories as they had been at the time it occurred. I believe that individuals who have unresolved dissociative disorders are candidates for further revictimization as adults. I hope Jean's book helps those individuals to recognize that healing is possible.

JACK M. REITER, M.D., P.S.

PREFACE

WHEN I WAS DIAGNOSED WITH MULTIPLE PERSONALITY DIS-order (MPD), I was shocked. As I looked for answers in books, articles, and films, I found that most of the available literature on this condition portrayed people living bizarre, dysfunctional lives. It was difficult for me, as I'm sure it is for most people, to relate to the abnormal behavior thus depicted. The majority of us with MPD are living, working, and functioning on relatively "normal" levels. As I went through my healing process, I felt it was time to change the publicized view of MPD as a psychotic malady, and present it as the recovery from post-traumatic stress syndrome that it is.

In my research I also found that most prior information came from a doctor's point of view and rarely touched the emotional level of the patient. What I've given in this book is an insider's view of living with MPD, and also of healing, from a fairly sane, stable perspective. Certainly there were difficulties to be overcome in the process, and painful situations that had to be handled, but there were touching and humorous aspects as well.

Psychiatrist Jack Reiter, who wrote the foreword, encouraged me to write to help other MPD patients, particularly
those who were in denial. He asked me to meet with one of
his patients, Jolene. Jack gave her one section of my manu-
script to read. I watched Jolene carefully. She shuddered as
she finished. Then she offered me her hand to hold, and said
(of her abuser), "It's just like that. He told me the same
things. *I* was wicked. *I* was going to hell. I didn't know this
happened to other people. I didn't know it was real." For Jolene and others, I needed to write of my experiences, not
only of the actions, but what went on *inside* my head, my
feelings, reactions, fears, and escapes.

There are some graphic scenes of abuse in the book.
These are needed for the reader to understand the trauma
that drives a mind into fragments. However, this book is not
about abuse but about hope. In support/survivor groups, I've
heard the same question over and over—Can I ever be well?
The message I try to bring in person and in writing is to have
faith. My conviction is that God brought me through that
horrific time by giving me the *ability* for multiplicity. I believed in myself, that I had the strength to overcome the fear
and pain of childhood memories, with God's help, and with
the support and guidance of my doctor, my family, and my
friends. To heal, you must have faith.

Unlike many who have suffered dissociative problems, I
was blessed in finding a loving, kind, understanding husband, who helped me survive the reintegration process, and
two wonderful doctors who facilitated it. Locating the right
individuals to support and aid us is sometimes as difficult as
the healing process itself. I thank God I was given the help.

I want to offer hope to victims of sexual abuse as well as
to their families and friends. I encourage these folks to continue seeking guidance from the many highly skilled therapists available, whether psychiatrists or psychologists, who

have worked with sexual assault and especially with dissociative disorders, which so often accompany sexual abuse.

Finally, I needed to take the reader beyond the disorder
through the entire reintegration, to allow more understanding and acceptance of this disorder and the transition to
being well. The progress to wholeness may be slow and
sometimes painful, but it's worth the effort—I've never
been happier in my life. If I have related my internal strug-
gles with the conflict resolution that led to becoming well
and whole, I may provide patients and professionals an insider's view of how the process worked. I trust that *Silencing the Voices* accomplishes this.

God bless you.

JEAN DARBY CLINE

ONE

T HE DOCTOR'S CHAIR SEEMED UNCOMFORTABLY HARD AS I
started relating my dream: "I was in an old English garden
whose giant hedge maze had overgrown. Like a frantic Alice
in Wonderland, I ran through its tangled corridors, searching
for her. I heard the light, sharp clicking of my shoes along
the broken slate pathway and snagged my sweater on a
reaching branch. Then suddenly I choked on my breath as I
heard his heavy footsteps, close by, much too close on some
parallel pathway.

"I turned the corner and saw my sister, Tanya, sitting on a
small green park bench at the end of an open area, her dress
ruffles partially hiding the ornate bench legs. She was a picture postcard of a white wedding dress in a quaint green garden. But my fear quickly replaced admiration of her beauty.

" 'Tanya!' I screamed. She did not hear me—she heard
only his approach. She jumped up and tried to scurry around
the bench. He ran toward her, a huge knife poised above
him. Grabbing her arm, he stabbed deeply into her chest.
She fell across the bench as he withdrew the blade. He disappeared quickly around the hedge, his footsteps fading

away down a distant path. Blood raced across the white dress, down the wrought iron, and pooled beneath the bench. I dropped to my knees where I stood. I felt exhausted. . . ."

I did feel exhausted. I was staring into the purple pattern of my dress, my eyes unfocused. My neck muscles were grasping onto my head and shoulders as I hunched forward, head slightly bowed. Without further movement, I rolled my eyes upward to steal a glance at Jack listening intently to my dream. However, a slight irritation rose as I saw his familiar face, unconcerned, looking down at the tablet as he made his notes. I made a conscious effort not to let a flicker of the anger pass across my eyes in case he looked up just at that moment. He must make a good poker player. He could sit there with his dispassionate stare as his patients poured their blood on his carpet, and yet he could spy the smallest nuance of a change of thought or emotion from a new look in their eyes. That's probably what made him a good doctor, too.

"What are you thinking?" he asked in his usual calm tone. I had let a tiny smile twitch the corners of my mouth with my last thought.

"Where did that dream come from?" I demanded, irritation returning stronger.

"Where do you think it came from?" he volleyed the question.

Obediently I bounced back inside my head. I had had these dreams many times, not the same dream, but variations on the same theme—two sisters in trouble or mourning the death of one another. Ann and Tanya weren't the names of anyone I knew in real life, but each was always one or the other, sometimes me, sometimes the object of my fears or pain. Often there was a "good" and a "bad" sister, usually when it involved death; the good sister, rarely me, died and I cried over her grave or tomb.

I had written some of the dreams down and sent them to

Jack. I never determined their meaning. It was more like watching a movie where I identified with the main character but only sensed an active participation. I experienced fear and exhaustion, but never the true horror or anger over what I saw. It was that it's-only-a-movie attitude that prevailed beyond the dream.

"What are you thinking?" He brought me back.

"I don't know. . . ." My standard answer dropped carelessly from my lips. I sighed the same frustrated sigh my youngest daughter had at her pediatrician's office a couple days ago. I recognized it. She had asked him, "Can't you just cure my cold?" I felt the same frustration—*Can't you just cure my neurosis?*

"Well, we'll need to get into this more next time," Jack stated, meaning our time was over. As he put away his notes and got out his schedule, he asked, "Are you planning anything special for Halloween?" His voice was clearly changing to a cheerful tone. It was always the way he ended a session, small talk to grab you back to the here and now, reminding you there was a world outside the confines of your head.

I struggled with the transition. I couldn't focus on Halloween—I had been living it.

"I don't know . . . nothing special."

It was unfair. My mind needed to probe the dream. I needed . . . Halloween? How could I think about Halloween?

"The girls will all go trick-or-treating of course, but I don't know what they will be wearing." I began tripping over my words, trying to refocus my attention. "I never plan these things very far ahead. I always sort of whip costumes together in the last week or so." My arm and neck muscles were beginning to unknot and my lungs responded gratefully as I drew in a long breath.

"How about two weeks from today at two o'clock?" he asked, penciling me in before I could answer.

"Sure, sure." It really didn't matter. I was hooked on this therapy. Even though it seemed endless, I held on to the hope that somehow the craziness could be cleaned out of my head.

As I walked down the broken concrete steps from the old house, I looked around the street for my car. An anxious thought pinched me: Where was it? I often forgot where I parked my car. Sometimes I couldn't remember whether or not I had even driven. But sometimes, worse had happened: I would suddenly find myself somewhere and not know how or when or even why I was there. I wondered if other people lost their minds occasionally or was it simply another personal aberration?

Oh, no, there was my ugly blue wagon, parked along the side street behind a huge, unkempt bush. My muscles untwined a bit more.

The cars on Capitol Hill were always squeezed together so tightly no one could exit a parking space without backing up at least three times, even on this quiet little neighborhood street. Huge yellow and brown cottonwood leaves had nearly covered my windshield in their hurry to finish autumn. I had to postpone my exit ritual long enough to brush them off the driver's side. I didn't mind. I loved "the fall, the mist and all . . ." I tried to remember the poem, but it escaped me.

I wove my way back to the freeway through Seattle's narrow streets. My mind explored my dream to see why "my sister" was being pursued. I tried to see the face of the predator, but it would not focus. A light rain began to fall and my windshield fogged up like my dream. A cottonwood leaf from the passenger's side entangled with my windshield wiper as I tried to clear away the sprinkle. I wished I had a wiper blade in my head.

All right, so I couldn't see the attacker. I would concentrate on the sister. I have three sisters, but none of them fit into the dream.

All three of my sisters were beautiful young women, any one of them more lovely than my Tanya. Still, I didn't feel their presence in my dream. Why?

It's their age. The answer crept up from my tight boots. I remember now in the dream the clicking heels of my black patent leather shoes as I ran from something more sinister than a frenzied pack of Wonderland cards. I wore the sky blue dress bought for my first junior high dance, so close to Alice's English pinafore. I was a child in my dream, running to warn my older sister. But in real life I didn't have one; I was the eldest.

My head shook involuntarily, as though dislodging a fly that had landed on my ear. I answered the movement angrily, "I can dream up anyone I want. Maybe I *wanted* an older sister."

A car swung in too quickly in front of me and I jerked forward to stomp the brake. The stubborn cottonwood leaf brushed across the windshield, still clinging to the wiper. Its companions were long ago blown off along the highway.

"Do you think you're going to something better?" I asked the leaf. I wondered if I was. Hank would be waiting for me at home. What mood would he be in today? Sometimes he took an interest in my sessions with Jack. Other times he was furious about the money he thought I was wasting. I'd been to other doctors in other states; they hadn't solved my problems with depression. Hank said a thirty-four-year-old woman should not be spending hundreds of dollars a year and her time analyzing her childhood when she's got three kids to feed.

I shook my head. I didn't want to think about dealing with Hank yet, no matter what his mind-set. I wouldn't be home for another half hour. I moved instead to my dream. . . .

• • •

I tried to envision Tanya again in the white ruffled gown. Was it a wedding dress? My own wedding dress had been a simple white silk gown, street length, with a high-collared lace overblouse. It wasn't the dress in the dream.

Was it one of my sisters'? Sandra hadn't bothered with a formal dress and Tina wasn't married, and wasn't likely to be, judging by her treatment of the men in her life. But Ailene, yes, Ailene wore a long, white wedding gown.

I smiled as I thought of Ailene's wedding. To me, it was the single most successful family affair we'd ever had, although Ailene disagreed with me.

Ailene's new husband had been around so long, even our dad had accepted him, as demonstrated by Dad's penchant toward yelling at him with the same vigor as his other children. But on the day of this wedding, both Dad and my husband, Hank, were in rare good form, neither seeming to be the angry people they usually were.

The one blowup that day had happened at breakfast. Dad had decided to do his famous pancake breakfast bit for everyone in the house. He did make good pancakes, but you'd better be there when they were hot. My girls learned the hard way. They didn't come down to the table on time. Dad began yelling up the stairs at them. Hank, who had no qualms about destroying his larynx screaming at them, took exception at anyone else's anger toward his children. A shouting match began between Hank and Dad. I heard them from the third floor and rushed down to see what was happening. Later, when my mother complimented me on how well I had handled both Dad and Hank, I got confused; I thought the battle had ended before I got there. But the rest of the day had gone smoothly.

Both the wedding and the reception had been held in our parents' home. The grand old brick mansion was built around the turn of the century by a doctor for his son. The house had been decorated in every corner for the ceremony. The living room spanned the full width of the house, perhaps forty feet, with a fireplace that could shame a baker's oven. Mom had placed dozens of flowering plants and Boston ferns in the huge room, sandwiching in chairs wherever they could fit. A makeshift altar with candles and bouquets was placed in the center before the fireplace.

I tried to draw a parallel to the dream garden. But no, the dream garden was wild and neglected. The living room, filled with wedding greenery, was warm and inviting, bursting with sunshine from the French doors on both ends of the room. Ailene had floated down the main staircase into this room, her father at her arm. Ailene was certainly no terrified Tanya.

Sandra and I opted for none of this wedding formality; neither of us wanted to be "given away" by a father from whom we had finally escaped.

As I pulled off the freeway, I thought again of Hank. He had helped me escape. I remember with gratitude the last blow I ever received at my father's hand. It was perfectly timed for Hank.

Hank and I had gone off together on Memorial Day. Dad had insisted that we not drive very far because of the heavy traffic, but we ignored him and drove over three hundred miles to Wisconsin for the day. It was midnight when we pulled up in front of the house. I knew I was in trouble. All the lights were off except Dad's, next to his chair in the living room. I barely said good-bye to Hank as I ran up the front steps. Frantic with fear, I unintentionally left my purse on the seat of the car.

As I rushed into the living room, Dad rose from his chair, his anger clearly visible, "Did I or did I not forbid you to go driving off somewhere today?"

"Dad," I pleaded, though I knew he was right. "Nothing happened. Hank is a good driver."

He stepped between me and my escape route up the stairway.

"I called Hank's home and his mother told me you went to Wisconsin! How could you—"

The rest of the sentence was lost as the back of his hand hit my face. I reeled back against the piano, striking my head on the corner of the old upright. Out of the corner of my eye, I saw Hank stepping into the front doorway, my purse in his hand. Although tears began to blur my vision, I watched as Hank dropped my purse, and in one swift movement leapt into the room, grabbed my father by the neck of his shirt, and yanked Dad's face down.

Dad stood a good six inches taller than Hank and outweighed him by fifty pounds, but there was no mistaking the sheer terror in his eyes as Hank yelled into his face, "If you ever strike her again, so help me, I'll *kill* you."

He hung on for a brief moment, glaring into Dad's eyes to assure himself there was no misunderstanding of his message. Then he pushed him away and ran to hold me. He cradled my head on his chest as I cried. When I finally looked up, Dad had gone without another word.

Since that day, if physically threatened, I had only to say, "I'll tell Hank," and Dad would back off.

Okay, I had to admit as I pulled into our street, Hank was unpredictable, but he'd saved me from a lot of pain in the past. What would today bring?

I pulled into the drive. I still hadn't resolved my cryptic dream, but now I had to move into the wife and mother role.

Being a wife and mother for this family hadn't been easy. For over twelve years Hank and I had struggled. I'd insisted he stop his excessive drinking before we married, pointing out that he was headed down the same road as his alcoholic father. Although he had complied, his temperament remained volatile. He could be so charming if his friends came to visit, but when they left, he could explode at me because he didn't like the dress I was wearing or what I had served for dinner. Unless I was cooking or cleaning, he wanted my undivided attention, whether it was to play cards or sit beside him while he watched the endless Westerns on TV. He had demanded so much of my time and energy that as our three girls came along, things gradually worsened. I feared his jealousy of our children was growing.

Hank's volatility extended into all parts of his life. He quit job after job, usually finding fault with his supervisors or the company. Paranoia became his middle name. He was convinced that his bosses were out to undermine his performance, or that they would take all credit for his accomplishments. Quite often, he would pick a fight with some manager and walk off the job with no notice. He moved us from place to place, deserting one good position after another. I wondered how he ever got hired the next time. No one seemed to check references.

Hank had been to four different schools under the GI bill, but never finished even a two-year degree. At each school he attended, he found problems. He had no self-confidence.

"This school is just a paper mill for diplomas. If I can make straight A's here, anybody can. No one would respect a degree from here," he said. So before he could complete a course of study, he would quit and find another job or another college, usually in another town. With each move I fought back financial disaster. Fortunately, I had always been able to secure well-paying positions and continue to support us. Well, except in Florida.

The pain of my time in Florida drove me to see Dr. Jack Reiter in the first place. I couldn't get past the anger of the whole thing. I had gone for psychiatric help in my early

twenties and shuddered at the memories and the thought of
ever returning. However, as much as I wanted to avoid seeing psychiatrists again, it was obvious I needed help to get
over the ordeal of my Florida experience.

Florida had been a nightmare from the start. Hank could not
find another job and we needed to move again. This time I
suggested we go a long way. I was anxious to live in the
state that had been my childhood vacationland. However, I
had trouble getting a job on the Gulf Coast, and accepted
one in Jacksonville, a town that I had never seen. What I
found was not included in my vision of Shangri-la. Though
the streets were clean and sunny, lined with swaying palms,
the days there were too typical of the tropics. The weather
was constantly muggy—in the summer, it was hot and
muggy, in the winter, cold and muggy. Nothing ever dried.
Children couldn't go barefoot because the ground was in-
fested with ringworm, pinworm, all sorts of horrible worms.
Each day I had to inspect the yard for scorpions and snakes.
Twice I called the sheriff to get rattlesnakes, and once the
game warden to remove a misguided alligator.

And bugs. Bugs were the bane of my entire existence
there. I went to the grocery store and then carefully picked
apart each and every box and bag looking for the inevitable
oat bugs. Flour and cereal, nuts and bread, everything had to
be sealed into jars and plastic containers. And each day
when we went to use any of it, we had to check again. I tired
of the joke about extra protein in my breakfast bowl when
the oat bugs or roaches floated up through the milk. I wondered how anyone could live there and why I had stayed so
long.

I made a few friends at work, but none of them socialized
with us. Our neighbors were elderly couples with their own
social groups. With my parents and closest siblings living
over a thousand miles from us, I was very isolated.

We lived close to a road where two young girls had disappeared on their way to the corner grocery. I scheduled my work start time late so that I could see Erin and Teresa to school safely. Hank stayed with Melissa during the day. He worked third shift and with my late departure, we managed to overlap the child care, but it meant the girls and I were alone at night. It worried me.

Then my worst nightmare happened. The girls had been asleep for hours. I saw Hank off to work at eleven o'clock and crawled into bed myself. I awoke when I heard his boots in the hallway. As I shook the sleep from my head, I wondered why he'd come home so early. I knew I hadn't slept a full night yet. I pried open my eyes to peek at the window. It was still dark.

As he entered the bedroom, I rolled over to face him.

"Hank?"

But it wasn't Hank. Quickly my mind raced to the nightstand. On it lay a hammer I had used to fix the curtain rod. Also on it was my clock. It displayed 3:05 in bright red numerals.

There was no time to move. The stranger's hand was on my throat before my body could respond to my brain's command to reach for the hammer. I couldn't breathe.

"Don't yell. You have three little girls who will be next if you make one sound."

Oh, no, not my girls! What could I do?

I must have been choking. He let up slightly. I grabbed his arm with both hands and tried to push him away but with little effect. He was incredibly strong.

"Don't fight me. So help me, I'll kill you and all those little girls, and you won't be around to do anything about it."

My arms began to ache—I could neither push nor release him. My body wanted to fight with all its might, but my mind screamed *He'll kill us all*.

He leaned over the edge of the bed, his fingers still anchored tightly around my throat. With the other hand, he pulled down his pants and underwear, threw back the sheet, and yanked up my nightgown.

"No!" I began to fight again.

From his shirt pocket he whipped out a small switchblade. Its sharp edge popped into view inches above my face.

"Do you know how many pieces I could make out of you in two minutes? Then I'd have to pick one of those little girls for this."

My hands dropped to the bed and I grabbed onto the sheet, making fists. He climbed quickly onto me, but I could not fight back. I kept thinking that somehow I had to save my girls. Was there any way I could reach the hammer?

All the time he kept whispering to me, "I've watched you every day, going to work, coming home. I've watched those girls too, going to school, coming home. I know everything about you and him. I know he's gone all night. You're here for me. I knew I would have you one of these nights. See, I was right. Here we are."

His breath was thick with stale tobacco and some alcohol. It wasn't beer. I didn't know what it was. *Get away from me!* I just wanted it to be over.

Suddenly he relaxed slightly and my arm shot over to the nightstand. He grabbed it. I couldn't stretch far enough anyway; the hammer was out of reach.

"I told you not to fight me. I told you."

"I'm not. I'm not. My arm was hurting."

"Oh, no. I saw what you were trying to do. You were reaching for this hammer, weren't you?" He picked it up in one hand and raised it above my head as he slid off the bed.

"Please don't kill my girls. I don't care if you kill me. Please don't hurt them." *They're so little and helpless. Oh, God, please help me.*

"I'm not going to hit you. This is your hammer. I have my own weapon. Turn over."

I rolled over on the bed and listened as he redressed. Suddenly there was a violent pain between my legs.

I screamed involuntarily. I whipped around and saw him holding his open blade.

"That's so you won't want anyone else for a while until I get back."

I cried with the pain and could form no words as I watched him run from the room, and heard him race down the hall and out the back door.

Oh, God! Oh, God! He's gone. What have I done? What can I do?

I rolled back and forth on the bed in pain and panic for a couple minutes. Then some inner force numbed my emotions and I leapt out of bed.

I rushed into the bathroom to check my wound. He had stabbed blindly, cutting a small gash into the vagina. The cut was small but was bleeding terribly. I felt faint at the sight of the blood running down my legs and ankles onto the floor. I gripped the edge of the sink.

Don't pass out, whatever you do, I told myself. *Don't pass out.*

I held a sanitary napkin on the area until the bleeding stopped. Then I ran lukewarm water into the bathtub and sat in it. My head was pounding, and my panic was returning. What was I going to do? I vacillated between anger and fear.

Hank would think this was my fault. I didn't fight the intruder. I let it happen. . . .

Damn it. It wasn't my fault. How had that depraved creep gotten in? I probably left the back door unlocked. If Hank realized that, he'd ask me why I didn't invite the slime in, or he'd ask me if I did. I didn't know how I was going to handle Hank.

I slipped down into the tub and cried. Why wouldn't Hank be understanding? Why couldn't he come and hold me, comfort me? I knew he'd be angry instead. I felt helpless and alone.

Slowly I climbed out of the tub and dried off. I'd have to be strong. I'd have to handle this alone. Wrapped in the towel, I ran down the hall and checked the back door. It was standing open. I closed and locked it. I checked the front door; but it was locked. As I returned to the bedroom, I realized that I had to hide everything, everything—the sheets, the blanket, my clothes. I wouldn't tell Hank. He'd only blame me. Things would be even worse if he knew. What was I going to do? I had to go to the doctor. What if this cut got infected? God, what if he had some disease?

Don't panic. Don't panic. At least I had an IUD. I wasn't going to get pregnant. I'd go to the doctor in the morning. Hank wouldn't know. Nobody would know. It'd be okay.

Get a new nightgown on. Change the sheets. Clean up the bathroom. Go to bed. Everything would be okay.

Before I crawled into my bed, I went into the girls' bedrooms and checked each one. They were still sleeping quietly; angels were blessing their ignorance. Thank you, God. They're okay.

When morning came, I couldn't guess when I had fallen to sleep. Erin and Teresa were up and fighting in the bathroom over the soap. Melissa was still asleep. I hurt all over. As soon as I stood up, I knew it was a mistake. My head began to pound again. I felt overwhelmed, weak, and ill. I wondered how much blood I'd lost. Then Hank came home and somehow we made it through the morning rituals. I hated him for making me live this lie, but I knew I couldn't trust him with the truth.

I pretended to leave for work, but I went to a doctor across town from my regular doctor. He was embarrassed hearing my tale. He was embarrassed examining me. I was sure he had never dealt with a rape victim before, or at least not one that had been stabbed too. He couldn't wait for me to leave. I felt like a leper. Why were there so many jerks in this world? It made me angry that I hadn't gone to the hospital and asked for someone who dealt with rape victims. Why wasn't I thinking clearer? Couldn't I find someone who cared about me? I fought back the tears.

I told the doctor that I didn't want my husband to know, that he would blame me for not fighting. The fact that I "let" this happen to me would be more important to Hank than any reason I could give him for not fighting. I hated having to tell him, but I couldn't afford the pain if he called Hank. However, the doctor seemed pleased that he would not also have to deal with this leper's husband. He gave me some medication and I fled from his presence.

The wound healed, but the terror went on. I lived on the edge of my nerves, afraid of the man returning, afraid of Hank finding out. In the weeks that followed my attacker did return, only to prowl my yard at night. I called the police several times. Each time I considered disclosing my ordeal to Hank, but I was afraid of his reaction. Finally, one night, shortly after Hank had left and before I drifted to sleep, the man came into the backyard and scraped his fingernails across the screen on the window closest to my bed. It was too much to bear; I'd have to tell Hank.

In the morning, I took the girls to school, sent Melissa into the playroom with her blocks, and pulled Hank aside to explain what had happened. He was as furious as I thought he would be.

"If you didn't fight to prevent being raped, then how were you going to prevent him from hurting the girls?"

"I wouldn't have let him hurt them, Hank."

"Right. What would have kept him from killing you afterward and then attacking the girls? You're disgusting."

"I know. I know," I said, shaking my head sadly. I felt defeated and betrayed. I didn't want to accept Hank's judgment, but my living nightmare had to end.

As Hank dictated, I went alone to the police station and explained it to a very sympathetic detective. I hid under the wide brim of my red hat, controlling my emotions carefully as I explained what had happened and why I had not reported the rape before then. But the officer saw through my facade. He tried to help me in every way he knew. After a couple of weeks, he spotted a man who looked very much like the description of my attacker, living one street away, only a block from my house. He drove me there when the man was working out in his yard. However, I could not be sure of his identification, so I could not have him arrested.

"I can't accuse him. What if I'm wrong? I'd rather let the guilty man be free than pick an innocent one."

The detective was frustrated with my lack of conviction, but said he would watch the suspect at night and try to catch him in my yard. He also trained me to use the .38 Hank bought for our protection.

"If he comes to your door, shoot him and drag him into the house," the detective told me. "Make sure he's dead and *in* the house before you call us. No one will fault you after what's happened."

I nodded agreement, but I was appalled.

I didn't shoot him, but I did see him again at my back door. I sat up nights with the gun in my lap, waiting in fear for his return. Lack of sleep and constant worry began to drive me into a state of paranoia. Stress made it so hard to think, I could barely function on my computer programming job. Finally, one day at lunchtime, I went out to the parking lot and found I could not round the corner of the building and cross the parking lot in broad daylight until someone I knew came into sight. I ran to my car and drove away in panic. I never went back. I could no longer work at all.

Rather than being sympathetic to my condition, Hank seemed pleased to be in complete control of my life. He moved us from the house to a dilapidated little box of a cottage on the north side of town, but didn't have a telephone installed. He rented a postal box to hide our new address. Shortly after our move, a letter was forwarded to the box. It read "Gene, where r u? I must have u again." Cutout newspaper letters were glued to a plain piece of white paper, and it had been folded into thirds and mailed in a plain white envelope to our old address. Hank took it downtown to turn it over to the detective.

I'm not sure what effect my rapist had tried to achieve, but for me, it was *traumatic*. When I first saw the letter, I sank into the couch in shock. He had found me again, even if only through the mail. I couldn't be safe anywhere. I could no longer leave the house at all, except to check the yard for snakes and scorpions so the girls could play outside. I used the side door to slip unseen into the backyard. I couldn't go to the store. I couldn't go to the laundry. I slept with a loaded gun buried in my bed. No one knew where I was or what I was doing, except Hank. Without a telephone I had no contact with my family or anyone outside my house.

I withdrew into my own world of terror.

In sharp contrast, Hank was delighted. He did the shopping and the laundry, only occasionally coaxing me along with him. He loved being the sole provider for his troupe. He loved having his wife and children at home all the time, anytime he came there. He loved coming and going at will, with no responsibilities for baby-sitting or anything beyond the shopping and laundry. He hated company and now he had us all to himself. He refused to see how miserable my life had become.

My days were filled with staring at the windows and doors in constant tension, between the times I was getting the girls ready for school and feeding them when they came home. When Hank wasn't sleeping during the day or gone to work at night, or doing the shopping or laundry, he played cards with me. I was totally isolated and unable to do anything.

Then into my life came my next-door neighbor, Sally. She came over to see me and I unloaded my worst fears and experiences into her apron. She seemed to take it all in without condemnation of any kind.

"Isn't there somewhere else you can go?" she asked after several weeks of support. "You must have other family somewhere you can go to."

I didn't want to go back to the Midwest, to either Hank's or my family. Where could I go?

Seattle. My sister Sandra lived in Seattle. There I would be so far away from the rapist, he would never find me. Hank wouldn't want to go, but he would go because I had to leave. Sandra would support me until I could get a job in Seattle. Yes, I'd go to Seattle.

"We are not going to Seattle," Hank told me when I announced my decision. "I have a good job here, and we have a nice little house. We're happy. We're not leaving."

"*You're happy*," I screamed back at him. "I'm not. I am leaving for Seattle with or without you. I have to get out of here. I'm going."

Hank knew I meant it. He reluctantly agreed to help get us ready. We sold many of our things and shipped others, in thirty-five UPS boxes, to Sandra and her husband in Ballard, a section of north Seattle. I packed up the girls and drove them to their grandmother's house, where they would stay the summer until I could get a job and find a house for us. I drove by myself to Seattle. It was several months before Hank joined me there.

Seattle was a freedom unknown. I wandered the streets alone, unafraid for the first time in nearly a year. Every mile on the way out there had put another mile between my assailant and me. I knew he would never find me. I was free from the terror that had confined and controlled me. For weeks following my arrival, I felt as if I had been taking some magic upper drug. Slowly, though, the euphoria was replaced with anger. As I thought about my "lost year" in Florida, the attack and my pain and isolation, my anger became focused at God. How could He have let this happen to me? What had I ever done that He would have let this happen?

All my life I had participated in church activities. I felt it was important that my children have this same rock of faith that had guided me in my life, but I had lost it. My anger was destroying my relationship with God. Even after the girls joined Hank and me in Seattle, I found I could not go to church, not even to take them. For almost a year, I quit church altogether. I became a workaholic, pouring all my energies into my job. But I needed my faith; I longed to fill the emptiness my anger had created. When I finally forced myself to go to church, I sat in the sanctuary and cried. I felt no remorse for my anger and no forgiveness for my sins. The pastor noticed me, and on our second visit, he pulled me aside after the service.

"There's cookies downstairs," the pastor told the girls. "Why don't you go down and get some and let me talk with your mother for a bit?"

As they left, the pastor took my arm and guided me into a small room off the sanctuary.

"Is there anything I can do for you? This is the second time I've seen you crying in church."

There was something so endearing in his voice, so caring. I instantly trusted him, but I wasn't sure I could tell him all that had happened. I chose my words carefully. I did want his help.

"I've been through a terrible time in my life," I told him. "I can't explain it, but somehow I blame God for what's happened to me. Even though my life is better now, I'm so ridden with guilt and anger, I can't find comfort, not even here in church."

The pastor sat down beside me. Taking my hands in his, he said, "I can't take away the pain, but maybe I can tell you a story that will help you as much as it's helped me for many years."

He looked past me out the window, his mind's eye focusing on a landscape hundreds and hundreds of miles away.

"As a young man, I was in seminary in a small Kentucky college. Every Sunday morning and Wednesday evening I held services in a tiny church about sixty miles south of the school where they didn't have a minister. The narrow road to the church that I had to travel wound through the mountains like a snake, taking every possible curve and valley. Each time I drove it, I thought it must have been built by a drunk. Then, my last year there, a newly licensed pilot offered me a flight over for one trip. I jumped at the chance to see my treacherous trail from the air.

"However, I found I'd been mistaken about the road. From above, I could look down on the whole terrain. The road, cut through the mountains nearly two hundred years before, must have been laid out by a master road builder. It was the only way that could have taken me through, yet the builder had not had the benefit of the aerial view."

He turned slightly and looked into my eyes, as he continued, "I realized then that our lives are a lot like that road. We may go into some awfully deep valleys and turn a lot of steep curves, but remember that we don't have God's view of our life. It may be that you are traveling on the only path through it—God alone sees it from above."

His words touched my soul and slowly I began to stop hating God for what had happened to me. After I told the pastor a bit more, he suggested that I get some counseling from a professional that dealt in assault.

Soon afterward I talked to my sister Sandra. Where could

I go for help? I was afraid to pick someone without a referral.

"Try Jack. I think you'll be impressed," Sandra said. She was seeing a psychiatrist, Dr. Jack Reiter, while dealing with the breakup of her first marriage. She called Dr. Reiter and gave up her appointment so I could get in quickly to see him.

Jack was my answer. Unlike the doctors I had dealt with years before, Jack was a facilitator, not a director of my therapy. He asked me vague, general questions, rather than direct ones, allowing me to talk about where I was in my life as well as what had happened in Florida. As I became more comfortable with my relationship with Jack, it became easier to talk about the more difficult episodes. It had taken many sessions before I could dump out my experiences in Florida, but eventually I had one tearful session with Jack. I ended up physically aching as horribly as I had the night of the rape.

I thought that would be the end of my dealing with psychiatrists. However, I continued to be plagued with chronic depression and unexplainable disturbances in my head. I confessed to Jack that I sometimes heard screams in my mind, but there didn't seem to be a pattern to the when or why they occurred. My dreams were filled with violence, more often of children than of my life as an adult. Sometimes I woke in the dark after dreaming some horrid drowning or fire, and could not sleep again that night. Jack taught me how to capture the dreams by lying in bed with my eyes shut when I first woke up and rethinking the dream. Then I could sit up and write the key points on a notepad beside my bed. So I continued seeing Jack and sending him my dreams.

During this time, I also tried to get more involved with the church. I joined the choir, worked with the Christian Education Board, and volunteered for service with the huge incoming Southeast Asian refugee community. Between my job as a computer analyst, my husband and children, and my outside activities, I tried to eliminate my depression and drive my problems from my mind. As I struggled to get on with my life, my church became once again a place of refuge, strength, and spiritual renewal for me.

TWO

Hᴀɴᴋ ʜᴀᴅ ɴᴏᴛ ʙᴇᴇɴ ʜᴀᴘᴘʏ ғᴏʀ ᴛʜᴇ ғᴏᴜʀ ʏᴇᴀʀs ᴡᴇ'ᴅ been in Seattle. He continued to quit jobs, fall into deep depressions, and even threaten suicide. Whenever I suggested he go see Jack or get some other help, he became angry and blamed me for his condition.

"Why did we have to come to Seattle anyway?" he would ask me. "Besides," he would add, "You're the one who's crazy. Haven't you been seeing psychiatrists ever since we got married?"

At least for now Hank was working. As I drifted off to sleep, I wondered how long it would last.

A soft whimper broke through to my consciousness. My half-awakened ear listened for a repetition. When it came, I yawned and forced my legs from under the blankets.

"I'm coming, sweetheart, just a minute," I called quietly. Poor baby.

As I entered my daughter's room, she sat on the edge of her bed, looking small and dejected.

"Go into the bathroom and wash up. I'll change your bed."

Her drowsy body staggered slowly out of the room. I pulled another gown and panties from her dresser drawer and stepped into the hall.

"Here, honey, put these on after you wash up."

She hadn't quite reached the bathroom door. Her pained face grimaced deeper at the effort of the few steps back to me.

After she closed the bathroom door, I opened the hall closet and took out clean sheets, a blanket, and a large plastic pad. I sighed and shook my head. What makes a child a bed-wetter?

My own fear and embarrassment sloshed quickly back into mind. As a child, I had avoided slumber parties and friends' camping trips, frightened of an "accident."

I was jabbed by the memory of my own pain at ten years of age. It had to happen with popular Emily Hillebrand, who I was sure had shared my disgrace with all her friends. Although Emily lived on the same block, she'd never been to my house. Her family was obsessed with neatness; I hid the mess and noise of mine by never inviting her there. My mind picked away at the pain.

Unexpectedly, one summer day, Emily had asked me to accompany her mother and her to their cabin at Paw Paw Lake. With my mother's permission, I filled a paper bag with clothes and ran down to Emily's house. Mrs. Hillebrand answered my knock and sent me upstairs to find Emily.

I went into Emily's bedroom. Pairs of shoes were aligned beneath the edges of the smoothed blue and white bedspread. Matching striped curtains hung at the windows. On the dresser a huge mirror reflected her hairbrush, combs, and a cut-glass bowl of hair ties and barrettes arranged on white lace doilies. I flushed with the thought of my own bedroom, littered with clothes, books, papers, and junk.

"Oh, there you are," I said, as I found Emily in the adjacent playroom, reading a book.

Although it was a summer Friday, Emily had on a light brown dress with gray eyelet sewn around the sleeves and decorating the scalloped hem. Her skirt flounced out from two or three net half slips. She was wearing bright white saddle shoes and socks with a tiny gray lace trim adorning the turned-down tops. I felt shabby in my black pedal pushers, faded pink blouse, and bare feet.

"Gosh, I didn't dress up. Are we going out, or just up to the cabin?"

"No," Emily said, looking at my feet. "My mother just thinks girls should look like girls, not boys. I don't care, though. You can wear whatever you want, so long as it's clean."

"So when are we going?" I didn't want to talk about my clothes.

On the way to Michigan, I began to worry. I was going for the weekend. I'd be sleeping overnight. What if I missed? But I hadn't wet my bed for a long time. Surely I could make it for two nights more.

When we got to their cottage, Mrs. Hillebrand made some popcorn and gave us small glass bottles of soda pop. I ate the snack, but barely sipped enough of the soda to wash it down. I was determined to have a dry weekend.

Emily decided to sleep in with her mother and gave me her cot in the opposite bedroom. I went to the bathroom last thing before I went to bed.

Early in the morning, I heard a pan clink in the kitchen at the other end of the cottage. I opened my eyes to bright light streaming through white, sheer curtains. I pulled back the sheet and light flannel blanket. Dry. Good. I slipped around the corner into the bathroom and sat on the toilet. As I began to urinate, I jerked up awake in Emily's bed.

No! It couldn't be. It was too real. As I sat in the wet bed, the vividness of my former waking faded into the dream. The blue and yellow flowered curtains and spread assured me that my mind had tricked me again. I stood next to the bed and ripped back the undersheet. The wet spot was already soaking into the mattress. I couldn't simply cover it up and pretend it wasn't there. I would have to sleep in it that evening.

Oh, no. What was I going to do? I had to tell Mrs. Hillebrand.

After I pulled the upper sheet and spread well back from the spot, I grabbed my clothes bag and rushed toward the bathroom. Once in the hall, I peeked into the other bedroom. Emily was alone, still asleep. Mrs. Hillebrand must really have made the clink. Good. I could talk to her alone.

After washing and dressing, I tiptoed to the kitchen where Mrs. Hillebrand was cooking.

"Mrs. Hillebrand?"

"Oh, good morning, Jean. Did you sleep well? Were you warm enough?"

"Well," I paused, wondering if she would understand me, "I'm sorry, but I had an accident." I wished I were dead or on a desert island, or at least home in my own kitchen.

"Oh?" she questioned.

"Oh," she understood.

"An accident? What kind of an accident?" Emily's voice burst in from behind me.

Mrs. Hillebrand answered softly, "Sometimes people have trouble controlling their bladder at night."

Emily didn't need any more. She ran to face me, her fisted hands on her gowned hips, and screamed into my face, "You peed in my bed?"

I fled onto the back porch. No one followed. As I sat weeping on the stoop, I could hear Emily's now squeaky voice and Mrs. Hillebrand's soft reply, but I tried not to comprehend their words. I studied the cattails at the edge of the lake, appearing through the morning mist and my tears.

So many years had passed and I still ached. I tried to shake away the memory with the folds of the top sheet over my daughter's bed.

A huge piece of dryer lint flew through the air as I snapped the sheet. Instinctively I caught it with my left hand. As my fingers closed around the bit of fluff, a scream resounded from somewhere deep inside my head. *Lord, please don't let the craziness come tonight.*

Black-and-white snapshots of memory flashed too quickly to be seen. I closed my eyes to stop the flashing.

I saw a picture of myself as a child, standing before the washer in the old laundry room, small and alone, a bundle of soiled sheets in my arms. Then a second picture snapped into mind. I could only see the corner. A child's arm was reaching out from under some dark thing; I couldn't tell what. The hand was grasping, clutching onto something soft and fluffy . . . lint.

I opened my eyes and stared at my hand. As I slowly uncurled my fingers to reveal the handful of lint, I heard the scream in my head again. I shuddered. I didn't know why. I didn't want to know. I dropped the lint into the wastebasket and rounded the bed to smooth the sheet.

Across the hall, I could hear little Melissa snoring. The muffled sound of running water stopped. I hurried to spread the blanket before my daughter returned.

As she entered the room, her half-closed eyes glanced up once and her mouth moved noiselessly. A grateful sigh escaped from her as she slid under the covers. I brushed the hair back from her cheek and gave her a quick kiss.

I stepped into the hall, and as I turned off the light, I caught one more glimpse of the lint in the wastebasket. This would surely bring me more nightmares. I shuddered again.

Over my shoulder, I could see the black-haired head nestled down, already sleeping.

The bed-wetting incident was all but forgotten by the time I saw Dr. Reiter again. Instead I began to explain some of the history of my mental health and my other doctors.

"I'm sure the doctor in Indiana thought I was insane. I don't know what he thought was my problem, but I'm sure he thought I was insane."

"Why?" Jack asked. He settled back comfortably in his leather chair and rested his Birkenstocks on the ottoman. His turtleneck pullover and cabled sweater made him look even more relaxed. If he lit up the huge pipe on the desk, he would have looked like a farmer at the end of a day's labor, instead of a doctor in his office. I didn't mind. The informal atmosphere made it easier to relate.

"He was always giving me potent drugs to try. Once I took some lithium and it dropped me to the floor. Actually, it was more like the floor simply came up and hit me in the face; I had no sensation of falling. But I'm sure he wasn't alone in his assessment. Both he and the doctor in Chicago ended up putting me into the hospital more than once. I probably deserved it. I probably am nuts."

"You're not nuts," Jack responded in his usual monotone whenever I said anything like that.

I ignored his remark. "I do remember that the doctor in Chicago made several comments about how bright he thought I must be, because I solved problems in my dreams."

"What kind of problems?"

"Well, once I dreamt that I was in an elevator shaft on top of the elevator. I didn't know how to get into the elevator or out of the shaft. I didn't know how I got there either, but you don't think about that in a dream. Anyway, the elevator was going all the way up. When it reached the top, I would be crushed by the ceiling. So I looked up and saw that the two cables that operated the elevator went up about eight or ten feet higher in a narrow shaft beyond the ceiling. I decided that if I stood between the cables I would be wedged up with them but not crushed to death. The doctor seemed amazed that I would figure that out in a dream."

"And what did you think?"

"I explained that I solve problems for a living. As an analyst on computer systems, I have to look at alternatives in design and political situations all the time. I think it just carried over to my dream. I suspect I was in a tight spot at work and figuring out how I was going to resolve it *without getting killed*, as it were."

"Could be." Jack nodded.

"Anyway, that doctor scared me."

"Scared you?" Jack picked up his notepad.

"Yes, I thought he was pretty benign until the first time he hospitalized me. Then I found out he was a major advocate of using shock therapy on his depression patients. I made him promise and Hank promise that they would never use it on me. I wanted to keep my mind and my teeth. I watched his patients come back disoriented and unable to remember who they were for days."

"Why were you hospitalized?"

"I was hospitalized in Indiana twice, once in the mental ward, but both times it was for severe depression. However, the first time I was hospitalized in Chicago was confusing. The doctor said I was depressed, but I don't remember going to the hospital or anything before being there. Then I was so desperately isolated." I shuddered as the memory replayed in my mind.

"Oh, why won't they just let me die? Why won't they just leave me alone?" A woman was crying fitfully.

I tried to shake myself awake, but I wasn't dreaming. I

opened my eyes to stark white bed linens. Beyond my bed was a door surrounded by pale peach-colored walls. Where was I?

"I don't know why my teeth hurt so bad," a second woman's voice complained.

"Oh, I know," a third woman answered. "Mine hurt something terrible for a couple days. Now they feel loose, like they're not really mine."

All the time, the first woman was sobbing in the background.

Slowly I rolled over in the bed and surveyed the room. There were four beds, one in each corner, except mine, which sat out a bit to allow for the door. Next to each bed was a tall table on rollers. The two women commiserating were sitting on the edges of the beds opposite each other. Across from me, the third sobbing woman sat in her bed like a small frail child, her arms wrapped around her knees. On one wall was a clock and on the opposite wall were two windows with bars on the outside.

Oh, my God, I thought. It was a mental ward. I was back in some mental ward. What happened?

Just then, a tall, blond nurse pushed open the door with her hip. In her hands she carried a plastic tray with a stack of paper cups, a large stainless pitcher, and several short cups like small cupcake papers. "All right, ladies, it's time for your medicine," she announced officially.

"Where am I?" I asked her quickly.

She ignored me. I hoped she simply hadn't heard me. As I waited for another opportunity to ask, I watched her work. She set her load down on one of the tray tables and poured a bit of water from the pitcher into one of the cups.

"Here you are," she said, handing the cup and one of the small containers to the woman who was holding her jaw in her right hand.

The woman rubbed her jaw one last time before she took

the two offerings and complained loudly, "My teeth feel like they've all been pulled out and stuck back in. Why do they hurt so bad?"

The nurse had picked up the pitcher, but she set it down again and rested her hand on the woman's shoulder. "It's not unusual for your teeth to hurt a bit the first couple days after a shock treatment, but they'll be fine in a few days." She turned slightly to the other complainer and asked, "Isn't that right? Aren't your teeth feeling better now?"

The second woman nearly leapt from the bed. Her mouth worked the words through her thick lips as though she was afraid she would really lose a tooth. "No. They're not okay. Oh, they don't hurt anymore. Now they feel like they're going to fall right out of my mouth, they're so loose."

The nurse pushed her gently back onto the bed. "Here, here. They'll be okay. Just relax and take your medicine. In a day or two, everything will be back to normal."

I wondered what normal was. These two women had been through shock treatments. I felt my own teeth with my tongue. No, I hadn't been shocked.

After dispensing the second woman's medicine, the nurse walked over to the sobbing woman, leaving her tray on the table.

"What's the matter, dear?" She sat down on the edge of the bed and tried to take the thin woman's hand.

The woman jerked back violently, her long dark hair flinging back to expose her reddened face. "Leave me alone. Leave me alone. Why won't you just let me die?" She put her head down on her arms and wept, shaking her whole body with each sob.

Suddenly the nurse grabbed her and hugged her tightly, saying, "Don't cry. It's okay. Everything's going to be okay. Come on, now. You're okay."

I had expected her to push the nurse away, but instead she relaxed like a small baby in the nurse's arms, crying quietly.

"There, now. I want you to take your medicine and sleep a little while, okay?" The nurse continued in a soothing voice. Slowly she slipped her hug away from the woman's embrace and moved quickly to the medicine tray.

I looked at the other two women. They had taken their medicine and were back to moaning over their teeth. They were oblivious to the third woman and to me.

When the nurse had gotten the weeping woman to take her medicine, she tucked her carefully into her bed. She continued to speak to her quietly and reassuringly as she worked.

When she finished, I expected to be given something next, but the nurse picked up the tray and started for the door.

"Wait," I demanded. "You have to tell me where I am. How did I get here?"

The nurse looked at me with the same sympathy as the weeping woman, and said with much the same soothing tone, "You're in the hospital, my dear. You'll have to talk to the doctor when he comes in." Then she quickly disappeared out the door.

Talk to the doctor? When will he be in?

The first woman's husband came to see her, as he apparently had every morning. His wife didn't recognize him and it frightened her.

"Why can't I remember anything? I know you say you're my husband, but I don't know who you are. I don't remember who I am. I can't remember anything. Nothing. Nothing." She started to cry as her husband led her from the room.

"Oh, you'll remember sooner or later," the second said after they had left. I thought at first she was talking to me, but she never looked at me, as she continued talking and walked out of the room, "Why, I've had lots of these shock treatments and I wish I could forget forever, but things keep coming back as terrible as ever. And boy, my teeth feel funny. . . ."

I felt disoriented, almost senile. A short time later another nurse came and took me to the ladies' room, where I had been assigned a clothes locker. This nurse was just as non-committal about why and how I got there before she disappeared.

I dressed and went unaccompanied back into the hall. I wandered about the ward as if I were in some dream world. No one spoke to me at all. I wondered where Hank was and if there was a phone so I could call him. In the recreation room sat a small piano and I played it for a while. Then I found a patients' kitchen and ate a few chocolate chip cookies. Finally I discovered a sunroom filled with hanging plants and several rattan couches and tables. I sat in the sunroom alone until a nurse summoned me for supper, which I ate in my room with the other three women, none of whom spoke to me. After supper, a nurse brought me a red capsule, which I obediently took and went to bed.

For three days I continued this routine, wandering about aimlessly in the ward, speaking with no one. I avoided my room as much as possible. The third woman never left the room and was constantly crying or sleeping. In either condition, I didn't want to disturb her.

Finally on the third evening, Hank came to see me. I dragged him out to the sunroom where I could be alone with him. He gave me a loose hug and a quick kiss before he sat down. He looked about him uncomfortably. I wondered what he was thinking.

"Where have you been?" I demanded.

"I had to take the girls to Indiana and then I've been working and sleeping."

"Do you know what it's like here? What happened? How did I get here?" I was panicking, "You have to get me out of here, Hank."

"I don't know what happened. You didn't come home from work Tuesday and that night the doctor called me and said you were here. I didn't know what to do." Hank shook his head and looked around again as though he was afraid someone would see him here. "What do you want me to do?"

"Look, Hank, the doctor has not been here to see me at all. I saw him once as he was going into one of the treatment rooms a couple days ago, but I couldn't speak to him. You call him and tell him to get me out of here."

"Okay. Okay." Hank was eager to get out himself.

The next day a doctor visited the weeping woman early in the morning. "Now then, we're going to take you in for a shock treatment this morning. You're going to feel a lot better afterward," he assured her.

The woman had ceased to care one way or another. Her thin face was puffy from days of tears and drugged sleep. Her long hair was tangled and dirty. Why hadn't anyone been taking care of her, I wondered. A nurse came after the doctor left and took her out to get prepared.

I sat in the room alone for the first time. I decided I would stay and enjoy the quiet.

It was nearly three hours later that they brought the woman back from treatment on a gurney. Her puffy face was now very white and there were large circles slightly indented on her temples. They moved her limp body into the bed and left her. I fled the room. I wondered if the place was designed to make people become nuts, rather than help them recover.

That afternoon, my doctor came to see me. I was ushered into a small consultation room where he was writing on another patient's hospital chart. "Well, Mrs. Marshall, Hank called and said you were ready to go home. What do you think?" he asked, without looking up.

I was amazed. How could he put me into the hospital,

keep me there for four days without a word, and then ask me what I thought about going home? Had he had me watched or what?

"Of course I want to go home. I do need to ask you something."

"What's that?" he asked, looking up from the chart.

"Doctor, why did you put me into the hospital in the first place? What happened?"

He gave a quick frown and then relaxed. "At about ten o'clock Tuesday night, the Evanston police called me and said they found you sitting alone in the park, crying. You had one of my appointment cards in your wallet, so they called me. I had them bring you to the hospital. When I saw you were so deeply depressed, I admitted you."

"And now?"

"And now you look fine and I think you should go home."

"Did you tell Hank that?"

"No, I just told him I would call him after I saw you today."

"I mean, did you tell him how I came to be here?" I wanted to know if Hank had lied to me.

"No. He didn't ask, so I simply told him you were here and would probably need to be here for several days. I'll call him and say you can go home today. I do think you should take a few days off and relax. You were pretty overwrought Tuesday. We should work out the issues that had you so depressed."

I wanted to ask more about what happened, but I was afraid. I didn't want the doctor to know that I couldn't remember anything at all about that day or why I had been so upset. He might realize that I was as crazy as I knew I was.

I shook my head and looked up at Jack. He had been silently watching me sift through my memory.

"So what are you thinking?" he asked calmly.

"Oh, just now I was thinking what my Chicago doctor had said the day he released me the first time. He said he could see that I was over my deep depression and I'd probably be happier at home. But of course I wasn't."

"Why not?"

"Well, that's another strange story. Hank had taken the girls down to his mother's in Indiana. So there was no one at our house when Hank took me home. He apparently thought I needed some peace and quiet—so much so, he went back to Indiana and left me there alone."

"Right from the hospital?" Jack seemed surprised.

"Yes, he basically dropped me at the door and disappeared. The first day wasn't too bad, but there was no food in the refrigerator. I had no money and no telephone. I carried pop bottles down to the local store and sold them and bought some apples. I don't remember much after that, until I found myself in downtown Chicago, wandering around the streets as everything was closing up. I thought I was going to be attacked and ended up screaming and the police carted me back to the hospital. It's still pretty confusing."

I was confused. The harder I thought about those days, the more I wanted to forget them altogether. A small buzzing began in my brain, making it more difficult to think. I had glimpses of memories in Chicago that didn't seem to be mine, like walks on the beach that I never took, and days that had disappeared from my calendar. There was a strange young man who used to come along the sidewalk below my window at work there. If I looked out, he blew kisses to me. I had the eerie feeling that I knew him better than I should, but I wasn't sure why. I dreamed about him being in bed with me. I shook my head.

"What are you thinking?" Jack caught the gesture.

I sighed and shook my head again.

"I can't imagine," I tried to sort my thoughts and avoid revealing the last ones, "why Hank left me there in the first place. I desperately needed someone to comfort me and make me feel secure. Maybe he didn't realize I was penniless, but he knew there was no food in that house. He'd been living with his mother."

"I thought he was working in Chicago. Isn't that why you went there in the first place?"

"Yes." I said, but shook my head no. "I went, but I shouldn't have gone. I did go there to be with Hank all right, but he was furious when I moved into Chicago with him. He preferred commuting home to Indiana on the weekends over living with us all the time. And I have to admit, we were happier too, for the most part. I know Hank didn't want us in Chicago, because once I got a good job, rented out our house in Indiana, and found a place in the Chicago area, Hank quit his job and moved back with his mother in Indiana."

"So why did you go to Chicago in the first place?"

"I had to get away from his mother." I felt a tinge of guilt and with irritation pushed it aside. "You have to understand. I had no trouble leaving my mother, none at all. She missed me—her cook—but I was free. But not from Polly, Hank's mom. From the day I married Hank, she wanted to rule our lives, and Hank would let her. He bought a house just a block and a half from his mother's. She went with us on every vacation after Erin was born. I remember just before Hank and I were married, she told me, 'At your age I had three kids and had to haul water up from a well a block away and I thought nothing of it.' I agreed. I told her I wouldn't think anything of it either. Whoosh!"

I passed my hand over my head, just as my comment had flown by Polly. Jack laughed and I relaxed a bit.

"Don't get me wrong," I said, the guilt slipping back. "Polly is a dear soul and I owe her a lot. She never had a mean thought in her whole miserable life, but she was a lousy mother. Yet she drove me nuts telling me how to raise my kids. Ask my sister Sandra; she can't stand the woman. You know, I brought Sandra down one summer to watch the girls, just to give me a break from Polly.

"But moving to Chicago was a mistake. Hank hated living with us then. He couldn't stand the baby's crying and he didn't want to do anything to help. That's why he had wanted his mother so close by. She could step in and take his share of whatever responsibilities he might have had with the babies. It wasn't so bad once the kids grew older." But I sighed, thinking of Hank's poor relationship with the girls now.

"When I left the hospital the second time, I moved back from Chicago into his mother's house for a while. Our house was rented out then and I didn't have anywhere else to go."

I thought about the first week I was back in Indiana. That strange young man had called me at Polly's house and asked for me by name. I told him he had the wrong number, that I didn't know him. He had sounded so desperate, so totally crushed. I felt guilty. I tried to shake the feeling again.

"So what happened?" Jack asked.

"I went back to work at my old job, and immediately plotted to move to Florida. I figured if Hank could decide to run off to Chicago, I could move us farther away.

"I never saw another psychiatrist after that, not until I came to see you. Doctors and hospitals would become terrible memories of my past. I figured I would live with my insanity. I had all these years. I could manage. I probably wouldn't be here today if it were not for the disaster that the move to Florida turned out to be. I wouldn't care to see the inside of another mental ward in my life."

"Well, I don't think you're likely to, but you do need to work through what really happened to you. We don't have time today, but you think about it, okay?"

As Jack handed me an appointment card, I wondered if I could keep from thinking about it. My life in Chicago had been so bizarre. There were too many time lapses, too many strange happenings. Who was the young man I'd seen out the window? Somehow I felt he was tied up in my hospital stay, but I didn't really want to know.

THREE

A COUPLE WEEKS LATER, THE NIGHT BEFORE MY NEXT AP-
pointment with Jack, I spent the afternoon and evening with
a couple of friends in Seattle. As I headed home, I admonished myself. It was so late. I wished I hadn't stayed so long.
I should have been home hours before. At least I had called
Hank to get the girls to bed. The freeway traffic was thin-
ning out and I exited, making it one less car.

How I loved this exit. As I went down the hill, I could see
the whole little town below. The city businesses were closed
for the night, but the streetlights glowed up from the dark
valley. All the roads up the hill on the other side were visible patterns of light. I could hear a train whistle far off,
howling down the valley like a lost coyote. It was almost unreal how alone I was, a couple miles from home, hearing the
whistle blowing at night.

I needed to get home and sleep to get ready for Jack in the
morning. He wasn't going to be very happy with me; things
had been going pretty well since I last saw him, with nothing too disturbing to tell him in any case. I thought I would
talk to him about something pleasant instead, maybe about

my grandmother and the wonderful summer I spent there. She was such a good person and loved me, but I avoided my grandfather most of the time. I was sure he loved me too, but he didn't have much patience with little kids. Undoubtedly the role model for my father, I chuckled.

Jeesh, I was going to get caught at the railroad crossing by that train. There wasn't another car or soul around. Were my doors locked? Yes, I usually had them locked. Why had I spent so much time with my friends? I felt as if I never had enough time to see them, but I had stayed so late.

The train seemed awfully long. The endless freight trains probably ran at night so they wouldn't hold up the car traffic during the day. The streetlight on the other side of the tracks flickered between each passing car like a strobe. The field on my side of the tracks had been cleared out to put in a parking lot. An old granary and warehouse sat on the other side, making a wall of darkness except the flash as each boxcar passed.

Oh, my God! What was that on the pavement? It looked like a hand. It couldn't be. It just couldn't be. *You're seeing it in your mind, Jean,* I told myself. It wasn't really there. It couldn't be there. Open the door and go see.

No. I looked away. I couldn't look back. I wouldn't look back.

It was the insanity again. I knew the hand wasn't really there, yet some part of me felt I'd seen the hand before. Where? *Think. Think, Jean!*

I was certain there was no severed hand lying on the pavement next to my car, but why was I seeing it? The train was coming to an end. I'd drive away and not look back. There was no hand on the pavement.

Oh, no. I could still see it in the rearview mirror. No, no, it was just the pavement, I calmed myself. Going over the tracks was bumpy. I didn't really see anything.

I drove around the block to go back over the tracks again.

If the hand was really there, I'd drive over to the police station and tell them. I didn't have to do anything.

Suddenly I felt terribly cold. I began to shiver.

I'm going home. No, I've got to go look. I'll see there's nothing there. Okay, here goes. Here's the track crossing again. Now, look. *Look*.

The dark pavement was bare. What had I been thinking? Why did I see it? I needed to call Jack, but I couldn't call him; it was the middle of the night. Besides, I'd see him in the morning.

I went home, hoping that Hank was gone to work. He'd be mad that I hadn't arrived before he had to leave, but I didn't want to deal with him. With him gone, and the girls asleep, I could try to figure this out.

Hank's car was gone when I drove up. The house was mostly dark. Why didn't Hank ever leave the porch light on for me? Only the little lamp in the living room was on and it hardly shed enough light for me to unlock the door.

Stop shivering, I told myself. The air wasn't cold.

Once inside, I turned on the kitchen light, walked down the hall, and pushed Melissa's door open a crack. She was sleeping. Good. I'd go down and check Erin and Teresa.

I turned at the staircase and went down.

"Mom? Is that you?"

"Yes, Erin, it's me. Why aren't you sleeping?"

"I was, but I heard you come in. You slammed the front door."

"Did I? I'm sorry. I didn't mean to wake you. How did everything go today?" I pushed the door open and sat on the edge of her bed. I tried mentally shaking off the edgy feeling that the sight on the pavement had given me.

"Not too good. The bus didn't stop to pick me up again and I had to walk all the way down to the school. I wasn't late, though."

"Well, it's good you weren't late, but did they tell you why the bus didn't stop again?"

"No, I didn't know who to ask."

I gave her a quick squeeze. "Well, I'll have to go down there tomorrow and have another talk with the transportation people again. I'd like to go break their kneecaps into splinters and have them walk a couple miles a day. Stupid jerks."

Time and again I had explained to the transportation people what Osgood Schlachter disease did to an adolescent child—how knee and shin bones became brittle and cracked; how running or even walking any distance could cause small slivers of bone to separate and jab the surrounding tissue. I prayed Erin would grow out of the disease soon as happened with many child sufferers. They had agreed to bus her door-to-door, but there were different bus drivers and one of them in particular refused to stop for her.

"Oh, Mom, don't get so upset. Just tell them to pick me up so I don't have to walk down that long hill."

"I'm sorry, honey. You get some sleep now, okay? I want to check on Teresa."

"Mom, I wanted to tell you. Teresa had another fight with Dad tonight. It really wasn't much. Teresa was doing her origami on the piano upstairs when Dad came in. He got on her case about getting paper scraps all over and down in the piano. After he yelled at her, she picked up everything and went down to her room. But she wouldn't come up for supper or anything."

"Poor Teresa. Well, she probably shouldn't have been cutting paper on the piano."

"But, Mom, the piano was closed anyway."

I sighed. What could I do? When I wasn't home, I couldn't tell if what Hank did was reasonable or not. Teresa left little messes all over as it was. The kids liked to play upstairs so they wouldn't have to be down here with Hank. He practically lived downstairs with the television when he wasn't working.

"Get some sleep. It's late, Erin."

We said good night and I slipped down the hall to Teresa's room.

Teresa was wrapped tightly in her bed, the covers up under her chin. Her round, sleeping face with dark brown curls bordering her cheeks and forehead reflected the hall light like a cherub from some Renaissance painting. I walked over and kissed her. She stirred a little but slept on. I had to make sure Teresa got a good breakfast the next morning. She would be starved, poor kid. I'd have time. I wasn't going in to work until after I saw Jack.

I'd even have time to run over to the administration building and chew out the transportation folks again. Why they couldn't understand that a child with Osgood Schlachter disease shouldn't be made to walk half a mile to catch a bus to school was beyond me. I tried not to think how it must be for Erin, her leg bones, particularly her knees, splintering and stabbing with every step.

Oh, Jean, I scolded myself, don't go working yourself up again, but I was grateful for any distraction from my earlier horror. You're tired. Go to bed. Don't dream.

Morning came and I sneaked out of the bedroom, leaving Hank asleep. I preferred his working the three-to-eleven second shift over the eleven-to-seven third shift, but third shift made it easier for him to be here with the girls if I had to be gone in the evening—probably not easier for the girls, but certainly for me.

I woke the girls and made breakfast. After sending Teresa and Melissa off to school, I drove Erin down to the junior high. Then I went off to fight the dragons at the administration building. Once again they assured me that the bus route had been changed to pick up Erin right outside her home, and no, they didn't think it was reasonable that she had to walk to school. Sigh.

I was going to be late again. I always started out that way, with plenty of time to get to Seattle. Then I rushed about doing what seemed important at the time, until I didn't have enough time left to get to Jack's for the start of my appointment. Maybe the traffic would be good to me.

I had to talk to Jack about the hand. I was sure it wasn't the first time I'd seen it, but where?

Jack beckoned me into his office. "So how's it been?"

"I was going to tell you that the week went pretty well, but last night I had one of those weird experiences again."

"What happened?"

"Well, I was driving home and when I got to the railroad crossing, I got caught by a train passing and stopped to wait. Then I looked out my window and right next to the car on the street was a hand."

"A hand? By itself?"

"Yes, it was severed and just lying in the street." I shuddered at the thought of it again. "But it wasn't really there."

"It wasn't there?"

"No, I knew when I looked away, it was my insanity."

"You're not insane."

"I know, I know. Insane is a legal term. Anyway, I thought I would drive around the block and look again. I knew it wouldn't be there."

"And was it?"

"No. I had seen it in the rearview mirror as I was driving away, but when I circled the block, it was gone." My head was buzzing its little interference again.

"What are you thinking?"

"I . . . I thought I had seen it before. It scared me. I don't know why. It was so horrible."

"What did it look like?"

"What do you mean? It was a hand."

"Was it a man's hand or a woman's hand?"

I closed my eyes. The buzzing was getting louder. It was hard to think over it. I pictured the hand. Was it a man's hand? No, it was shrinking down in size, smaller and smaller.

"It was a child's hand."

"Your hand?"

"No." I remember seeing it. Where? Stop this damn buzzing and let me think!

"Jean, when you were a child, were you hysterical?"

"Hysterical? No, I don't think so."

"I think you were. When did you see this hand before? You were a child then, weren't you?"

"I don't know. I . . ." The buzzing had become deafening. "I was thinking about my grandparents when I saw it."

The railroad tracks, it was the railroad tracks.

"I saw it by the railroad tracks."

"When?"

Grandpa's car was closing in around me. I closed my eyes and I could smell it. The brown-striped seats with leather cords around the edge were under my feet. The floorboard was swept clean. The small, hard steering wheel in my hand steadied me as I leaned to see. Outside there were lots of people running back and forth, yelling to one another. Policemen and firemen were pushing people on the sidewalks. In the intersection was a huge, black train engine, its wheels dwarfing Grandpa's car. I looked through the split windshield up at the top of the engine and down to the bottom of its wheels. The street beneath the wheels was red. Then I glanced beside the car. There it was. My eyes were glued to it. I couldn't look away from it. An amputated child's hand lying there alone.

"I remember now, coming back with my grandfather from his office in Chicago. We had to stop by the railroad tracks.

There had been a terrible accident. Blood had splashed all over by the tracks and the street. A lot of men were picking up things with pieces of newspaper. My grandfather told me to sit down and look at my feet. He got out to talk with one of the men."

"What did you do?"

"I couldn't sit down. I wanted to know what had happened. I stood up on the seat and looked out the window. There was that hand." I saw it so clearly in my mind. It was grotesque, lying there alone, severed from the child who owned it. I shook my head, but the image was so fixed I couldn't free it.

"How old were you?"

"I don't know. I'd guess about four, maybe younger. I'm not sure. I remember, though, I stood up on the seat to see, so I had to have been pretty young."

"Did you find out what happened?"

"Yes." The image slipped away as I remembered my grandmother's kitchen. "I was hiding in the kitchen when I overheard my grandfather telling my grandmother about it later. They were in the dining room. They thought I was out in the yard, I think. He said that a train had come through right after school let out. It's an odd intersection with five streets that meet in the middle. Then the railroad track runs through the middle of it. Anyway, there had been a patrol boy at one of the crossings. A little girl ran past him into the street. Apparently the patrol boy ran out to grab her and they were both pulled under the train. I guess the men were picking up pieces of the kids with the newspapers."

I shuddered again and hung my head. I didn't want it to be real. It was so ugly, so terrible.

"So last night you saw the hand again?"

The buzzing had faded to a gentle roar. I could hear my heart throbbing in my ears. I must have nodded, because Jack didn't ask me again.

"Have you had other experiences like this?"

"I don't know. I don't think so." The buzzing was dying away at last. I took a breath and looked up at Jack. He was wearing his poker face again.

"What are you thinking?" he prodded.

"I've always been afraid of being alone."

"Why?"

"Oh, I don't mean being alone, but being left alone. I was thinking that I had several scary things happen in Chicago. The train accident. I couldn't take my eyes off that horrible little hand. Then Grand Central Station."

"What happened in Grand Central Station?"

"Nothing really happened. Once I thought I was left there alone and it scared me so much."

"Tell me about it."

"It was when I was going home from my grandmother's. It might have been on the same trip as the accident. In fact, I think it must have been. I remember being about the same age. My father had come to get me and we were going to go back on the train. I wanted something; I don't remember what it was, but I wanted it enough to put up a stink. My father kept telling me if I didn't shut up, he would leave me there to find my own way home. Then all at once, he was gone. I wandered around the place for a while and couldn't find him. I stood by one of the benches and cried, and then began screaming because I knew I was lost forever."

"Where was your father?"

"I don't know, but he must have been watching and hiding from me, somewhere close by. When a woman came up to comfort me, he suddenly appeared and waved her away. Whenever I get into a big open place like a stadium or the railway station or airport, I start to panic again. I'm pretty sure it ties back to that."

"Nice guy, your dad."

"I don't know. I've sometimes threatened my own kids

when they were little that if they didn't come along right then that I would leave them."

"And did you ever leave them?"

"No. They always came when they saw I meant it. Of course I never really meant it, so what does that mean?"

"But your father really left you alone."

"Not for long, I'm sure. And I know now that he was close by, but I didn't then."

Why defend him? He had scared the living daylights out of me. I thought back on the train station. I looked up at the high ceiling, at the air ducts and lights. I looked around at the people running to catch their trains or browsing at the newspaper stands or buying flowers. There wasn't anyone I knew in sight. The place was so big and I was so little. I was lost and alone. I walked around the benches and lockers. I couldn't find my daddy. I didn't know how to get home or back to my grandmother's. Why had I been bad?

That's it. I was bad. I made my daddy leave me. It was my fault. That's why I defended his actions.

"To a little child being lost is pretty frightening."

"I know, Jack. I remember being terrified. I guess I felt guilty about being naughty."

"Scaring a very small child for being naughty is cruel. You can't blame yourself for everything that happened to you."

"No, I suppose not, but I did feel guilty."

"Well, you shouldn't. Getting back to the hand you saw, can you think of any other times you saw something that wasn't there?"

"Well, once there was a fire."

"What happened?"

"Actually it happened a couple different times. I can't explain what happened with any of them."

I stared at the rug. Fire always frightened me. I had always been able to cope with most emergencies, but never

with fire. I wondered if my house would burn down someday from someone's careless cigarette. Would I stand by and
watch it or go up with it? If I told Jack everything, one of
these days he was going to lock me up somewhere and
throw away the key.

"Jean, what about the fire?"

"Well, the first time was when we were living on Webster
Street. I guess I was cooking, but I'm not sure. Anyway, a
pan on the stove burst into flames and I couldn't move. I
stood there screaming. My mother and my brother, Matt, ran
into the kitchen. Matthew grabbed the pan off the stove and
threw it into the wastebasket in the corner. Then he dragged
the wastebasket out the back door with the broom handle
and dumped it off the porch. My mother was so proud of
him, but she chewed me out for standing there and doing
nothing."

"You were scared of the fire?"

"Yes, but it's not just that. I . . ." Jack sat there waiting
while I tried to pull my thoughts together. I knew what I had
related was what really happened, but it wasn't what I had
seen.

"I was standing next to the stove when the flames seemed
to fly up from the pan. The wall caught on fire and then the
door. Then the ceiling. The whole room was on fire around
me. I couldn't move. There was fire everywhere. Suddenly
it was all gone and there were my mother and Matthew both
yelling at me. I didn't know why. I really didn't know what
had happened until later."

"And later?"

"Late at night I went down and turned on the kitchen
light. I remember standing there looking at the walls and
ceiling and wondering why nothing was scorched. The walls
were light blue then, I think. There wasn't any sign of the
horrific fire I'd seen. I knew then that I was really crazy."

Somewhere inside my head I could hear myself laughing.

As many times as Jack told me that I wasn't insane, I knew I was. We played this game of hide-and-seek. Could I pretend to be sane long enough to leave his office? Could he continue to ignore all the crazy things that went on in my life?

"How old were you then?"

"Let's see. My father's accident happened when he was painting the kitchen pink, so it had to be before that. I was about twelve when it was painted. So I must have been eleven or twelve when I caught the kitchen on fire, or thought I had."

"You said there were other times?"

"One other time I had a grease fire in my kitchen. I saw the wall catch on fire and I knew the house would burn down. I stood there and screamed. It was Hank that ran in, put the pan in the sink, put a lid on it and the fire went out. I remember the same amazed feeling as I looked at the wall and ceiling and couldn't find anything burnt. I did actually have a grease fire once that seared the wall, burnt up the cooking utensils hanging there and smoked up the whole kitchen. Hank put that out too. He even scrubbed down the walls and ceiling to get rid of all the smoke damage. But this fire happened long after the one that simply appeared to be out of control."

"How did you feel when you saw the fires?"

"I guess I thought I was going to burn up in them."

"Why didn't you try to run away?"

"Somehow I always felt I would burn up; that's how I would die. And of course I've always had the fear I'd burn up in hell. At least I remember many times that my father threatened that I would."

Jack shook his head.

"Can you think of any time that you were really in danger from a fire?"

"No," I answered, searching his ceiling for any memory.

"I've had dreams about fires too, but it was always someone else that burned up."

"Next time you have a fire dream, write it down for me."

"Okay."

It was several weeks later that I sent Jack a trio of my nightmares, one of which was about fire with my mind's fictional siblings Tanya and her sister.

In the first dream, there were two sisters playing in their bedroom. The room appeared to be my room in our housing project home. One of the sisters was tired and curled up on the bed to sleep. The other girl took a jigsaw puzzle to where the hall opened into the living room, and poured the puzzle on the floor. She sat cross-legged on the floor and began to put it together. It was a picture of Jack and the Beanstalk. After she got the border done, she couldn't decide whether to fill in the giant or not.

Just then the giant marched in the front door and kicked the pieces down the hall. The girl ran into the bedroom to get her sister, but she wasn't there. Instead the bed was made up and smooth as though she had never been there at all. Where her doll bed had once been, there was a crib and a baby sleeping in it.

I added a comment to the dream for Jack, that the house had been one from my childhood, and that Sandra's crib had been added to my room when she was born.

In the second dream, I was in the living room in our old house on Webster Street, where I was sitting at the table writing in my diary. Sandra was playing the piano and my mother was in the kitchen. Suddenly when I looked at the diary, I saw that it was actually another book and I was writing all over it with a red crayon.

I was surprised and flipped through the pages. Every page had been written over in large crayon numbers and letters. They were not words. They were like a code we used to use in games of deciphering. I couldn't understand any of it and I couldn't remember writing it. I closed the book and looked at the cover. It was John Steinbeck's *To a God Unknown*.

I threw the crayon into the wastebasket and hurriedly put the book into a slot in the library shelves in the dining room.

No, I can't do that, I thought. If my father sees it, he will think one of the little kids drew in it. I didn't want them to be punished, so I took it back and dropped it into a paper bag. I took the paper bag into the kitchen and dumped coffee grounds into the bag. My mother smiled and thanked me for helping her. Then I felt guilty and began scraping dirty plates and putting them into the sink.

In dream three (the fire dream), Tanya was sitting in a room with a stone floor. She was sewing an elaborate design into some material, possibly canvas, which was stretched over a loom.

Tanya's sister Ann ran into the room. She was frightened and told Tanya that she must run away somewhere. Tanya was not frightened and continued working.

Suddenly the double doors into the room flew open. A huge rubber ball rolled into the room and close to where Tanya was working. She stood up and placed her hand on it. It burst into flames and her dress and hair caught fire.

Ann grabbed Tanya and dragged her from the room. She had some difficulty because Tanya was trying to pull her tapestry off the loom, even though she was on fire.

In the hall, Ann wrapped Tanya in a rug and put out the flames. Everything in the room had burnt up, but since the walls and floor were stone, the fire could not spread and nothing else in the castle was hurt.

Tanya looked like a charcoal statue, but she was not in pain. Her sister told her that nothing could hurt Tanya and she would look okay again. The only thing she had to do was grow her hair long again because the fire burned it short.

Tanya cried because her design was gone and she could never make it right again.

Later it was time for dinner and everyone was going into the great hall to eat. Tanya didn't want anyone to see her, so her sister Ann wore Tanya's long white gown and pretended she was Tanya. She was afraid that everyone would know that she was Ann, and not Tanya. However, when her father asked where Ann was, she laughed and told him that she had gone out. She thought, too, that it was funny that she told him that she (Ann) had gone out, when really the fire had gone out.

I thought about the dreams as I sealed the envelope to send them to Jack. I hoped that Jack and I would discuss these dreams the next time I saw him, but I really didn't expect it. Whenever we got together, I rarely remembered to bring up my dreams. There was so much going on in my real life—Hank and the girls, and me, grappling with my state of mind.

Later in Jack's office, I recalled a dream from earlier in the week, in which I was walking across a floor covered with wet varnish.

"I know the nightmares of the sticky floor come from the horrible memories of my father's accident. It wasn't varnish: it was blood. Of course in the dreams it was disguised as varnish. I have a lot of guilt over the accident." I shook my head. Why should I feel guilty? It was a terrible accident, but not my doing. Had I wanted it to happen?

"Why do you suppose that is?" Jack questioned.

"It's because of what happened the day of the accident. We had such a blowup, I imagined that I had killed my father." A shiver ran through my arms as I thought of the day.

"How did you think you killed him?"

"Let me start at the beginning. Dad was painting our kitchen pink and kind of a sickly maroonish purple for the cupboards and trim. The evening of the accident Dad was doing some painting. But before that, we had a battle at supper." My mind was drawn easily back to the day.

I had tried to locate my younger brother Mark before supper. I had made macaroni and cheese and peas, food Mark hated. There wasn't anything else to fix. I needed to warn Mark first or he was sure to get Dad mad, but I couldn't find him.

As I finished setting the table, Dad came into the kitchen.

"Where is everybody? Let's eat," Dad said as he pulled his chair out.

"I'll call them."

"No, I'll get them," he said, heading for the stairs. Leaning against the bottom post he yelled, "Come and get it before we feed it to the hogs."

I smiled, wondering if he meant himself.

As I looked at the table, I thought there must be something else I could put out that Mark would eat. Apples. I took a few snow apples out of the crisper. In the knife drawer, most of the knives were dull or rusted, but there was one large meat carving knife that was sharp. I selected it. After preparing the apples, I put a bowl of them on the table and left the knife on the counter.

"Where's Mark?" Dad asked as he plunked down in his seat. The other kids had gathered on the benches opposite Dad; Matthew grabbed the chair closest to the back door.

"He's outside somewhere," Sandra offered. "I saw him in the vacant lot earlier."

Dad glared at her, "Well, where is he now?" as though she had some crystal ball, or he was upset for getting yesterday's news.

"I don't know." Sandra slipped down slightly in her seat, as if being smaller was a defense.

Dad made some grumbling noise and began to dish out the macaroni on my plate and reached for Sandra's plate. On each plate he dumped a scoop of the macaroni and the peas. As he finished with his own plate, Mark slammed the porch screen door and Dad looked up.

"Mark! Why didn't you come when I called? Now, go wash your hands."

Mark tried to explain that he was down the block as he hurried up the stairs, but Dad was not listening. I wished Mark had not heard Dad's call at all; he would be unhappy with supper.

As Mark zipped into the kitchen and sat in the chair next to Dad, he watched Dad plop macaroni onto his plate.

"Yuck!" Mark exclaimed, shooting an accusing look at me. Dad proceeded to serve up peas and looked at Mark angrily.

Mark said, "I'm not eating that."

"That's what we're having for dinner," Dad growled.

"Well, I'm not!"

Oh, Mark, I begged silently, don't push it; just eat a little, or don't eat, but shut up.

Dad suddenly grabbed Mark's plate and threw it toward the sink, yelling, "Fine. Fine. Don't eat it. Don't eat anything, then!" He had aimed for the sink, but in anger his judgment was off, and the plate struck the edge of the sink with a loud crack, and bounced back. Peas and macaroni exploded over the kitchen floor, rolling under the table.

Mark sneered at Dad, obviously satisfied with Dad's failure, "And who's going to clean that up? Not me. You made that mess."

My mind cried out, Oh, no, Mark, no!

It was too much. Dad swung his huge hand across and smacked Mark's smirking face, snapping Mark's head back violently and flipping his chair. As Mark fell, there was a terrible thud of Mark's head cracking into the stove and a maddening crash as Mark, the chair, and whatever Mark could grasp off the table struck the floor. Mark's wail pierced my ears and I screamed.

I stopped and looked up at Jack.

"I'm not really sure what happened next. What I remember so clearly couldn't have been real, Jack. I was so frightened and angry, I don't know what I did."

"Tell me what you do remember."

I focused again on Mark's crash.

I turned away and looked across at the counter. There on the counter was the huge knife. Suddenly I jumped from my seat and grabbed the knife.

"I'll kill you, so help me," I screamed. "You won't keep doing this to the kids. You are dead!" I jammed the knife into Dad's back and he slumped into his plate without a sound.

I bit my upper lip as I avoided looking at Jack, and then said, "I know that didn't really happen—my father's still alive and I'm sure I never stabbed him."

"Go on," Jack encouraged me. "What happened next?"

Suddenly I was sitting upright in my own bed with Sandra sound asleep beside me. Did I have a nightmare? It was very late; all the other kids were in bed too. Mom's typewriter was clicking away in the corner of the living room. The smell of fresh paint convinced me that Dad was in the kitchen painting. I had curled back down in bed when there was a tremendous crash.

Dad emitted a terrified scream. Then he called to Mom, "Help, honey! I've nearly cut my arm off!"

I bolted up in bed and froze. I couldn't move. I couldn't speak. My fingers gripped the blanket and I couldn't release them.

I heard her chair fall as Mom flung it aside. Then I heard another thud, followed by what I thought was Mom scrambling from falling as she ran through the dining room.

"I'm coming! I'm coming, honey!" she called, as she rushed to the kitchen.

"Oh, Fred! What can I do? How can I help?"

"Get Matt, quick. We've got to stop this bleeding."

I listened to her steps as she ran through the kitchen and living room, and flew up the stairs.

She screamed for Matthew, actually began to shriek, before she reached the top. I stared as she ran past in the hall, her whitened face frightening me more. "Quick. Get up. Your father's had a terrible accident. Quick! I need your help!" Then she dashed back to the stairs.

I listened as Matthew leapt from his bunk and raced through the hallway and down the stairs behind Mom. I still could not loosen even one finger. My whole body was rigid.

"His arm is nearly cut off, Matt. He's bleeding so badly. We've got to stop it somehow." Mom was panicking as they ran to him.

"Oh, God, Dad! What do we do? Mom, call an ambulance." Matt was wide awake and taking charge. "Here, Dad, take this towel and put some pressure under your arm."

"We need to make a tourniquet," Dad told him.

"How?" Matt answered, "there's not enough arm left above the cut to tie it off."

Mom was on the phone, "Please. Please hurry. He's bleeding so badly, we don't know how to stop it."

My mind was shrieking, What can I do? I should be down there. I can't move. I can't move. Oh, God. Please help them. Don't let my father die!

Tears began to run down my frozen face as I listened. I could hear Matt and Mom as they struggled until nearing sirens drowned out the noise of the kitchen below me.

Lights flashed through the windows in the opposite bedroom.

"Okay. Okay," a policeman's voice was saying. "Bring the stretcher on in. Okay, what have we got? Move these chairs. We need to get a stretcher in here."

Another voice joined in, "Oh, we've got to get that bleeding stopped quick. He's lost an awful lot of blood already."

"Get a tourniquet on it," a third voice instructed.

"We tried," Matt said.

"Okay, move back now. We've got him."

There was a shuffling sound of chairs and equipment moving.

"How'd this happen?" one of the voices asked calmly. "Don't talk. Your wife can tell me."

Mom answered, "He was painting above the back door. I guess he stepped down from the ladder and caught his foot on the edge of the wastebasket. Then he must have lost his balance and fallen. As he fell, he threw his arm out and crashed through the window in the back door. He must have come down on the glass." Her voice was strange and squeaky.

"Okay, we're done here. Let's go. One, two, three, up. Okay, let's roll. We'll call the hospital on the way in. Come on, now, move!"

"Matt, you stay here. I'll call you as soon as we know anything." The voice was Mom's, giving instructions as she ran out the door with the policemen.

"'Bye, Dad," Matt called weakly after them.

The whole crowd left hurriedly. I heard the front door close, then the sirens as the ambulance left. Then silence. I took in a slow breath and listened. Where was Matt?

Then I heard his bare feet on the wood steps, slowly climbing up the stairs. When he reached the top in front of my bedroom door, my mouth opened. "Matt?"

He stepped into the doorway. The hallway light shone on his blood-covered hands, arms, and pajama legs.

"God, Matt. Is Dad going to be all right?"

"I don't know," Matt said, his shocked, pasty face still, his gaze barely moving from his bloody hands. There were no tears.

"I have to clean up now," he said quietly, moving methodically toward the bathroom.

What had happened? I needed to know. My frozen arms and legs relaxed and I slid out from the bed.

"Don't go down there," Matt warned through the open bathroom door. He had pulled off his pajama shirt and was soaping his arms. "I've got to go back and close the kitchen doors so none of the kids see that."

"I'll do it," I called back to him as I rushed down the stairs. I had to see. I had heard it all. Now I had to see.

As I rounded the bottom of the stairs and looked into the kitchen, I felt ill. Before me the kitchen was coated in spilled paint and blood. So much blood. It had spread from the corner where the accident happened to well under the table. Splashes of blood and paint, mixed with broken glass and horrible, tiny bits of tissue, appeared on the walls, the ceiling, the floor, the door, the stove, and the tablecloth.

I spun away from the sight. My stomach spun faster. I stepped across the doorway and pulled the door, closing it behind me. I leaned against the door, struggling to keep the contents of my stomach down. I stared at the pattern the gurney wheels had made across the carpet. *Dear God, please let him be alive,* I begged.

Suddenly Matt was standing before me. I hadn't heard him come down.

"Are you okay? You need to go to bed," Matt said to me. "I need to make sure the dining room door is closed too." I was amazed by his strength and control.

I prayed all night for my father and for forgiveness for having been so angry with him.

In the morning, Matt and I got Mark, Sandra, and Luke ready for school. I changed Ailene's diapers and dressed her. We wouldn't let anyone go downstairs until we all went down. Then Matt slipped in and out of the kitchen, getting milk, cereal, bowls, and spoons to feed us in the dining room. He explained what had happened and warned everyone to stay out of the kitchen.

No call had come in the night. When the baby-sitter, Bessie, arrived to take care of Ailene, Matt explained the situation to her, and left for school. I couldn't go. I had to know what was going on. Why didn't Mom call?

Bessie took Ailene upstairs and played with her as she cleaned. After a while she came back down and told me, "I gotta clean up that mess, Jean, 'fore your mom gets home."

She went into the kitchen.

"Lordy, Lordy!" I heard her cry. "I never seen so much blood! How is that man alive?"

I wondered if he was. *Please, God. Please let him be alive.* My skin felt cold.

"Jean?" Bessie called to me. "Go down to the basement and bring me a bucket, would ya, honey? I gotta get this glass picked up."

I hated to leave my vigil of watching the road out the front window, but I jumped up and opened the kitchen door. The smell of the paint and blood were overpowering. Bessie was squatting beyond the pooled blood, picking up bits of glass and dropping them into a paper bag. She looked up as I came in. Her face was no longer deep brown. It appeared covered with ashes, deep wrinkles carved into it.

"I don' know if I can do this, child," Bessie said, shaking her head as she stood up. "I jest keep thinking about that po' man and all this blood he lost here. It makes a body sick."

She was nearly staggering as she came toward me, her huge body shifting with each step.

"I'm gonna go on up and play with your sister fo' a while. Maybe later I kin do this."

"Bessie," I hugged her as she reached me, "I'm going to work on it a little. If I can get some of it, maybe you can do the rest."

She nodded quietly and went on to the stairs.

Staring at the floor, I felt ill too. How was I going to do this?

I picked up the bag to get the big glass pieces first. I stepped gingerly out on the dried blood. It wasn't dry; it was sticky. My sneaker stuck in it and made a horrible snapping sound as I lifted my foot. *Oh, dear God, help me,* I prayed. *Give me strength.*

I fled to the basement to get a bucket and as I came up, I spied the mop in the stairwell.

That was it. I'd dump water over the mess and mop it up. I'd have to watch out for the glass, but if I could get the mess off the floor, the rest would be easy. However, I worked for several hours. I only nicked my hands in a couple places, but as I was extracting one splinter, I noticed three little holes in my left palm. I wondered how they got there.

Bessie lumbered downstairs and opened the kitchen door a crack, asking, "I gotta git this baby some lunch. Kin I come in yet?"

"Yes, Bessie, I think I've got most of it. We'll have to throw this mop out, though. It's full of glass splinters."

"I don' think your po' mom will care. You sure been hard at it." Bessie shook her head. "I'm sorry, but ya know it was makin' me sick."

"I know, Bessie. I don't think I can do much more. I don't know how to get the paint off the floor." I felt weak and tired. I wanted to go back to my window and sit.

"Have we got any soup and crackers? I got to feed this young'n 'fore I do anythin' else."

After lunch, Bessie put Ailene down for a nap and went to work on the kitchen. I played some records on the phonograph, but stayed by the window.

About two o'clock, a police car pulled up in front of the house. An officer jumped out and ran around the car to open the door for Mom. They stood by the door and spoke a couple minutes, both of them nodding and shaking their heads through most of the conversation.

He's alive, I thought. *I know he is. There's something about the way Mom is standing there talking with the policeman. He's got to be alive.*

Suddenly Mom turned and started up the front steps.

"Bessie, Mom's here," I called to her. I held my breath, waiting for Mom to come in and tell me for sure.

"Oh, that po' woman," Bessie answered, leaving the kitchen just as Mom opened the door.

"Oh, Bessie!" Mom cried, as Bessie clutched her into a crushing hug. "He's going to live, but they're not sure they've saved his arm yet. They had him in surgery for hours."

"You po' thing. You must be exhausted. Come sit down. I'll make ya some coffee. Have ya had any food? I'll make ya some soup."

"No, no, Bessie," she sighed. "I don't want anything but sleep. I need to lie down for a while."

Suddenly she saw me. I was still sitting at the table. I couldn't move until I knew for sure whether or not he was alive.

"What are you doing home from school?" she asked angrily.

I didn't understand her anger. I was terrified that my father had died. No one had called. I sat the night and day through not knowing.

"I . . . I had to help. I didn't know what had happened."

"Well, you should have gone to school." She turned back to Bessie. "Did everyone else go to school?"

"Yes, ma'am, they did." Bessie seemed surprised too. I thought she was going to say something in my defense, but Mom interrupted her.

"Is Ailene sleeping?"

"I put her down, and I hadn' heard a peep from her since."

"Well, I'm going up and lie down a bit." She looked down on me as she reached the landing, "You should have gone to school." Then she disappeared up the stairs.

Oh, Mama, why can't you see how frightened and ill I am, too? I put my head on the table and wept.

Bessie came over and put her arm around me. "It's okay, child. Your mom's so tired and worried about that po' man, she can't think of nothin' else."

"She never called me, Bessie," I sobbed. "I never even knew if he was alive. How could I go to school?"

Bessie patted my head. "I know, I know, child. But he is, so stop your worrying." She went back into the kitchen.

I dried my eyes and shut off the record player. Then I became angry with myself. Why should I be crying? I wasn't the one who was hurt. Mom had been up all night at the hospital. No wonder she was angry with me. I should be helping her. I would help her. I'd keep the kids quiet when they got home and I'd make supper. . . .

I looked up at Jack. He was shaking his head.

"I felt so guilty," I told him. "I didn't do anything right. I didn't help when they needed my help, and I didn't go to school like my mother expected me to."

We sat in silence for a moment or two.

I fought back my tears as I added, "But I needed her too. All I wanted to know was that he was okay."

I sat quietly for a few minutes, calming myself and trying

to think about the scene at the dinner table. Finally I said, "I didn't kill my father, but it seems so real, even today. I can still see that butcher knife on the counter. I can still feel my hand closing around it. I was so angry at my father for hitting Mark and hurting him the way he did. I wonder what did happen."

"Think about it the next couple of weeks and we'll try to sort it out," Jack advised me, putting down his notepad.

He added, "I think the three holes in your palm might be a good clue. Try to remember how you got them."

The next time I saw Jack, we began back again with Dad smacking Mark. I closed my eyes and pictured myself sitting on the bench next to Dad.

I looked over at the counter. There lay the huge knife. I wanted to kill Dad. I wanted the violence to stop. How could he be so cruel? But I couldn't do anything. I looked down at my hands. The fork in my right hand had pierced the skin of my left. I couldn't even feel it. My hands shook as I removed it and slid it onto the table. The three tongs of the fork left three small, bloody holes in my palm.

I jumped up and ran around the table where Dad was dragging Mark up from the floor by one arm.

"Stop that racket and clean up this mess!" he demanded.

"Come on, Mark. I'll help you," I said, sliding myself between Dad and Mark.

I rubbed Mark's head as we both cried, squatting down to gather up the peas and macaroni. Mark put the plate in the sink when we were done and went upstairs. I went back to my place at the table, although I didn't want to swallow another thing. Everyone was eating slowly and silently.

"Well," Dad said, as he finished his dinner, "who else is going to be a member of the clean plate club?"

I nearly threw up.

• • •

"I guess that explains it." I said to Jack. "I didn't kill him, but I surely wanted to. I wanted to so much and yet, when he nearly died, I felt guilty. You know, I still feel guilty every time I see him sitting at a piano with his crippled hand."

"You needn't," Jack stated flatly. "Children take on guilt for things for which they have no responsibility. You had every right to be angry at what had happened earlier in the evening, and you didn't cause your father's accident."

This placed one piece in the giant puzzle in my mind. I looked at my hand. There was no scar, but it seemed that I could still see the three little holes in my palm.

FOUR

Pastor Dave was a lifeline for me, a solid base of God, tender and human and vulnerable, and most of all, understanding. He was the one person in my insane world that I trusted to remain steadfast in his kindness no matter what I told him.

One Saturday afternoon I met with the choir director at church to practice. I had decided to sing a solo at church the next day. She was going to accompany me on the piano. I had chosen a song called "Something Beautiful" as it had words that I thought were appropriate for my mental condition.

While we were practicing, Pastor Dave came in from his office and sat in the back of the church. He never spoke during my rehearsing, but applauded after we had finished. The choir director left and I asked Dave if he had a couple minutes for me.

"Sure," he said. He came up to the front of the church and sat down on the steps that led up to the pulpit and choir platform. "That song will work great right before my sermon tomorrow. I'm going to be speaking on trust and surrender."

As I sat down on the steps beside him, I looked quickly around the church for any signs of other people, but I was certain we were alone; there had been no other cars in the parking lot except his, the choir director's, and mine.

"Dave," I pleaded in near desperation, "I want to tell you why I picked that particular song."

He nodded.

I pulled my knees up a step and rested my elbows on them, cradling my chin in my palms. I sighed and explained, "There's a perfect line in that song for me, the one that goes 'All my confusion He understood.' I only wish I could understand."

"What's the problem, Jean?" Dave leaned forward and gently pulled my right hand from under my chin. He was a great believer in the comfort of touching.

Gratefully I clasped his hand in mine. "I don't know, Dave. You know I've been going for mental therapy for years and years. I think I've got something straightened out and then I get hit with some other memory. I can't believe I'm just crazy."

Dave laughed sympathetically. "No, I wouldn't think so."

"I have a good doctor I like and trust," I assured him, "but it's been pretty difficult lately. Whenever I have a hard week after one of our sessions, he tells me I'm getting better. He thinks a lot of what's wrong with me is involved with how violent my childhood was, but, Dave, in spite of everything my Dad did—hitting us and yelling—all of us seemed to grow up okay. I mean, none of us turned out to be druggies or alcoholics. We didn't provide any out-of-wedlock babies or end up in jail. All my brothers and sisters graduated from high school and went on to college, just as I did. It's simply that sometimes I get so tired of dredging up all my pain and seeing how it's still affecting me."

"So why do you keep going?"

I felt my security slipping away. I didn't want to tell him the particulars Jack knew.

"Dave, I know there's some horrible stuff that went on with me, material I'm blocking out mentally. My sister Sandra has a memory problem too; she can't even remember anything about the house we grew up in. We used to laugh about her poor memory, but now we know better—she can't remember because it's too terrible to remember. Anyway, I don't know what happened to me either, but I get little pictures in my brain sometimes, little snapshots that flash by, accompanied by horrible screaming. I used to pass it off as insanity and I figured I would have to hide it from everybody. However, Jack—that's my doctor—is certain they are real memories and that eventually I'll have to deal with them."

"Well, how can I help?"

"Oh, you're already helping," I smiled, squeezing his hand. "I guess I only needed you to know I had this internal conflict waging. Somehow, I think it will work out. I guess I need to listen to your sermon tomorrow."

Dave laughed. Then he took my other hand in his. "Let's pray together, okay?"

We bowed our heads where we sat on the steps and Dave prayed aloud, "Our Father, be with Jean in her battle for mental health and inner peace. Strengthen her to handle whatever she must deal with. Bring Jean and her family the support they need for one another. Bless Jean and be with her now and evermore. We ask in the name of Your son, Jesus. Amen."

"Amen," I answered. Then I offered my silent prayer of thanks for Pastor Dave.

Sunday, my sister Sandra abandoned her regular church to come to hear me sing. Her husband and son were gone for the weekend. After church, the two of us escaped to her place to work on a jigsaw puzzle and talk.

Sandra was five years my junior, but closer to my age than my other two sisters. We had shared bedrooms from the time she was born until the day of my wedding, and we had fought and laughed and cried together all those years. Now we were both trying to reexamine our childhood and solve some of the problems our adult lives had inherited.

Over the past couple of years, each of us had discovered independently, and then together, so many of the same traits. We couldn't stand to cry in front of anyone. That came directly from our dad, who wouldn't tolerate it and "would give us something to cry about if we didn't shut up." We were both afraid of anger, anyone's anger. Neither of us knew how to deal with it—whenever we had seen our dad angry, he was out of control and someone ended up getting hurt. Finally, we confessed that we both fought for our own self-respect. Had we been so completely programmed to feel worthless as children, so that even when we succeeded, it wasn't good enough?

We cleared some papers off the dining room table and Sandra tossed the tablecloth aside. I talked to Sandra about my mixed feelings for Dad, as we turned over the pieces of the Springbok puzzle of Saint Basil's Cathedral that Sandra had brought out.

"Each of us girls went through what I would call the 'favorite child status,'" I told Sandra. "I don't think the boys ever had Dad's attention, except when there was a job to be done. But for each of his daughters, it seemed to last from about age five to maybe age ten or eleven. It was that period of our lives when Dad seemed to take a special interest in only us."

"Except Tina," Sandra interjected.

"Oh, I guess I wouldn't know that for sure. You guys

moved away the year I got married and Tina was only four. Ailene was the favorite child then."

"And she stayed Dad's pet until she got disgusted with him and stopped going places and doing things with him. Tina was always the brunt of Dad's criticism, never his little darling."

"Well, I was busy with my own problems, so I lost track of what happened once you guys moved. Anyway, I remember being the favorite child so clearly, and losing it so painfully. I came down sick when I was eleven. At the time they thought it was rheumatic fever. Dad took me off to the hospital, saw the nurses tuck me into bed, bought me a blue bunny that played Brahms's 'Lullaby,' and walked out of my life forever. When I came home from the hospital, he didn't have the time of day for me and you were the light of his life."

"Oh, yes," Sandra agreed. "I didn't lose him quite as dramatically as you, but it did seem to happen suddenly. In fact, I think I abandoned him first. I made a good friend—you remember her—Sally Kindell? I began to escape from home and spend as much time at her house as possible. I suspect Dad just picked up the next girl in line and began taking Ailene everywhere with him."

"Yeah. I think all of us made good friends and our own escapes over the years. It was too hard to be at home so much of the time."

As we turned the puzzle pieces, we shoved the border to one side, sorted the sky from the church pieces, and reserved a small section of the table for those little pieces that pretended to be border, but usually ended up in the middle somewhere. I thought the Springbok company must keep people up nights thinking of ways to trick puzzle workers.

"The problem with this is there are so many blue pieces for the night sky and the shade doesn't change enough to section it off," Sandra complained.

I ignored her and went back to our discussion. "Jack thinks much of what is going on with me, and with you for that matter, involves Dad and his treatment of us. I have such mixed feelings about him. It's such a love-hate relationship. I abhorred all his violence and yet all the time I was home I somehow wanted to recapture my favorite-child status."

"I know what you mean." Sandra nodded agreement. "Dad could be so charming and wonderful, but remember when he took his little darlings around and showed them off, he was also seeking out the praise and glory from having his beautiful little ones."

"That's probably true, though it pains me to accept it. I tried to believe he thought of me as something special, but given his treatment when we weren't being shown off, I suspect you're right. There were no special favors for the favorite child in the house. There, you were one of the many, underfoot and always in the wrong."

"I keep remembering how he always sought out the store manager whenever we went to Krogers grocery, just to hear him say, 'What a beautiful little girl you have, Fred.' He always reminded me of Little Red Riding Hood—'What big eyes you have, Grandma.' I don't believe the man ever spoke to any of us directly, though." She looked up from her sorting and we both laughed.

"No, but I liked the manager," I commented. "Our lives were so bereft of compliments, except at school, of course. I recall one semester—working so hard and making only one B and all the rest A's. While the teachers loved me, all I heard at home was why hadn't I made an A in that last class. I wanted to give up altogether."

"It was always that way," Sandra agreed. "We were competing against Mom and Dad and they both graduated at the top of their classes. Wasn't Mom valedictorian or was she salutatorian? But Mom did give out compliments on report cards. I think you just remember Dad's complaints, because we tried so hard to please him and never could."

"I don't know." I tossed a misplaced border piece over to Sandra who nearly had the bottom edge worked. "Whenever I get caught up in thinking how mean Dad was, I try to recollect all the fun things he did for us."

"Like what?" Sandra looked up suddenly. I had to remind myself that her loss of memory blocked the good as well as the bad.

"There are three things that stand out in my mind: trips to Florida, Christmas tree cutting, and raking leaves in the side lot and singing as they burned."

"Yeah, sure, trips to Florida," Sandra groaned sarcastically. "I remember them well. I had to ride in the front seat and stare out the windshield to keep from throwing up. And it took them a long time to even admit I got carsick; everyone got mad at me. Then, of course, Dad was so comfort minded—'What do you mean you have to go to the bathroom? I stopped three hours ago; why didn't you go then? No, I'm not stopping again until I get to Chattanooga!' "

We burst out laughing and I dropped a puzzle piece on the floor.

"Yes, well, there was that." I chuckled as I crawled under the table. "I do remember wrapping up cans of pop in our sweatshirts, to try to keep them cold for an hour or two. Then when we drank them, we wouldn't have to wiggle, waiting for the next restroom stop. We'd be close enough for his next stop by then."

"No fair hiding pieces," Sandra teased. "It's hard enough as it is."

"I wasn't really thinking of the trip down to Florida, though," I replied, as I retrieved the piece. "I was thinking about the fact that Dad was willing to pack up the whole brood and haul us down for a vacation in the sun. And likewise, hauling us out to the tree farm at Christmas. We'd tromp through the snow-covered woods in search of the best Christmas tree, which he would ceremoniously saw down. Then we'd all sing carols in the car on the way home."

Sandra shook her head. "I guess I do have to give him that, but you have to remember that these were things he liked to do too, not just things he did for his kids."

We worked the puzzle silently for a while as each of us meditated on our feelings. I knew I was up against the same duel of emotions Sandra was—both trying to justify and accept Dad's violent behavior, while at the same time rationalize away the good into some egotistic motive. Somehow, neither of us could make a black or white silhouette of the man. Like everyone else, Dad had many complex facets.

Then Sandra sighed, looked up, and changed the mood. "Time for my daily Pepsi. Even when I'm dieting, I allow myself one. Do you want one?"

"Sure, why not." I followed her into the kitchen and stopped to look out across the valley from the window. "Someday, I'd like to have a view like this."

"Someday, I'd like a view of the house I spent the first fifteen years of my life in," Sandra countered.

"You could have it today, if you want to work that hard."

Sandra paused and leaned on the open refrigerator door. She pursed her lips, as though they might utter an agreement before she could make the mental adjustment. Finally she swept two cans from the shelf and swung the door closed. "Sure. It's time to go home."

We deserted the puzzle and pulled up chairs at the kitchen table. I looked at Sandra as we opened our pop cans and took a first long swig. I had always admired her long, dark hair and almost Indian-shaded skin. My own hair had been blond, practically until I went into junior high school, and then had turned such a mousy brown, but she had been born beautiful. Dad's grandmother had been a Shawnee Indian and Sandra carried Great-grandmother's physical heritage more than any of his other children.

"Well, where do you want to start?"

Sandra sighed and bit the left corner of her lip. "I guess I'll have to tell you what I remember first. Whenever I think about our house, I am skipping home from school. I do remember the elementary school distinctly. Then I come to our front steps and go up to the porch. I can open the screen door and walk into the enclosed porch, right up to the front door. But then Mom opens the door and I can't go in. It's almost like she fills the whole doorway and blocks me, so that I can't even look inside."

All right, I told myself, let's proceed, Dr. Jean.

"Okay, that's a good place to start. Pretend you're coming home from school, but Mom is gone off to her friend's house and nobody is home to answer the door. I'll walk you through the house once the door is open."

Sandra took another long drink of her Pepsi as though fear had suddenly dried out her throat. She swallowed heavily. "I'm coming home, up the steps, onto the porch, and open the door. What do I see?"

"Directly in front of you is Dad's chair. It's got a wood frame and dark, almost maroon, cushions. A little to the left of it is a small wood table, carved like three wood scallops with three spindle legs connecting the top and bottom shelves of the table. There are magazines and newspapers stacked on the lower shelf and a lamp on the upper. Picture this, there's a path we made around that table and Dad's chair to avoid stepping in the little skin flakes Dad left on the floor from picking his legs and feet."

"Oooo!" She shuddered at the thought. "I remember. Oh, that was so gross!"

"Beyond that was the kitchen door, which was usually open and pressed against the wall behind Dad's chair."

I continued to walk her through the house on the main

floor and on through the upstairs. Finally I thought about the basement. "Okay, now let's go downstairs."

"I guess that's what frightens me most," Sandra admitted. "It was always dark down there and seemed to be Dad's domain."

"It was. He kept most of his tropical fish down there. Sometimes he had twenty or thirty tanks of them. He had his model railroad trains on a table in the center of the big room on a huge plywood board. And, of course, there was the furnace room where he went to read his dirty magazines."

"His dirty magazines?"

"Yeah. He kept them hidden among the newspapers. He used to sit by the warm furnace on the stacks of papers and look at them by the hour."

"I guess I didn't know, but I never wanted to go to the basement. I always felt like he was down there somewhere." She waved her hands as though shoving away a ghost.

"And then the laundry room was down there, next to and behind the stairs. I had to go down quite often, to wash sheets. I wet the bed, remember?"

"Remember?" she cried in disgust. "I shared a bed with you, *remember*?"

"Oh, yes. I'm sorry."

"I can picture the basement layout as you describe the rooms, but I still can't make myself walk down the stairs."

I glanced out the window. The blue sky was darkening and edged with gray.

"Well, I'm sorry," I said, looking at my watch, "but it's late and I need to head for home."

"What? And leave me with all that blue to work?"

I finished my pop and laughed. "You can do it. They haven't made a puzzle yet that could lick Sandra." I wondered if we could piece our lives together as well.

As I drove home, I longed for another chance to work with Sandra. We needed each other to gain our sanity.

FIVE

Jean hadn't seen Jack for quite some time, but she was due here today. I sat in the car outside his office. Could I pull it off? Would he think I was Jean? If only I could remember more of what she did here. I knew I shouldn't be doing this, but I had to know what they had in mind for me. Jean had never really been aware of me, but I had made her life pretty difficult sometimes. I didn't feel too remorseful, though— she had made mine impossible, whether she was aware of me or not.

Well, Jody, here goes nothing, I thought, as I went into the old house. I was early. The front room looked like a waiting room, covered in faded green wallpaper. It was full of chairs, some soft living room type, some straight hard backed. There was one middle-aged gentleman sitting in a corner, looking over a magazine. He didn't seem to be reading, simply fingering through it, glancing at the pictures impatiently. I picked a stuffed side chair along the opposite wall and wished I had waited in the car, but it was cold outside.

Shortly Jack appeared at the entrance of the room. "Jean? Come on in now."

I went into his office. Opposite his desk were three chairs. I wondered which chair she usually sat in as I chose the far left chair facing the desk. As soon as I sat down, I was sure it was the wrong chair. Would he notice? Jack cozied into his leather one and picked up a clipboard with papers attached to it.

"Well, how have you been?" he asked.

I gathered my coat closer around me as I replied meekly, "Oh, okay, I guess." I tried to sound like her—what did she usually say?

"So what's been happening this week?"

This week, this week, where had I been? My mind fought for an answer.

I've only been here today. Why didn't I think this out a little better before I came here? Why did she come here? What would she ask? What did they talk about?

"Nothing much. Are we getting anywhere?" I asked.

"What do you mean?"

I crossed my arms tighter and tried to look more confident. "I mean what is this all about? What do you expect me to get from coming here all the time?"

"Well," he answered slowly, looking into my face, "we want to find out what the source of your depression is, and then, hopefully, we can help you overcome it. What do you hope to get out of coming here?"

Why did he always answer my questions with a question?

"I don't know." A feeling of frustration was coming over me. "I just want to know what's going on."

He had been staring at me intently. He sat forward in his chair and asked, "You're not Jean, are you?"

I drew myself back into the chair and cleared my throat, "This isn't as easy as I thought it would be."

"What do you mean?"

"Well, I've always fooled people—they don't see any difference. But with you, well . . . I just don't know what to say."

"Who are you?" He had the look of someone who had just won a chess match.

"I'm Jody."

"Where's Jean?"

"I don't know. Off somewhere. Maybe she's asleep." I didn't know what to tell him.

"When are you Jody and when are you Jean?" He seemed fascinated.

I blurted out my confession. "I don't know. Sometimes I get control, and when I do, I try not to give it up. Jean was planning on coming here today, so I came instead. I thought it would be a good chance for me to find out what you guys did here. I didn't know it would be so hard to fool you. I didn't think about what I would need to say. Is that how you figured out I wasn't Jean?"

"No," he answered, his smile softening. "It was a lot of things. Your hair is combed differently. You sit differently. Your facial expressions and your hand movements are different. You don't talk like Jean and you don't act like Jean."

I felt defensive. I had always been successful. Hank never noticed the dissimilarities and I had to put up with Hank every day, or at least whenever I had control. I bit my lip. Who was this person who could see through me so very quickly? I didn't trust him and yet I did trust him. What would his knowing do to me?

"Have you been here before?"

"No, I know about Jean coming here, but I haven't been here myself." I was irritated that he had found me out so quickly.

"Why are you here now?"

"Like I said, I just wanted to know what you guys were doing."

"But why?"

"Look, Jean does a lot of stupid things. Sometimes I can get her out of them, sometimes I can't." I was getting angry. Why was he questioning me? Why couldn't he simply tell me what was supposed to be happening?

"Stupid things like what?"

All right, I'll play the game. "Like marrying Hank!"

"Jean married Hank, but you didn't?"

"That's right. I wouldn't marry that man in a million years. He's a taker; he takes and takes, but never gives *anything*."

"But you live with him."

"Jean lives with him. I try to leave whenever I have control."

"And the kids?"

I started to say Jean's kids, but my heart softened; I loved those girls. I took them places when I could, to the zoo or the parks. I wasn't around or in control when they were born, but I remember all their little lives.

"Well, their dad doesn't beat them, but he isn't very nice to them either." I tried to skirt that question.

"I meant, are they your kids?"

"No." I let them go, however reluctantly.

"So, you only have you to watch out for?" He made it sound so selfish.

Why shouldn't I have only me to watch out for? Who else would watch out for me? Nobody I knew. I pouted. "Yes."

"So what do you do when you say you have control?"

"Well, I do things I want to do, whether it's going out driving or making cookies or whatever. Sometimes I do have to go to work and pretend I'm Jean, or she would get into trouble."

"So, you do look out for Jean too?"

"Yeah, I guess," I admitted with a sigh. I did have to keep her life intact or I didn't know what would happen. I never had control enough to create a life of my own. I know if I had control long enough I could have made it, and I sure wouldn't be living like Jean. There wasn't any way I could explain that to this guy, though.

"How do you get control?"

"I don't know." I really wasn't sure.

"Well, then, when do you get control?"

"Usually when Jean is very tired or totally stressed out." I could answer that one. "Right now she's having a blowup with Hank; she's actually considering divorcing the joker."

"Really?" He seemed genuinely surprised.

"I don't know. She thinks about it a lot, but she's so married to him, it drives her nuts, I think. She needs to lose that sucker."

"Can you transfer control back to her when you want to?"

"Yes," I answered warily. What was he up to now?

He answered my thought. "I wondered if I could talk with Jean."

"No. If I give her back control, she won't give it back to me."

"Does she know how to do it?"

"Shoot, no. She doesn't even know me." I stifled a laugh. "She wouldn't even believe you if you told her about me."

"Why not?" Jack looked skeptical.

"Why should she? She just thinks she's crazy. When I have control she loses time or days or whatever." I tried not to laugh again. Jean was so strange that way. She'd even heard me sometimes, but she wouldn't acknowledge me.

"Is there anyone else is your head?"

"I don't know. I don't think so. Jean sometimes gets very depressed or frightened and I call her the *other* Jean, but I don't think it's another person. Maybe, I don't know." I tried to remember Jean at her worst. I couldn't always see what was going on, like when she came here. Nowadays I didn't know a lot of what was happening much of the time. It was different when we were in school. Back then Jean was depressed a lot of the time, and I could make friends, go places, and do things.

"Would you let me talk with Jean?" he requested again.

I looked at Jack. I knew it would mean giving up control for the day. This guy would never be able to get it back for me. I hadn't even found out what Jean and he were doing here yet, but we seemed to be playing by Jack's rules.

"All right." I was tiring of the game anyway.

I looked down at my hands and concentrated. *Jean, where are you?* It was sort of like playing hide-and-seek in your head. Jean was off in one of the other rooms. This time she was a long way away. That was a bad sign. She must be very depressed. Suddenly Jean grabbed control.

I looked up. I was in Jack's office. He was staring at me with a strange kind of look. Where had I been? How did I get here? Was I asleep in his office? I tried to remember if he had used hypnosis or something. I often awoke without knowing how I got there, but this was the first time in Jack's office.

"See, I am crazy," I said with deliberation and total belief.

"No, Jean, you're not crazy. But we now know what's happening." He sounded equally determined to dispute my self-analysis.

"What?"

"I was talking to Jody. Do you know who she is?"

I looked quickly around the office. We were alone.

"No. I don't think I know anyone named Jody. I called my invisible friend Jody when I was a child, you know, like Christopher Robin's friend Blinker, or was it Binker? Oh, and some of the kids used to call me Jody in high school. What are you talking about?" I was feeling confused. The fog that sometimes floated in my brain seemed to be passing through again. "Was there someone else here?"

"Yes and no. What do you remember was happening here?"

I tried to think. It seemed so hard with this fog. "Well, I was sleeping, I think. I was dreaming about being here and hearing someone talking."

"What were they saying?"

"I don't remember. It was just a dream," I insisted. The whole discussion irritated me. I tried to think about what happened today and how I got here. I must have spaced out again. What happened today? Did I get my assignment done? Did I even go to work?

"What time is it?" I asked out of my confusion.

Jack gestured to the clock. "About four-thirty. What are you thinking?"

I looked at the venetian blinds. Through the barely open slits, the dark winter twilight was all that was visible. My head was going into a tailspin. Jack's office was the one *safe* spot in the world for me, and now I was going crazy here too. Why was this happening?

"Why am I so crazy?"

"You're not crazy," he said quietly, as though somehow he could see all the frenzied activity going on in my brain, and was trying to be the calm in the storm. "You have someone else in there, who sometimes has control."

"I don't believe that." It was frightening. My craziness was exploding right here in this office. What could it mean? Someone else in control?

"Well, it's true."

"Doesn't that prove my insanity?" I thought of a child-hood friend at school who was diagnosed as being schizophrenic. I pictured myself back in the hospital, drugged and shaking from the medication; was it going to be like that again? I had the strongest desire to pace around in circles. Sometimes that helped me think through problems and this was overwhelming me.

I must have looked terrible because Jack asked, "Jean, are you okay?"

"Yes . . . I just don't know what to think. You know I sometimes lose track of time. Sometimes I wake up and I don't know how or when I got there, but this doesn't make any sense." I wanted to get more air, but I couldn't seem to breathe.

"Jean, I haven't worked with many patients that have this type of neurosis, but it is a neurosis, not a psychosis. It's called dissociative hysteria. Most people call it multiple personality disorder. It happens when trauma occurs in your childhood that you can't deal with as a child, so you sort of wall it off to another person and go on with your life. Have you ever heard about or seen a movie called *The Three Faces of Eve*?"

"I think so. I'm not sure. I think I may have seen the movie years ago. I don't remember much about it. Why?"

"Well, you have the same type of condition as the woman in that movie. It was about a real woman who had three different personalities."

"And you think I do?"

"No, I don't know how many you have, but I met another one a few minutes ago."

"And you expect me to believe that?" I felt angry, but couldn't justify it to myself. "I know that I have been insane all my life and I know that I have done some pretty crazy things, but I would certainly know if there was anyone else in my head."

I didn't want to accept his explanation. I had always been in control of my life. One of the reasons I never drank alcohol was that I didn't like that feeling of not being in control. Insanity I could accept, but having someone else in control of me, I would never accept.

"Do you remember when we talked about the difference between a neurosis and a psychosis?"

"Yes, I think so."

"Well, you are not insane; you're not even psychotic. A psychotic person can't differentiate between reality and their delusions. You know you can never deny reality. You are suffering from a neurosis. And now that we know what it is, we can work on the why, okay?"

"No! I don't believe you." I tried to think of the different ways I had felt and why I would have been different today. Why would he have thought I was someone else?

"Where were you today?" He probed a tender spot.

My mind reeled again as I fought for an answer.

"Can you tell me where you were immediately before you came to my office?"

Why can't I remember? I can't remember. My mind was racing through a black hole. Where was I today? When did I get up today? Oh, yes, I remember that. At last I had some hook to hang on to. I smiled apologetically. "I don't remember right before I came here, but I do remember this morning."

"Tell me about it."

"Hank and I had a fight last night. It was about how he was treating Erin. It was a terrible scene. He got mad about my protecting Erin and undermining his 'discipline.' He thinks screaming and dragging the girl from the dining room table is discipline for not liking the way she eats spaghetti. When I tried to get her away from him, he broke up another chair. Anyway, everyone but Hank was in tears before the whole thing was over and I told him to get out. He left, but he came back later after everyone had gone to bed.

"This morning when I got up he started in where he left off, and I was too tired to deal with him. I told him to get out and get lost. After he left, I got the girls ready and on to school. Then I guess I went to work."

"You guess you went to work? Don't you know?"

"Oh, Jack, don't press me. I don't remember. I remember

driving to work, I think. I probably got so busy that I forgot. I have so much to do. I was recently assigned to a new project and . . . I don't know. I don't know." I was getting so tired I began to rub my face with both hands.

"It's okay. I was trying to see when Jody took over."

Jody. I recalled when someone had called me Jody. I was in high school. I was never very popular, but there was one clique of popular girls in my class that ran around together. Every once in a while, one of them would invite me to join them and go somewhere. I always felt like an outsider when I was with them, even though they treated me like one of the gang. They were the only ones that called me Jody. I never corrected them. I assumed that they had overheard my brother Matthew calling me JD and thought he meant Jody.

"What are you thinking?"

I sighed. I was so tired.

"I was thinking about when I was in high school and a few girls called me Jody. I always assumed they overheard Matt calling me JD. He said my initials stood for juvenile delinquent.

"The closest friend I had then was an exchange student from Turkey, named Dania. She had a lot of trouble in history and math and I would tutor her after school. Dania wasn't in any of my regular classes, but she was always passing me notes in study hall that only read 'Jody help me.' If I got caught with them, I would claim I didn't know who Jody was." I laughed nervously. "I don't know if they ever believed me or not, but I never got detention for passing notes."

"You enjoyed being Jody then?"

"No, I didn't mean that, but it did get me out of trouble in that one case. It's not that I minded going by Jody, but like I said, only a few girls called me that at school. No where else . . ." I drifted off, thinking about someone else, but not actually bringing him into focus.

"There was someone else?"

"No." I shook the thought from my head. I didn't want to remember. Somehow it felt better out of focus and out of mind.

Suddenly Jack changed the subject. "Jody tells me that you are thinking about divorcing Hank. Are you?"

"Oh." I searched for an answer. Divorce wasn't anything I could think about. Everything I'd been taught, everything I believed in, told me that you made your marriage work. It was up to you to keep it alive and well. But then there was Hank. I had sent him away angry again this morning. I wasn't even sure he would be at home tonight when I got there. Of course he would. Where else would he go? He needed me. He loved his kids, I told myself, but I wondered, thinking about last night. Why was he so hard on them? Why did he suspect everything and everyone? I was happier when he was gone. The kids were happier when he was gone. Somehow I had to make it work. . . .

"Jean?" Jack had been waiting patiently as my mind raced into furious circles.

Suddenly I thought about what Jack had said. "Jody told you?"

"Yes, she said thinking about it was driving you crazy."

I put my head into my hands again and tried to think. Thoughts of a possible Jody were pushed aside to think of divorce. When Hank was so unreasonable, I did think about divorcing him, but I would never be able to do it. I promised God as well as Hank that I would marry him forever. Even if I wanted Hank to leave, I couldn't break my promise to God.

"I don't remember what I told you. But I know that Hank loves me and I could never divorce him." Was I convincing myself?

"Jean, we don't need to talk about that right now. I wanted you to understand that Jody exists and she knows about you.

I wanted to know if you knew about her, and if you did, how much you knew."

"I don't know why this scares me, but it does. I don't believe there is anyone else in my head. I could believe that I act or react differently depending upon my own mood and tensions, but I don't think I have another person inside."

"I think we better set up another appointment for next week. I would like you to think about this and try to remember any dreams you have this week. It might help. How about next Tuesday at noon?" Jack was putting away his notes and scanning his appointment calendar.

"Jack, I don't know how I am going to exist until next week. I may have to write to you every day, all week."

"That's okay." He smiled as he handed me the appointment card. As I rose to leave, he gave me a quick hug. "You'll be all right. See you next week."

Without looking back, I walked out of the room and out of the old house that was his office building. I watched my feet as I half stumbled down the steps into the twilight. Then I looked up and around the street. My car was nowhere in sight.

Oh, God, how did I get here today? I couldn't remember. I turned left and walked down the street about halfway down the block.

As I walked back to the corner where I had begun, tears began to form. I crossed the street, checking out the rows of cars on either side of the side street as I crossed. I walked past several more old homes, their lights spilling out windows, across small box porches and onto the lawns. Soon it would be too dark for me to see the colors of the cars. *Where was it? Why did this happen to me?*

Suddenly I spotted my old car across the street, neatly squeezed between a dented, rusty pickup and a worse-looking VW bug. I wondered how I ever got it in, or how I was going to get it out now.

I crossed the street, unlocked the car door, and slid into the front seat. I felt exhausted. I leaned into the steering wheel, causing the horn to blare. I jerked up and locked my door. I sat in the car trying to think. I needed to get home and fix supper, but this appointment had put my head into such a spin I could hardly move.

After several tries, I eased the car from the parking place and headed for home. I should have called. Hank would undoubtedly be there with the girls. How would they all be? I didn't think I could stand another night like last night. What was I going to do? Hank needed to get counseling. I couldn't let him stay with the girls, not with the way he'd been. It seemed to be getting worse and worse. Whatever I had to do, I was too tired to deal with anything tonight, but it absolutely had to get better.

Within the hour I pulled into our driveway. I drew in a long breath and opened the front door. The girls were playing a game of "Sorry" on the kitchen table. Hank was nowhere in sight, but his car was in the carport.

"Where's your dad?" I asked the girls.

"Mom! You're home." Erin jumped up and ran to greet me. "Dad's downstairs watching TV. We're starving. Did you bring anything to eat?"

"No, I have stuff here to fix. It won't take me too long. I'm sorry it's so late. You'll have to move your game into the living room."

"Oh, Mom," scolded Melissa, "all the men will slide around the board and we'll never get them all back in the right places."

I rubbed my hand in her long black hair. She looked like a pixie. Born prematurely, she never quite caught up to the size of the other little girls her age. Her two older sisters protected her from anyone who might pose her any threat. Erin was off to junior high now, but Teresa walked her to school each day. I loved them all so much.

"Don't worry, Melissa. You'll probably be done with that game before I'm ready to put dinner on the table. Only don't start another in here when you're done."

I fixed dinner and set the girls down at the kitchen table to eat. I made up a plate for Hank and poured him a glass of tea.

"I'll be right back," I assured the girls as I descended the staircase from the kitchen to the family room.

Hank was asleep on the couch. The TV was blaring some cops and robbers show. It irritated me and I wondered why he always had it on so loud. He had to have it on constantly. I set his plate on top of the TV to turn it down a bit. He didn't stir.

"Hank?" I tried to rouse him softly. I always dreaded waking him. Sometimes he came up fighting, actually striking out at some unseen enemy. I attributed it to his years in the service. Sandra told me that when she stayed with us she used to poke him with a broom handle if she ever had to wake him.

"Hank!" I called louder.

"What? What?" He sat up quickly from a sound sleep.

"I brought you some supper."

"Why?" He seemed to growl at me. I hoped it was from the sleep.

"I thought you should eat before it got too late."

"Has everybody eaten?" he asked in the same annoyed voice.

"No, the girls are eating now and I haven't gotten anything yet."

"Oh, so you wanted to make sure I ate down here tonight, huh?"

"No." I floundered. Had I wanted him to eat somewhere away from us? I wondered if I had subconsciously thought about it. "I thought you might want to finish watching your show, so I brought your dinner down to you. I thought I was being nice."

"Yeah, well, give me the tea. I'm dying of thirst."

He downed the glass and handed it back to me.

"I'll bring you another glass."

"Never mind. I'm coming up."

He took the plate out of my hand and slowly climbed up the stairs. I turned off the TV and followed him.

The girls had been laughing and talking, but as they saw him emerge from the stairwell, they quickly quieted.

Erin ventured a test question: "How was the show, Dad?"

He pulled up his chair and plopped his plate on the table. "What show?"

"I don't know," Erin answered, "whatever you were watching."

"If you don't know what I was watching, then why do you care how it was?"

"I was just trying to be nice."

"You're being nice. Your mom's being nice. You all kill me with your niceness. What were you saying about me before I got up here? I heard you laughing."

"We weren't talking about you. We were talking about Melissa and how we used to call her Frog." There was a touch of panic in Erin's voice.

I was proud of the way she tried to defend herself, but it upset me that she had to do it. Why couldn't he trust anyone, especially his own kids? And why would they be talking about him anyway?

There wasn't much more conversation through dinner except to ask for more tea or biscuits. I was grateful. I was also thankful that Hank was working third shift and would be leaving for work soon.

After the girls went to bed, Hank got ready and left for work. At least he didn't argue with me again. I pulled on my nightgown and crawled into bed. As I lay there, I wondered what I could do. I wanted to tell Hank to get help or get out, but I had tried that before. He would always say it was my problem, not his. I was the one going to a psychiatrist, after all. I was the one who was crazy, not him.

Was I crazy? Or was Jack right? Was there someone else living here in my head. What had happened today? Did I go to work? Who could I ask? Certainly not the kids. What was going to happen when I showed up tomorrow? If I didn't go in, did I at least call in? What was I going to do?

I slid out onto the floor, and kneeling, laid my head on the bed.

"Dear God, please let me sleep. I'm so tired. Please help me make the right decisions. Help me get through tomorrow, whatever it may bring. Please make some sense of this Jody business. Be with my poor children. Strengthen them and help them tomorrow and always. And be with Hank. Help him to get the help he needs. I ask in the name of Jesus, Your Son. Amen."

The morning came, and as I touched my feet to the cold linoleum, I felt as if I had caught a hangover from someone, the way you catch a cold. Somehow it didn't belong to me, this dizzy, unreal feeling that someone else had a grip on my life. I got myself to work, but I wasn't sure how I'd managed that. As the noon break approached, I couldn't stop thinking about yesterday's appointment with Jack. When my lunch hour was long over, I couldn't go back to work. I couldn't get my mind off the *other person*. I couldn't breathe. My subconscious was screaming.

Stop it. Stop it. I had to stop my panic. I'd drive a while, but where?

I hurried to the parking lot and retrieved my car. I followed I-5 as it went south through Renton, Kent, Fife, and into Tacoma. Suddenly a sign beckoned to me. Mount Rainier. I took the 512 exit.

For the next couple of hours I drove up through the foothills covered with ever denser forest. Why was I going? Was I running to something or away from something? Maybe both.

I didn't want to hear what Jack had said. Another person? How could that be? I had control. I had to. How could someone else be in control of my body?

Maybe Mount Rainier would be calm, stable, something larger than my frazzled mind.

As I pulled into the parking lot at the Sunrise Visitor Center, a sense of relief flowed across my nerves. Mount Rainier was so close I could nearly hug it. I got out of my car and walked a short way toward the mountain. The air here was always rain fresh, cold, and clear. Selecting a large boulder just off the path, I inched myself atop it and looked up at the mountain. The sheer beauty of white and grandeur stilled my searching soul for a moment. Here was the handiwork of God.

Beyond the path, through the alpine meadow, the hillside dropped down into scattered firs, their hunter green arrows poking up through the snow at the start of the glacier. Then the mountain rose thousands of feet.

I took in a breath and shivered. The wind was gentle, but chilled from the ice and the elevation. There was no sound but its shushing.

I looked down at my feet. Tiny yellow and purple flowers carpeted the sides of the pathway and gathered around my rock. I hoped I hadn't stepped on any of them. They seemed so small and insignificant, as I was to the mountain.

What was going on with me? I couldn't have "Jody" living inside of me. Jack must be wrong. She didn't exist. *Does she*? I asked the mountain, but the wind brought back no answer.

As I thought back over my life, I felt that I had constantly needed to be someone else. I had always felt insufficient. I was never good enough; I never did enough, not for my parents, my husband, and even now for my children. Jody was my escape as a child. I made her up when I was desperately lonely. She was my invisible friend who comforted me when I cried by the river. She wasn't real. She couldn't be.

Control. Don't lose control. Breathe. Be aware.

I shivered. What did Jack say before I left—give control back to Jody? Never. She's not real.

The sparse clouds shifted slightly and the sun's reflection on the ice struck my eyes suddenly. I turned from the glare and gazed into the valley.

To the mountain, I was a flower. To the valley, I could be a giant, with my foot crushing a hundred firs in a single step. Who was I anyway?

I remember Melissa asking me the same question.

It had been on a particularly bad day. I needed to pick up some groceries. I went to the bank to withdraw some cash and was informed that the account was already overdrawn.

Hank, why do you do this to me? He would get money from the account whenever he wanted any, even if there were checks outstanding, and I was left scuffling with our creditors. *Oh, Hank,* I thought in disgust, *you remind me of the lady in a joke, asking the bank how she can possibly be out of money when she still has checks left. Darn you, Hank.*

Entering our front door I couldn't resist yelling, "Hank! Where are you?"

The three girls were playing Monopoly on the dining room table. Melissa answered, "He's in the family room, Mom," and in the same breath, "What did you bring us?"

"Nothing," I snapped. I flung my coat and purse at the couch. "What did you expect?"

She suddenly cowered in her chair. "What's wrong, Mom?"

The movement made me flash back on my sister Sandra when she was frightened. Melissa was so like her: small, dark complexioned, and helpless looking. I was instantly remorseful.

"I'm sorry, honey. I didn't mean to yell at you. It's your dad I'm angry with."

The girls eyed me with suspicion as I went into the family room and closed the door. After a general row over finances, I left Hank with his television and went to cook. When supper and homework were finished, I sent the girls to bed. Hank had retreated back to the family room. Melissa put on her nightgown and came into the living room where I had curled up to read a book.

"Mom," Melissa pleaded, "I'm still hungry."

I was instantly agitated. "What? Why do you wait until you're supposed to be in bed to ask for something to eat?"

Melissa began backing off, waving both little hands as though she were erasing what she had said. "I don't really want anything, Mom. I just thought I did."

I plummeted into low mode. Wasn't I a rotten mother? Here was my little girl being sent to bed hungry, and with such angry words. I dropped down and hugged her.

"I'm sorry, Melissa, I didn't mean to be so angry. We'll get something, okay?"

I cut up an orange for her in the kitchen, and as I watched her eating it, I soared into my high mode. Wasn't she the most beautiful little girl in the world with her long, dark hair and big, black-brown eyes? I brushed her hair with my hand.

She looked up at me coldly and said, "I don't know what you are. First you're mad, then you're sad, and now you're happy. Who are you really?"

I didn't know. I couldn't tell her.

• • •

I still didn't know. I looked back up at Mount Rainier and squinted. That day with Melissa I had been unstable, but I hadn't been another person.

I was cold. I had to go back to the car and warm up. What time was it anyway? I turned my wrist to see my watch. Four-thirty? I had to head home.

I hopped off the rock and tried to avoid crushing any of my colorful kindred spirits. As I reached the car, I turned again to stare up at the mountain. There were some things permanent in my world.

I hoped it wouldn't blow up like Mount Saint Helens merely to prove me wrong.

The car was sun warmed inside. I was surprised at how wonderful it felt. I had gotten colder than I had realized. As I drove back down the mountain, the warmth lulled me into a calm.

Jack doesn't know everything. He can't. I've been me all my life. I've had so many difficulties. I was only stressed out when I got there yesterday. I don't know why I couldn't remember, but lots of people don't remember parts of their day. It just passes, like driving in a car for a long distance. You don't see whole towns you go through. Or even driving home from work, suddenly you can find yourself turning onto your street. Then you realize you don't remember much of your journey since you left work. You've been thinking about something else, and all at once you're home.

I knew I was telling myself lies. I didn't know where I'd been for a couple of days. Suddenly I was in Jack's office and he was telling me he'd been talking to someone else inside my head. It was all too crazy.

SIX

"SO JODY, YOU'RE BACK. WHERE'S JEAN?" JACK SMILED knowingly, as I plunked down in the wood chair furthermost from him.

"Do you really care?" I knew he and Jean were up to something. I needed to know what.

"Yes, I do. How is it you're here today?"

"Whenever Jean's severely depressed or confused, I get a lot more control. So I decided to come here again and amuse myself with your smug little smile. What makes you so sure it was me when I walked in the door?"

"Jody, as I told you last time, the differences are significant. The most obvious thing is your hair."

"Oh, yes. Jean always pulls it back or lets it hang so . . . so . . . I don't know, I can't stand it." I pushed the sides back over my ears. "I like to part it in the middle and have bangs but not too close around my face. I just didn't think about it. Most people take no notice. Anyway, would you like to tell me what you have planned?"

"Planned? What do you mean?"

"Don't start with me. I know you and Jean are trying to figure out a way to get rid of me."

"Get rid of you?"

"And don't play dumb with me. I know you talked to her about me last time after I gave her back control. You're trying to get rid of me. It took me nearly two days to get it back again."

"How could we get rid of you? You're her or part of her. I'm trying to figure out how you became two people. There's no plot to get rid of anyone. Why are you so angry?"

Why do I feel so threatened? I'm part of her, she's part of me. But I'd gladly get rid of her and live my own life. She didn't know about me, but she'd been trying to drive me out for years. She destroyed my relationships with other people and interrupted my activities if she got control. But of course she didn't have the same advantages that I had. I knew she existed. I could play with her, talk to her, give her control anytime I felt like it. She thought she was totally crazy until Jack came along. Poor Jean.

"I'm not angry at you. I'd just like to have a life of my own."

"When did you join Jean? What's your earliest memory?"

"I don't know who joined who, but I do have some very young memories of her."

"Tell me about them."

"Her dad was a sicko. He liked to lay in bed naked and bring her into bed with him. He told her she couldn't tell Mommy about it; it was their secret. Of course she felt guilty about it."

"So you were there too?"

"No, I wasn't. I wouldn't have anything to do with that man."

"But you're part of her, so her dad is your dad."

"No, he's not. Forget it, okay? I'm sorry I ever said anything."

"Okay, but it gives me a clue. So tell me about your life now."

I shrugged. "What's to tell? Jean ruins everything I try to do." I stared at the ceiling for a while. I could have had a great life without Jean and especially without her husband.

"What are you thinking now?" Jack asked.

"Uh," I hesitated. I wondered if I should tell him. Oh, why not? "I was thinking about a time I played a trick on Jean." I smiled, thinking of poor confused Jean, caught up, embarrassed to death. Then I frowned, thinking how it had been the end of my relationship with Edward.

"Want to tell me about it?"

"It's all rather complex, actually."

"I don't mind. Why don't you tell me?"

"Well, I told you last time. I didn't marry Hank."

"Yes, you told me."

"So I'm not married, you understand?" I felt very angry. He was going to be like Jean—accusing me of immoral acts. Of course, she didn't know it was me; she thought it was her insanity that created my relationships with other people. I hated her. I hated her self-righteous little attitude.

"Okay, you're not married. Jean's married."

"Don't forget that, okay?"

Jack nodded his head and looked down to make some little note on his notepad. I could just imagine what it was— "Jody's not married, Jean is." Ha.

"Go on," he prodded.

"I can't stand Hank. Do you know what he's like?" I didn't wait for Jack's answer. "He's like a spoiled child who always has to have his way. The best of everything for him— the best shoes, the best clothes, the best car; his time, his food, his everything. He doesn't even acknowledge his own kids' needs. Everything is for him. Did you know that he wouldn't even attend his own best friend's wedding because he didn't like the dress Jean was wearing? Appearance is everything. He couldn't have *his* wife show up at the wedding looking anything less than perfect."

"But you said you weren't married to him?"

"No, no I'm not. But Jean is, so I can't get away from him. However, I try to make my own life when I can."

"What do you mean?"

"I mean . . ." I paused and tried to think how to tell him. I'm not Jean. I'm not. But I want the same kind of things she wants—warmth, someone who cares, someone to love, to be loved. Hank was incapable of those things. I tried to tell Jean. I tried repeatedly. I felt sad. I didn't want to hurt Jean. Sometimes I got angry with her. She could be so stupid. Hank didn't love her. Oh, he needed her all right, but he couldn't love her. He was incapable of love. He only needed someone to be his second mommy. He treated her with the same contempt as a spoiled brat. How I hated him. Why couldn't she see that there were other men out there? People who could care. People capable of love and warmth . . . and decent sex.

"Do you want to tell me about it?" Jack broke into my stream of thought.

"It's simply that I can't stand Hank. I found my own men."

"Your own men?"

"Well, yes. A couple of them, actually, but one at a time, though."

"Of course," Jack answered smugly. I could learn to hate him too.

Why don't I just tell him? Who the hell cares anyway? It was a long time ago. Edward had been dead for years and who knew where Brian was now. Erin knew about Brian, though. I let her see him kiss me once. That was stupid of me. I tried to deny it, but I don't know if she bought it or not. She was so young. Do I feel guilty? Yes, I broke Brian's heart. It wasn't my fault, though; it was Jean's. She always broke up everything.

"What are you thinking?" Jack broke in again.

"I don't know. About everything, I guess. Jean always destroyed my relationships with other men. I guess I picked a married man first because it was safer."

"Safer?"

"Well, I couldn't have him calling for me at home with Hank there, could I?"

"I guess not."

"Hank would have killed me. He wouldn't have known it was me, but he would have killed me anyway. I share this body, you know."

"You think Hank's that violent?"

"Oh, come on. Anyway, dating a married man made it so much easier to sneak around Hank. Besides, there wasn't much of a chance that Edward would leave his wife and run off with me."

"Edward?"

"Yeah. Edward was the first guy I ever dated after high school. He needed someone to listen to him and give him a little more in bed than he could get from his spouse. He wanted more respect than he could get from her too. Everyone wants to think someone else thinks the world of them. Although I do think Edward might have contemplated leaving his wife for me if Jean hadn't ended our relationship."

"Then how would you have handled it with Hank?"

"I don't know. I don't actually think Edward was the one I wanted to be with the rest of my life. I needed him the way he needed me. I don't know how I could have gotten Jean away from Hank, either."

I shrugged my shoulders as I thought of Edward's departure.

"Want to tell me about it?" Jack seemed to read my mind.

"I was thinking about the first time I put Jean and Edward

together. It was also the last time I had him. After that, I tried to keep her out of my relationships."

"What happened?"

"I thought it would be a joke. Maybe I thought if she could see what it was to have someone really love her, she might leave Hank. I don't know. It was funny at first."

"What happened?"

"Well, I was about nineteen when I started dating Jean's boss, Edward. He was married and twice my age, ugly as sin, but sharp and refined. He was also sensitive and caring, something Hank doesn't have a clue about. He was from England originally, and before the war he was a cab driver. He used to tell me that no matter what he did, whether he was a pilot or a bank manager or whatever, his wife always thought of him as an ordinary cabby. I felt sorry for him at first, although I was attracted by his sheer intelligence. Then I found out that he was also a marvelous lover."

My mind wandered off to the time we had met in a high-rent district of town and sat in my car talking. Somebody had seen Edward run along the yard from his car to mine, and they had called the police. An officer had arrived with his flashlight and asked to see our identification. Edward had been scared when the patrolman told me that he knew my dad and asked if my dad would approve of my seeing someone twice my age. I got pissed and told him it was none of his business or my dad's. He told me to get out of there and go home.

"So what happened?"

"We went up to Edward's cabin on one of the small local lakes. There wasn't another house nearby, but Edward would hardly put on a light in the cabin. He was afraid one of his neighbors might see it and come over to see who was there. I guess most of them knew his wife pretty well. Anyway, we went into one of the bedrooms and put on a little light in one corner of the room. With the shades drawn, it was pretty dark. We stripped down and were into a touching session. He always complained that his wife wouldn't let him touch her much; just do it and get it over with. Well, we didn't; we took our time. Then I got this idea that it would be fun to see what would happen if Jean found herself there. Maybe she'd even enjoy it. So I gave her control."

"What did she do?"

"She *totally* freaked out! I can't imagine what Edward thought. At any rate, she got out of there in a hurry and broke up our relationship. I could never get control again whenever he was around, not even to explain what happened."

"Why not?"

"I don't know." It maddened me when I thought about it. I wanted so much for Edward to know what had happened, that he hadn't done anything wrong, that we had been close. I remember when Jean saw him years later. He was sick then, dying of cancer, and looked all washed out. She looked dowdy that day, worse than usual, and he avoided her like the plague, not that it mattered anymore. Why couldn't I have gotten control? Why wouldn't Jean let me say good-bye to him?

"You look sad."

I shook my head to lose the thoughts. "I thought he was a neat guy. I don't think I've ever met anyone who has a sharper mind than he had. When he died a couple years after our breakup, I felt sad that everything had ended so badly." My irritation rose again. "I simply wish Jean would have left well enough alone."

"Sounds to me like you gave her the option."

"I guess that's what makes me so mad. It really was my own fault. It did seem like a good joke at the time." I stuck out my lower lip the way I usually did when I was mad.

"So now what are you thinking?"

"It isn't fair. I need to be close to someone. Jean has

Hank, for all the good that will ever do her. She has no right to take away my chance at finding love."

"You said there were a couple men?"

"Yeah. Brian was the other. He was much closer to my age, actually two years younger. He wasn't married, and even though he knew Jean was, he didn't care. He loved kids and I'm pretty sure if I could have gotten Jean away from Hank, he would have married me. I met him in Chicago, shortly after Melissa was born."

"Chicago?" Jack looked more interested than he usually did. I wondered why.

"Yeah. What's so special about Chicago?"

"What do you know about Jean's ending up in the hospital there?"

Oh, he already knew part of the story.

"Well . . ." I pondered how much I should tell him. What the hell? It was so much water under the bridge now, who would care? "Jean was headed for that crack-up without my help."

"How do you mean?"

"She was totally overloaded at work. Melissa had just been born with a medical problem that required surgery and the baby cried all the time. Jean had trouble juggling child-care, conflicts at work, fights with Hank. What can I say? Problems and stress . . ."

Jack nodded his head once.

"Anyway, I met Brian on the commuter train one day. We began seeing each other evenings after Hank went to work. Jean worked late so much of the time. Brian used to meet me after she got off. The only problem was that he often got there early and blew kisses to me from the sidewalk below. That always confused and frightened Jean. Once when Hank had to work on Saturday, I took the girls and we went down to Brian's house. We pretended to be just friends, but when the girls were looking at his goldfish, we hugged and kissed.

Teresa and Melissa were too young to remember, but Erin saw us at least once. I was sorry about that. I didn't want to upset her."

"What about the hospital?"

"Yeah, well, that was the end of my time with Brian. Jean was working overtime. . . ."

"Jean," a co-worker called for attention. "Isn't that your friend out on the sidewalk?"

Jean started to say no, but I grabbed control.

"Yes, thanks. I have to get going now. He's got my supper."

I leaned toward the window and saw Brian standing on the sidewalk across the street. He usually went over there to catch my attention, because, from there, he could see me through my office window on the third floor. It was quite dark out, but the thoroughfare was well lit and he stood right under a streetlight. I blew him a kiss and looked quickly to see if anyone else had seen me. Several people had been working overtime with Jean, but they were still busy and no one had noticed.

I turned back to the desk. I wanted to stack things up neatly for Jean, but I had no idea what all those papers and punch cards were or where they should go. The group had been working on a system conversion. I had been working on learning enough of the lingo to pass as Jean. I decided to leave the mess for her to sort out the next day.

I grabbed my purse and turned to leave. The co-worker called after me, "See you tomorrow, Jean."

"Yeah, thanks. Have a good evening." If there's any left for you, I thought. It must have been after eight then.

Brian met me at the door and whisked me up in a powerful hug.

"So, how'd the police academy go today?" I asked him as he put me back down.

"Pretty good, pretty good." Brian laughed. "My sergeant says I'm getting to be the best sharp-shooter he's ever had. I'm not sure how great a compliment that is; he could say it to everyone and mean it, no matter how badly they did."

I laughed. "Well, in less than three months, you'll be one of Chicago's finest in blue. I hope you know how to shoot."

I hated to think of Brian as an officer. I had an aversion to guns and the violence that went with them. However, he had gotten a job as a security guard, where he still worked part-time, and he fell in love with the whole idea of carrying a gun. As much as I disliked Brian becoming a police officer, I didn't have the heart to dampen his enthusiasm.

"So, what did you bring me for supper?" I could smell deep-fried something, as he picked up the two paper bags he had set on the sidewalk to give me a hug.

"Oh, greasy, unhealthy stuff that will make you fat and your skin break out, but I'm not going to give you any until you guess what it is." He began walking down the street, holding the bags away from me.

"Sounds so appetizing. Where are we going anyway?"

"I know a charming little park about three blocks from here where we can dine in privacy and comfort on the table of our choice—the swings, the slide, or the merry-go-round."

"Oh, Brian, you're a nut."

We zigzagged up a couple of blocks and found the little corner park. It was less than two or three city lots, with a half dozen trees, two streetlights, and the three amusements that Brian had mentioned.

"You forgot the sandbox," I said jokingly.

"Oh, yes. However, as you will observe, my dear, there are no seats on the sandbox. So what's your choice?" He bowed slightly, waving his bag-filled hand out across the playground.

"Let's sit on the merry-go-round. At least it has a surface

to use as a table." As we walked toward the flat, round, wooden disk with its metal hand supports, I tried to guess, "What French-fried delight have you brought? Is it chicken?"

"No, but you're close."

"What's close to chicken? French-fried tuna? Chicken of the sea?"

Brian fell into his seat on the wheel laughing. "I have to tell you. You are so close. It's shrimp and French-fries."

"See, I thought it smelled a little fishy, but the fries confused me."

We ate our food and wiped up with the mountain of napkins Brian had wisely packed along. Afterward we played on the huge slide and swings.

Suddenly a car pulled up on the street and beeped.

"It's my brother," Brian explained, running to the curb. "What's up, Bruce?"

"I've been looking all over for you," Bruce yelled, his frustration showing. "The factory phoned and said the night watchman called in sick. They want you to cover security tonight. I told them I'd have you there by ten o'clock. You're ten minutes late now. Come on, hop in."

I had followed most of the way to his brother's car. Brian looked back at me with guilt.

"Don't worry about me, Brian." I answered his look. "I have my nerve gas sprayer and I'm less than a half-mile from home."

"You sure? Let me see it."

I dug the sprayer out of my purse and held it up for him.

"Okay." Then he gave me a long kiss and hopped into the car. As it drove away, Brian called back, "I'll call you tomorrow. I love you."

•   •   •

I tilted my head as I looked up at Jack. The pain was still there; tears just below the surface. "That's the last time I ever saw him." I sat back in my chair and crossed my arms.

"So what happened?"

Sure, you could give a damn about me and my feelings. It's Jean you care about. I sighed.

"The next thing I knew, Jean had grabbed back control. She didn't know where she was—although we were only a few blocks from work—and she panicked. Even though Brian had given me a nerve gas sprayer, she was afraid to walk anywhere at night alone. Then a police car came along, hauled her off to the hospital, and I guess you know the rest."

"It didn't bother you that Jean got in trouble over something you did?"

"In trouble?"

"What would you call being placed in a mental ward over confusion you created?"

It wasn't like that. Why did he make it sound as if I were the villain?

"I didn't plan it. It just worked out that way. I ended up the big loser in this, remember that. I'm the one who lost Brian."

"Can I talk to Jean?" Jack asked suddenly.

"No, you can't. I told you the last time it took me two days to get back control. Right now she's struggling around with what she should do about Hank and I don't want you to give her any advice. I want her to get away from Hank and I think she will, if you leave well enough alone."

"I'm not going to advise her one way or another. She needs to make her own decisions. You see, Jody, if I were to tell her, or you for that matter, what she ought to do or not do, it would relieve her from the responsibilities of her own decisions. That wouldn't help any of us. Can you see that?"

"Yes," I nodded, but I felt wary. I didn't trust him. He

wanted to give her back control, but why? I wasn't convinced he wasn't plotting with Jean. What could they do?

"I need to talk to Jean, get her views on what you related."

"Can you get her to give me back control?"

"I'm sorry, Jody, but I can't answer that. I doubt it. She still doesn't believe you're real. I'm hoping that some of what you've told me will hit home and she'll start questioning why it happened."

Damn. What if she does start believing Jack? What will that do? Right now it's easy to get control. But what if she refuses to believe him? If this ended anything like last time, brother. It could take me another two days of effort to get it back.

"Look, Jody. The only way I can help Jean, and you in the process, get better is to convince Jean that you're real and start dealing with where you both are. Please let me speak with her."

"All right. All right. But *try* to give me back control. Jean is so depressed right now. I hate to think what could happen."

"I'll try."

Jean, Jean, where are you? Come out, come out, wherever you are.

Not again! I'm in Jack's office. Why is this happening?

"Jean?" Jack leaned forward and looked into my face. "Are you okay?"

I put my head on my hands. I'm so tired. Why?

"Jean, I was talking with Jody again."

"No. I don't believe you. Why do you keep saying that?"

"Jean, I told Jody that the only way you and she are going to get better is if you can accept that she exists and start working from there."

"I can't."

"Jean, try to remember. Can you remember what just happened? How did you get here?"

"I drove here and I walked through the front door."

"No, you didn't. Jody did. Do you remember a guy named Edward? Jody was telling me about a nasty trick she played on you."

Edward. How could I ever forget Edward? He had been my mentor from the very beginning. When I came into the data processing department, there were about three hundred men and two women; the other woman was the secretary. Edward was so unlike most of the men there. He completely believed a woman could be every bit as intelligent as a man. He took me under his wing and taught me so much. He was the most brilliant man I've ever known. Together we developed a system software package that was so good I found it in use out here in Seattle more than a dozen years later. Our company must have sold it to the hardware vendor, it was that good.

"Do you remember Edward?"

"Yes, he was my first boss in DP—data processing."

"Jody says she had an affair with him."

God, why can't You wipe it all from reality? Edward was such a good man, honest to a fault, generous and kind. He loved his wife. He loved his kids. *Why did this happen to us? How did it happen?*

"Jean?"

"I don't know what happened. It was horrible. I was married to Hank. I would never do anything like that. I don't know. I don't know."

"Can you tell me what happened?"

"I was working with Edward, lots of overtime. We were struggling with the different machines' software, trying to come up with a way to move a lot of the production jobs from one vendor's machine to another quickly. It wasn't easy. The underlying structure was so totally different. We had to work a lot of overtime because the old machines were scheduled to be moved out. Anyway, we spent a lot of time together."

I tried to remember when it had started. There was a buzzing in my brain, something trying to surface and to stay hidden at the same time. I felt guilty, but I was also convinced that it wasn't my fault. I had always tried to be a good girl.

"This was shortly after I married Hank, before any of the girls were born. Actually, I'm not sure when it all started. I worked for Edward about a year before I got married. Hank worked second shift. He kept being upset because he might come home at eleven o'clock and I'd still be working. He used to joke about my having an affair with Edward. It made me feel very defensive. Edward did ask me to go out for a drink every once in a while. I never went, though.

"After a while, Hank began to get a little serious about the possibility that I was seeing Edward on the side. I kept telling him that he was being foolish. I'd tell him to look how much Edward had helped me; look how much money I was making on overtime. But I don't know. I kept remembering things that couldn't possibly have happened."

I tried not to shudder. I pictured Edward touching me. I tried to think about the computer room, the old coding sheets, anything to take my mind away from the picture.

"Like what?" Jack pressed.

"I don't know. Edward just said things, like inviting me to come out to his house to baby-sit. Once I went out there and found his wife had taken the kids to their cabin. I asked him why he did that. He told me that he knew his wife wouldn't be back until the weekend and we could have all evening to play. I made him take me home."

"Why would he do that?"

Edward, Edward, why did you do that? We worked so well as a team. We could have done so much together. After the last time, I had to ask for a transfer. I couldn't face him day after day, not after what happened. I wanted to cry. I had so much respect for the man.

"Jean? What happened with Edward?"

"I don't know. I really don't know. Somehow he seemed to change. He started touching me when we were working. He seemed confused when I got upset about it. Then one awful night—"

I couldn't tell him. How could I tell him? What would he think of me? I loved Hank. I would never be unfaithful to him. Never. God, I didn't do that. I didn't. I'm not that kind of person.

"One awful night you found yourself with Edward?"

How could he know? How could Jack know? I didn't tell him. I couldn't tell him.

"Jody told me that she played a trick on you and gave you control in the middle of a lovemaking session with Edward."

He does know. Jody? How can that be? Jody, Jody, of my childhood, how can you be me? I made you up. I made you talk; I made you answer. You're not real! It's craziness. It's insanity. I'm not here at all. I'm dreaming. I've gone crazy and all my worse nightmares are coming true.

"Jean, can you tell me what happened?"

"No. It didn't happen. It's craziness, that's all it is."

"No, Jean, Jody is real. It was Jody that was seeing Edward. She put you there. Tell me what happened."

I can't breathe. Please let me breathe.

"I don't know what happened. I sort of woke up and there we were, Edward and me. He was . . . he was . . ." licking my leg—I can't say it. I was standing up against the wall and he was kneeling in front of me.

"I began screaming and told him to get away from me. He looked so upset. He picked up his clothes and backed out of the room. I got dressed as fast as I could and ran out to his car. I didn't know where I was or how I got there. When he came out, I told him to take me home."

"What happened after that?"

"I asked for a transfer from his area the next day. He was very upset about it. He told me that we could still work together even if I didn't want to see him anymore. I don't know. I couldn't face him. I could hardly face Hank."

Hank had been right, but how?

"Jean, we're almost out of time. I want to ask you to do something for me."

"What?"

Jack got out of his chair and sat down in the chair next to me. I thought at first he was going to take my hand, but then seemed to think better of it.

"I want you to give control back to Jody."

"What?"

"Jody can give control to you. That's how you got here today. I want you to try to give the control back."

"What control? What are you talking about?"

"Can you close your eyes and try to relax and think of Jody?"

"No, I can't. Every time I think of Jody, I can't breathe. I made her up. She was gone with my childhood. Don't you understand? She's not real." My fists had drawn up with the tension.

"Okay. Relax now." Jack went back to his chair and picked up his appointment calendar. "Let's make an appointment for next week, okay? Are you doing anything special this weekend?"

Oh, sure, sure. Pull my guts out through my ears and then ask if I'm doing anything special for the weekend.

Jack handed me a card. I'm not sure I heard the day or time. I tried to look at the card, but I couldn't focus. I wanted to run out of the place.

When I reached the sidewalk, I stopped and drew in a big

breath. My car was parked in sight, but again I didn't remember parking it.

I thought as I climbed into the car, *I'm not coming back here. I am never coming back.*

I canceled my appointment with Jack, and for the next few months refused to set up another. I didn't want to accept his theory. I was always in control. Sometimes I forgot things, sometimes I said or did things I didn't remember saying or doing, but did I lose control? Could there be someone else in control of my body? Was that possible?

During the months I avoided Jack, I struggled with the concept of Jody. More and more I became aware of her presence in my life. As I thought of affairs with other men that I had broken up, it seemed possible, even plausible. I had tried so hard to be a faithful, loving wife. The Lord knew I wasn't the kind of woman who would have that sort of relationship outside my marriage. It made sense that "another person" had been making my life impossible. How many other things had "I" done that I didn't know I'd done?

Even in my day-to-day living, things had happened—arguments Hank said I'd had that I couldn't remember, meetings I'd missed at work for no apparent reason, and whole days that seemed to have been swallowed up and taken from my calendar. I was determined to find the truth about this Jody.

One Saturday afternoon, I took the girls to Woodland Park Zoo. I decided to try direct contact. If Jody existed, maybe I could talk with her. As the girls were entertaining themselves in the petting zoo, I sat on a bench in a quiet, bricked-in area just outside.

"Well, Jody," I said quietly aloud, "if you're real, talk to me. Why is it you know what's going on with me, but I never know what you're up to?"

You don't listen. You'd rather believe you're crazy, you silly witch.

Was that Jody, or was the voice in my mind created through my own imagination? What did *she* know that I didn't? What could I ask *her*?

I waited until an old couple strolling past were out of hearing range before I tried again, "Jody, do you know why I am afraid of fires?"

Only that your dad said you'd go to hell and burn forever. You still think you will, don't you? Oh, yeah, and you wished him there too, didn't you?

"What are you talking about? I never wished anyone would go to hell in my life."

Yes, you did. You were in junior high, walking home from school, remember? You saw him in the car with his girl-friend. You know you did.

If this was Jody, she had been right about my father. I had long forgotten the incident. I knew he had been running around with other women. My mother confided in me and I tried to console her. I hated to see how he was destroying her self-esteem. Then one day I had taken a different route home from school and there he was, sitting in a car, hugging and kissing some blond woman I'd never seen before. I wanted them both to die and burn up. I wanted it so badly, it seemed the car had burst into flames before my very eyes and I ran away. Just as I reached the corner, I looked back and was shocked to see the car sitting there, undamaged, its two occupants oblivious to my presence. Yes, I certainly had wanted them to go to hell—he said *I* would, and there *he* was, for a moment in the flames.

I stared at a crack in the sidewalk before me. I wondered how this memory had surfaced. Had there been someone talking to me? I felt dizzy. Was Jack right? Had I somehow divided as a child and become two different people in the same body? So much made sense with his explanation, but it all seemed so strange. What would have made this happen? And what was I going to do about it if it was true? Worse. What if it wasn't true? What if Jack was wrong? Am I really crazy in spite of Jack's opinion?

Oh, Jack, I've got to see you. I can't do this alone.

The following Monday, I called Jack and set up another appointment. However, he was going to be out of town and it would be several weeks before I could see him, but this had to be resolved. In those weeks, I tried more and more to converse with Jody in my head. Slowly I began again to hear her answers. Was she real or was I getting worse? I was anxious to talk with Jack, both excited and fearful.

Winter struck hard during the night before the appointment. The rain froze and light snow sugarcoated the frosted pavement. In the morning I was tempted to skip my appointment. I was used to a lot worse weather in the Midwest, but nothing I had experienced had prepared me to deal with the "black ice" of the Northwest. I was afraid I'd find some of those invisible slick patches on the long, hilly drive between home and Jack's office. But today I would drive very carefully. Now, if Jack didn't cancel my appointment. . .

Maybe he would. Maybe I wanted him to. It wasn't merely the treacherous roads. I was afraid of knowing, *really* knowing, that I wasn't always in control, that Jody was real. I looked at my left hand and remembered three little holes that weren't there. Yes, what the Jody of my mind said was right; I always believed I was crazy. It was easy. Stress could do anything to your mind if it got too bad, even make you see and believe things that didn't happen. Jody must be one more aspect of my insanity.

Was I more than one person? I searched back, looking for a clue. I had found myself in strange places and not known how or why. Did the "other person" take me there and give

me back "control." How was that possible and why wouldn't
I know?

I needed help, someone besides Jack. Who could I talk to?
Who could I trust with my state of mind?

Dave. Pastor Dave. He was the only person I knew who
would trust me completely. Right now that was even more
important than my trusting him. If he would go with me to
Jack's, I could prove this thing out one way or another. If he
saw and talked to this other person, this Jody, I would know
for sure. But would he do that?

Dave knew I was struggling with my illness. If anyone
would help me sort this out, he could and would. I put my
hand on the phone, but I couldn't quite make the call. Why?
Didn't I want to know? No, I didn't want to know.

Make the call, Jody was saying. You need to know I'm
real.

What did *she* want? Was it Jody? If it was, why did she
want me to know? How else could I handle this? There
wasn't any way to get better unless I knew what the problem
was and worked on it.

I forced my fingers to move.

"Dave?" I was startled when I heard his voice. Somehow
I had expected the church secretary to answer. "Are you
busy? Could I come by and see you for a little bit today?"

Sure. Sure. I could come. He was probably the most bur-
dened man I knew, but somehow he always had—no,
made—time for everyone who popped in with yet another
problem.

As I drove to Dave's office at the church, the day began
to warm and rain began to fall, washing away my worry of
the ice on the hills. If only I could stick my head out the window and let the rain wash away my insanity as well.

Dave sat next to me in his office.

"You know I've had a lot of mental difficulties the last
few years, and I've been seeing a psychiatrist," I started.

Pastor Dave nodded.

"I'd like your help. Could you go with me to my appointment with the doctor today?"

"How can that help? What do you need me to do?"

I leaned forward on my hands, pinching my nose with my fingertips as I looked at Dave's sincerely concerned face. I knew I could trust him.

"Dr. Reiter says I have multiple personality disorder. Do you know what that is?"

"I've heard of it."

"Well, I hadn't, or at least I didn't remember what it was until Jack said I had it. In any case, I don't know what is going on with me. I don't know if that's happening to me or not. I need someone who can give me a honest appraisal of what they see and hear. I need someone I can trust and who believes in me. You're the only person I know that fits."

"You know I'd do anything to help you, Jean," Dave assured me. "I haven't had any experience with multiple personality, but I'll do my best. Sure, I'll go with you." He gave my hand a squeeze.

"I can't tell you how much I appreciate your help." I nearly cried. Why God provided me with strong, loving support whenever I was in crisis was beyond my understanding, but it seemed as if He always did.

I called Jack to tell him about bringing Dave along. I was sure that Jack was glad I was willing to seriously consider his diagnosis.

The appointment with Jack was late that afternoon. As I drove there, I explained my fears.

"Dave, there are so many things about this that I don't understand. So many memories that I know simply aren't true. So many unexplained circumstances, I couldn't begin to tell you in the next hour. In a way, Jack's explanation of what's going on with me makes sense. But if it's true, and I do mean *if*, it's even scarier."

"What would you like me to do?" Dave didn't seem to be dismayed at all, just concerned for my well-being, as always.

"Jack says he can get Jody, that's what he calls the other person, to talk to you. Oh, Dave, this seems too incredible to be real."

"Take it easy. It's going to be all right." He put his hand over my tight grip on the steering wheel. Somehow just his touch made me relax a bit.

I sighed and continued, "I guess what I need most from you is some verification that what's happening to me is real. You're the one person I can trust to see what's going on and tell me when you know." Now I did feel like crying. I trusted my sister Sandra, too, but she would believe what Jack told her. Dave wouldn't be swayed unless he actually witnessed the changes.

As I pulled into a parking space outside Jack's office, my stomach began its nervous knotting. I wanted to sit there in the car and talk to Dave. I dreaded going into Jack's office.

"This is it?" Dave looked around the street. There was no sign on the side of the house. Only a small bronze placard that hung next to the door on the porch identified Jack and his associate's offices.

"Yes."

I had to go immediately or back out. I jerked open the door. As I forced myself out, the breeze that hit my face seemed almost warm. The rain had stopped and the ice beside the car had nearly turned to slush.

"I think we're just about on time," Dave commented, looking at his watch as he stepped out. He brought his head up into a large branch of a close bush and was rewarded with a shower of melting snow.

"Whoa. I bathed before I left this morning. I don't need this."

"That's what you get for watching the clock." I laughed.

It was a major relief. I wondered if he had done it on purpose.

As we walked up the steps into the house, I tried to distract my mind. I hated that shade of blue. Who would ever paint a house such an ugly color?

Once inside, my senses seemed to be raw, aware of every stimulus. I could smell the wood polish that had been applied to the dark wood handrails and doors, and the scent of the fresh coffee from the kitchen. I could hear the typewriter clicking away in the back office and children playing in an upstairs waiting room.

"Don't be so anxious." Dave squeezed my shoulder as we walked into Jack's waiting room. He could see my distress.

My eyes swept the room trying to decide where to sit, but before I could land, Jack appeared at the door.

"Hi. I'm Jack Reiter," he said, enthusiastically shaking Dave's hand. "You must be Dave."

"Yes, how do you do?" Dave smiled broadly.

I looked at the two of them together, the two people who had seen parts of my heart and mind that no one else had ever seen, and now what would they share?

We moved into Jack's office. Of the three chairs opposite Jack's, I took the middle one, forcing Dave to choose to sit beside me. He selected the one to my left, forcing me to be unable to look at both Jack and him at the same time. I was sorry I had made my choice.

Jack took about twenty minutes to fill Dave in on my condition. Of course I kept catching myself shaking my head. It was hard for me to believe. I wondered what Dave would think.

"I'll tell you one thing this has done for me," Jack told Pastor Dave. "It's made it possible for me to treat Jean again. For a couple of years of working with Jean, I was at a loss. I didn't know what was going on with her. I didn't know how to help her. It was very frustrating and I stopped seeing her for a while. She had been sending me dreams that were confusing, given Jean's persona. However, when I first met Jody, the dreams made sense; clearly they were the dreams of more than one person. I guess, in the back of my mind, I had been processing the possibility of multiplicity, though I hadn't yet made that conclusion. However, that part of the thought process made it easy for me to recognize and accept Jody the first time she came into my office."

Dave was very understanding. "I've known Jean for several years now. She's been a part of the church and involved with the refugee program. She makes friends easily and has a lot of them in the church. I can't say that I've ever seen anything 'different' about her behavior over the time I've known her."

"Jody may not be the churchgoing type," Jack commented. "In fact, I would be very surprised if she'd ever been inside of a church, that is, except with Jean. She has a different set of morality rules than Jean has, few responsibilities except to herself, and little connection with family. She hates Hank and claims the girls aren't her kids."

Finally Jack turned to me. "What do you think? Are you ready to let Jody talk with Dave?"

"To tell the truth Jack, I'm scared to death about it. I keep thinking that he'll think I'm acting this all out."

I glanced at Dave out of the corner of my eye. He was sitting forward in his chair, attentive, concerned, but not skeptical.

"No. Dave will see the same differences I've seen. I don't think there's any question."

I turned to look at him. "Dave, I need you to believe I don't know what's going on. I need your help, maybe more than Jack's right now."

Dave reached over and gripped my arm reassuringly. "There's no reason not to believe this, Jean. I came so I could help you."

"So now, Jean, if we could talk with Jody . . . ?"

I looked down at my hands. My palms were up and the fingers were loosely interlaced. As I bowed my head, my nose began to run slightly and I sniffed. The office was too warm.

Could I give control to Jody? Who was Jody? I felt too hot. I should have taken this coat off. Jody?

I looked up. *God, I'm tense. Oops, sorry God . . . Okay Jean, I won't blasphemize. I'm just tense and hot.* I loosened my coat and pushed the hair off my ears and fluffed it off my neck.

"Jody?" Jack smiled. "Do you know this guy?" He gestured to the fellow sitting next to me in his long dark overcoat.

Did I know him? I knew him from somewhere, a friend of Jean's. Oh, yeah—from church.

"I think so. Aren't you the church pastor?"

His smile was quickly overshadowed by a pair of frowning eyebrows. "So you're Jody?"

"Ah, yes, it's me, and Jack has painted such a lovely picture of me—selfish, uncaring, irresponsible—did I miss anything, Jack? Yes, I did forget something, but you're wrong, Jack, I don't have a different set of rules about morality. I just didn't happen to marry Hank, so I'm not bound by matrimonial law." I was too angry at Jack to be civil for Dave. Jack's implications that I was promiscuous hurt. I'd told him about Edward and Brian so that he could understand some of Jean's confusion. I had tried to help, and he had turned it against me.

"I'm not trying to be negative," Jack replied. "What I was trying to do was to point out the differences between Jean and you for Dave."

"Like what?"

"For instance, tell Dave about your family."

This was just great, I thought sarcastically. *Let's bring in the whole world.* I'd tried so hard to protect Jean, pretending to be her, so she wouldn't have everyone know what a nut she was. Now here was Jack hauling in Jean's pastor. *Oh, well, Jean, you asked for it.*

"Wellll." I drew out the word like Jack Benny. I turned slightly to face Pastor Dave and tilted my head to the side. "Let's see. Jean married Hank. I didn't. Jean had Erin, Teresa, and Melissa. I didn't. I'm not married; I don't have any kids. I don't have a job and I don't have anyone to take care of but me." I turned quickly back. "Isn't that right, Jack?"

"How long have you been around?" Jack ignored my snide reply.

"That's a hard question to answer. As long as I can remember." I was still irritated by his introduction of me to Pastor Dave.

"And how long is that?" Jack pressed.

"It's a chicken and egg question, Jack."

I glanced back at Dave. He was sitting forward, almost on the edge of his chair, straining to see my face as I bandied with Jack. He looked as though he wasn't sure about the whole visit. Maybe he was sorry he came at all. He didn't seem to have anything to say, but then I guessed that Jack was questioning me for Dave's benefit, so he wouldn't have to say anything.

"Okay, are you the chicken or the egg?" Jack asked.

Deep sigh. "Look, Jack, we talked about this before. I don't know if Jean was first or me. I do remember that it was Jean who played with her daddy and was guilty, not me. That was at about three, okay? I don't remember anything before that, but then I doubt if Jean can either. So, who's the chicken?"

"Well, can you tell Dave anything about your life?"

Looking up at the ceiling, I sighed again, leaned back in

my chair, and rubbed my neck with both hands. I rubbed my upper molars with my tongue. If Jack was looking for a confession of my sins to Pastor Dave, I wasn't going to offer it. I turned in my chair to face Dave. I pointed my left index finger at him like a small pistol.

"Listen," I said to Dave. "It wasn't my idea to come here in the first place. If you want a life history, talk to Jean. She and I have very little in common, except this body." I turned my hand and poked my chest with my left index finger. "Just because she has a job and works to support her kids—which *she* has to do because she's married to Hank, you understand—doesn't make her any more accountable than I am. Maybe I have even more responsibility if you really look at it. I have my own life to lead too, but I don't have the same opportunities Jean has. So I don't take her away from Hank and the girls. Nobody gives a crap if I'm happy in my life."

Dave seemed surprised and curious, but noncommittal.

Jack and I talked for the rest of the appointment time. I began to understand why Jack had let Jean bring Dave here. Jack was convinced that my life would be better if Jean accepted the situation and worked with me. Dave could provide Jean the assurance she needed that I was real.

Dave hardly said a word. I was sure he thought I was a self-centered witch, though I was just as sure he would never admit it. As we walked down the sidewalk, I realized that we were approaching Jean's car. Out of the corner of my eye, I watched Dave striding right along with me to it.

"I'm taking you home?" I left my mouth hanging open. Where was home?

"I hope you don't mind," Dave answered.

"No. No, not at all. It's just," I fumbled with how to ask him, "just that, well—I don't know where you live." I laughed nervously. What was he going to do with his new-found knowledge of me in Jean's head?

Dave laughed. "I didn't think about that. I came here with Jean. You don't share her information?"

"Of lots of things, yes, but not everything. I wasn't around today until Jack began talking about me, and I don't think I've ever been to your house."

"No. I guess not. Jean's only been there a couple of times. Head for your place and I'll direct you. I don't live too far from your house."

On the way home we talked some more about the differences between Jean and me.

"I'm sorry I was so bitchy in Jack's office. I'm not really like that usually. Somehow, he's twisted all around things I've told him. I love the kids, but they were born to Jean and Hank. Yeah, we shared this same body, and I have to tell you I did feel pretty stupid every time Jean got pregnant, but it was her. I didn't marry Hank. I can't stand the man. You should know; you've met him. He treats Jean like shit. I'm sorry. I shouldn't talk like that."

Pastor Dave smiled slightly and looked out the window.

"Look," I defended myself, "I believe in God as much as Jean does, but she is too deep into *religion* for my taste. I mean that God doesn't expect us to be perfect; that's what Christ was for, wasn't He? I know I'm not perfect; Jean just keeps trying to be."

"I'm curious though." Dave sounded almost apologetic. "Humm, do you mind if I ask you a few questions?"

"No—shoot. I didn't mean to be so blunt in Jack's office. He gets me pissed off sometimes."

"Well, Jean's told me about some difficult times while she was growing up. I'm wondering where you were during those periods."

"Dave, I don't know. I can't tell you where I was when lots of stuff happened. It's the same problem Jean has now. I lost time, days, back then, maybe months. I'm sorry I can't give you a better answer. Maybe if you told me what specific time or problem she talked about, I could figure out where I was then and what I was doing or not doing. By the time I was in high school, I had control more time than at any earlier period."

"That's interesting. How did you manage to go through high school?"

Uh-oh, here we go again, I thought—Jean's the responsible one. I smiled sheepishly. "Well, I have to admit it was Jean that got *us* through high school in terms of studying and grades and stuff like that. She's the one who could do the math and the English, and played in the orchestra and so on. But I did do some artwork, and I got us a lot of friends. I learned how to dance and drive a car better than she did. I dated guys in high school, while she had *a* boyfriend for a while. I know that all doesn't sound very important now, but it was back then."

By the time we arrived at Dave's house, I had hopes that he had a little better opinion of me than he had when we left Jack's office. I couldn't be sure. Jean would probably be angry at me, but she'd have to accept my existence and deal with it. I wondered what Dave would tell her.

It was nearly a week before I could meet with Dave again to see what he thought of Jody and me. He verified the differences in appearance and demeanor. Jody had been much more outspoken and confident than I normally seemed to be. He was very supportive and said he would follow up with Jack as well.

"It's quite something," Dave admitted. "I wasn't sure what I'd see when I went to Dr. Reiter's office, but it wasn't anything I could have expected. I was struggling through the session to accept what was going on. I'd heard of this sort of thing happening and I wondered, is this really what's going on? I was trying to comprehend it in my own mind, but Jody is so different from you, it's striking. I was a bit shocked at first in the office, but in the car on the way home, I could tell she'd been very angry with the doctor. She's real all right, and, as Jack says, you'll have to accept her existence."

At last, I began to feel that I had someone, someone outside Jack's office, who could aid me in this battle. I was grateful for Dave's understanding, but not the prospect of dealing with Jody.

SEVEN

FOR THE NEXT FEW MONTHS, I SAW JACK REGULARLY. HE called out Jody and I gave her control nearly every visit. He told me he was working to convince her that it would be better for both of us to cooperate. I began to hear more of Jody's comments in my head and some of the conversations that she had with Jack. But I was still struggling with my own belief that I was always in control and Jody was somehow a figment of my own imagination.

Jack confronted me with Jody's early memories of me.

"Can you tell me about your relationship as a child with your father?"

"I loved him very much, but I also hated him, well, at least a lot of the things he did. Sandra was five years younger than me. For a while I was sort of Dad's favorite. He took me everywhere with him. When I was eleven, I got ill and Dad began to take Sandra with him instead. I felt abandoned then."

"What about earlier?"

I withdrew into my youngest memories. I had been

naughty. My daddy and I played together. I knew it wasn't right, but I did whatever my daddy wanted.

"Jean?"

"I . . . it's very hard to talk about."

Jack waited as I decided what I could tell him. I was beginning to feel shaky. I tried not to let it show.

"My father was into nudity. He walked around the house with nothing on a lot of the time. He slept nude. He'd sit in the living room and read the paper nude. I was afraid to bring my friends home because I never knew what to expect."

I shifted in my chair. I didn't want to go into the details.

"And . . . ?" Jack finally pressed.

"Oh, Jack, it's so hard. I feel guilty, dirty. When Mom was gone, he used to pull me into bed with him. He liked me to feel him and he caressed me. He didn't hurt me or anything."

"How old were you then?"

"I'm not sure, probably three or so, maybe younger. I don't remember."

I felt shamed. I shook my head and put my hand over my mouth.

"What are you thinking?" Jack asked.

"He told me not to tell. He told me over and over. I knew it was wrong. I felt so guilty."

"A three-year-old can't be responsible for what her parent tells her to do."

My knees were weak and my head was spinning.

"I suspect this was about the time Jody came about," Jack said. "A very young child can't deal with sexual abuse."

"He didn't hurt me."

"Jean, do you think it's normal for a three-year-old to have sexual contact with an adult?"

"No. I just mean abuse seems too harsh a word."

"Abuse means misuse, improper conduct, harmful to the abused. You don't think that word applies?"

"Yes, . . . I guess . . . I guess it was abuse." I covered my face with my hands.

Jack eased me out of the issue before he sent me home, asking me about my job and the project I was working on. I dreamt horrid nightmares of fires and danger for several days.

My speculations about Jody haunted me. Jack knew details of my life experiences that I had not told him. It worried me.

Finally I decided I needed to haul my sister Sandra down to Jack's office with me. I explained to her what Jack thought was happening. I related Pastor Dave's visit, but emphasized how much more I needed her support—someone close, someone who'd known me all my life.

When we went to the appointment, Jack offered us tea or coffee. As I sat waiting while Jack got Sandra a cup, I wondered if this meeting was a mistake. What if the whole thing backfired? What if Sandra didn't believe me? I needed her. Who else did I have? Pastor Dave had believed what he saw and heard, but Sandra and I had been soul mates through so much. I had been as supportive as I could during her divorce and a new relationship she had developed with a fellow named Ben. I told her I would stand behind her decision whatever it was, and I did. When the rest of the family tried to talk her into sticking it out with her husband, Carl, I told her she had to do what was right for her. Well, not all the family; our brother Mark, bless his heart, had said, "Carl had his chance and he blew it. Let's hear it for Ben!"

Sandra had supported me during all my craziness too. But now she was going to see Jody. What if she thought it was me? Maybe she would think I was acting. I'd lose her trust. Maybe there was still time to end this before it started.

"You sure you don't want anything?" Jack asked me, as he handed Sandra her coffee.

"No, I'm fine."

Too late. I was committed to showing Jody to Sandra.

Why are you worried? Give the girl some credit. Sandra's always been there for you.

Were Jody's thoughts coming through? Okay, okay.

Sandra sat on the couch close to Jack's office door as he came in. She quickly moved to the chair opposite me, where she could place her coffee on the little table that separated our chairs.

"Well," Jack asked as he sat down, "what do you think, Jean? Can we talk with Jody?"

Right now? I was stunned. Somehow I had expected some time, some lead-in, something.

"I . . . I'll see. I'll see if I can get her." I was nervous, rubbing one hand against the other's knuckles, as though it were a magic lamp from which a genie would appear and take me from this awful situation. Could I do this? Jody . . . ?

I smiled and stretched a little, trying to loosen the kinks in my shoulders. Jean was really too tense. I pushed my hair back behind my ears and off my neck. It looked so much better that way.

"Well, well. Here we are again." I smiled at Sandra.

"Wow," she replied quietly, amazed. Then she tilted her head slightly, curiously, and with barely squinted eyes asked, "Again?"

"Sure. You and I have spent lots of time together, although not for quite some time." She'll remember me, I thought confidently. We were naughty together too much for her not to know.

"Can you tell me when? Give me an example?"

"Let's see . . ." I sat rubbing my palms on the wood armrests. "When we were both living at home, we did a lot of things together. Remember when it got really hot—I'd get you out of bed, and we'd drag the mattress onto the back upstairs porch?"

"That was you?"

"Yeah."

Sandra smiled broadly and her eyes reflected the memory. "I do remember pulling the mattress out on the porch. And I do remember you. Just now, it was the change in demeanor that surprised me. Jean was so tense, leaning forward, clasping her hands. When you appeared—leaning back, relaxed, fluffing your hair—well, that was the key for me. It was that single movement that I remembered seeing, reaching behind your neck and pushing up your hair."

I wasn't surprised. I had expected Sandra to recognize me.

"And you and I slipped out and climbed off the porch to go lie down, right in the middle of Logan Street and Miami Avenue at three in the morning one Sunday, only to say we'd done it."

Sandra shook her head. "I don't remember that, but we could have. So much of my memory is lost."

"Logan and Miami was the busiest intersection near our house during the day," I explained to Jack. "But Saturday night all the bars had to close at midnight for Indiana's blue laws, and nothing was open on Sunday. So by three o'clock in the morning, the town was deserted."

I looked at Sandra again. "Yes, Jean was little Miss Goody Two-shoes, and I was probably a bad influence in your life, but we did have a lot of fun, didn't we?"

"How do you think you were a bad influence on my life?"

"Remember how I used to take you and Mark down to the park early Sunday morning so we didn't have to go to church with Dad? I even brought the Bible with us so we could have our own little service in the band shelter before we went to the playground."

Sandra shook her head no. "I can't recall much of anything from my childhood years. I used to joke with the family about not being able to remember anything about the house we grew up in for the first fifteen years of my life. Now it's become a frightening problem. I don't know what secrets are blocked from my mind. I think seeing you and Jean as separate entities helps me understand some of what happened back then. Jean seems so obedient and responsible and you seem so . . . so free."

"I think working with you and Sandra together might help both of you," Jack said. I smiled at the prospect of spending more time with Sandra again.

"I never forgot the people next door with their dogs, though," Sandra said smiling. "You and I used to throw acorns off the porch into the yard and drive those dogs nuts, remember? That was you, wasn't it?" Now that Sandra realized what was going on, she seemed immediately to know when I'd been there instead of Jean. It pleased me to know that she accepted the situation so easily.

"Yeah, and we used to watch the people who moved in after those folks left, fighting in their kitchen. We could see down into it from our bedroom window." I laughed.

"What I recall most about you was being with your girlfriend Becky," Sandra said. "You used to take me with you, something Jean almost never did. You and Becky taught me naughty little songs like 'Roll Me over in the Clover.' We played fun games together. You say you were a bad influence, but what I remember is that you spiced up our lives, gave us the laughter."

"From my earlier meetings with Jody, I think it's safe to say that Jody was probably the healthier of the two, between Jean and Jody," Jack interjected. "I wasn't so sure at first, but Jean is very dependent and subject to depression. Jody seems to have a more positive outlook on life. I've gained a better understanding of Jody's relationship with other people than I had previously. Hopefully we can work this through so it's that healthier personality that survives."

"Certainly I have a more positive outlook. It's easy. You don't put up with all the crap people try to dump on you. If you don't want to be knocked around, you get the hell out."

"Listen," Sandra asked me, "was it you or Jean that used to hide in the closet with me?"

"Ha! It was me. We used to crawl into the big boxes of clothes in our closet and hide under the clothes, especially when Dad came looking for us."

"I thought so," said Sandra. "First we were scared. We'd be so quiet until we were sure Dad had gone downstairs looking for us. Then we'd start whispering and pretty soon we'd be laughing, until we got into laughing fits so hard we cried."

"Yeah, that was a lot of fun," I agreed. "We could hear him stomping back and forth, looking for one of us. He was sure we were there somewhere. He would even come into our room and look in the closet. We'd hold our breath and be scared to death. Then after he was gone, we'd giggle and laugh. It's a wonder he never did find us."

Jack had been sitting back enjoying our conversation, but he interrupted, turning to Sandra and said, "I think you can see the differences today. I think we'd better get Jean back now and see what she thinks."

I was sorry. I wanted to spend more time with Sandra. It had gone too quickly, but I understood the need to give control back to Jean. If we were going to work together to solve our life, Jean had to recognize me and what had happened. Jack had convinced me of that. Who knows, maybe we could get rid of Hank? So it was important for Jean to know that Sandra accepted me. I gave her one last smile.

Okay, Jean, your turn.

• • •

I slumped a bit in the chair, pressing the bridge of my nose between my thumb and fingers.

"Well?" I asked Sandra.

"Oh, I remember Jody and you as separate people," she replied. "We talked about so many of the fun things Jody and I did together."

"Like what?"

"Dragging the mattress out on the porch on hot nights."

"Yeah. I got in a lot of trouble over that," I said. I pictured Dad looking out his window and just barely seeing the corner of our mattress on the porch, followed by his screaming at me about getting the mattress all dirty on the bottom. I caught the flack, usually the back of his hand; Sandra was too little. But I smiled and shook my head. "So Jody did that, and not you?"

"Yup," Sandra said, smiling.

"So why didn't she stick around to take the punishment for it?"

"We overslept, I guess. I think she would have pulled the mattress back into our room if we had awakened earlier. She was good at hiding out and avoiding Dad."

"Yeah, we had to do a lot of that."

Sandra and I chatted for a while on the way home. Then we were silent as we each processed our thoughts of what had taken place. If I was really two people, which Sandra confirmed, how would I end up if I worked with Jody? I didn't understand the process. I was worried and sad. Jack had thought Jody was a healthier personality than I. Would she survive; would I? Tears began to cloud my eyesight.

"If Jody is going to survive, Sandra, what is to become of me? Will I just disappear?"

Sandra was obviously shaken and didn't have an answer.

In the weeks that followed, Sandra and I worked together on Sandra's loss of memory and my dealings with Jody. Sandra talked more about how Jody taught her to hide and run away from Dad. We shared books on recovery. Sandra lent me a copy of *Scream Louder*, a book on the experience and healing of an incest survivor and her therapist. One night as I was reading it, I became more and more depressed. It was not only that I identified with the victim, but more that I identified her father with mine. The parallel was easy. While my father was not an alcoholic, he was just as demanding as the man in the book, and just as unpredictable.

I recognized the victim's fear in the book. She was a child, what could she do? Her fears had been my fears. As a child, what could I do? We both had tried to second-guess our fathers. What rules had priority? Would I be punished for doing one thing, or should I do something else to prevent his displeasure, at the risk of being punished for that? I mustn't say the wrong thing; mustn't even look at him wrong or he might interpret my thoughts as disagreement. I had to look at him while he was talking and I'd better display the proper face—smile if I should smile; look submissive and obedient, even apologetic, if he was lecturing. Fear controlled my life then.

The more I thought about it, the more I understood why Jody had hidden and escaped from Dad and from my life in that household as much as she could. When she had been there, she had fought with him, as apparently she did with Hank now. Well, not right now. Hank was off to his mother's for the hundredth time or so, and only the girls and I were home. Our finances were a wreck, but I needed the break from Hank to deal with my mental welfare.

I put the book down and curled up in my bed. I was too tired to think anymore and went to sleep. . . .

I was three or four years old in my dream.

"Get your shoes and socks on," my daddy demanded.

"Yes, Daddy," I answered, afraid. Why wasn't I ready to

•

go? I ran back to my bedroom and found my little white socks on the floor. They were almost too small for me to get on, but I did. Where were my shoes? They weren't there. They weren't under my bed. In my closet? No. I began to panic.

I ran to my parents' bedroom and looked under the bed. I saw only Daddy's brown shoes.

"Jean, come on," he called down the hall. "We're going to be late."

What could I do? I'd wear his shoes. I pulled them out from under the bed and put my right foot into the right shoe. It was huge and my foot was so small. I put the other foot into the other shoe and tried to take a step. The shoe slipped off immediately.

Now what could I do? I couldn't find my shoes. How could I wear these? I stepped out of them and ran across the room to a laundry basket in the corner. I rummaged through it quickly, knocking some of the clothes on the floor. Oh, no! Now I'd have to pick those up too. I pulled out a big pair of white socks, threw them on the bed, and began tossing the spilled clothes back in the basket.

"Jean!"

Terrified, I hurried back to the bed and pulled the thick socks over mine, leaving a lot of the sock hanging off my toes to squish into the ends of the big shoes. I stuffed one sock and foot into the shoe and tried to tie it. I didn't know how, but I managed to get one knot. I could lift the shoe without it falling off.

Before I could get the second one on, Daddy stood at the bedroom door. "What the hell are you doing?"

"I couldn't find my shoes." I tried to crouch down to make myself even smaller.

Just before his huge hand met my face, I jerked myself awake.

•   •   •

Well, I was trying to put his shoes on; that was my first thought. I immediately tried to dismiss it. I was a very little child in the dream. Why wasn't my daddy helping to find and put on my shoes? Because he never considered a child as being a child?

Suddenly an incident I had discussed with Sandra came back to me. Dad had thrown a gallon of milk at her and Mark. She had been eight when it took place, Mark ten, and I was thirteen. Sandra was glad to have her memory validated. Now I remembered it with the fear and helplessness I'd felt.

I saw myself as a young girl at the keyboard of the upright piano. Dad came stomping into the house, his arms full of groceries and a couple gallons of milk in glass jugs. He was swearing about having dropped a gallon on the cement steps that led from the street up to the house.

I turned on the bench to face him as he passed through the living room. What should I do or say? Should I tell him I was sorry he dropped the milk? Should I offer to help him? That might make him turn his anger toward me. I bit my lip and said nothing as he hurried past me into the kitchen.

Suddenly I was more afraid. Sandra and Mark were eating grilled cheese sandwiches at the kitchen table. Mark might provoke Dad further.

"Why do you try to carry everything at one time?" Mark asked sarcastically, confirming my fear. "You always drop the milk."

Oh, Mark! I thought, why did you say that when you know how angry he is already?

Suddenly both Mark and Sandra screamed. I froze for an instant, and in that instant, there was a tremendous crash. Mark yelled again and kept it up, but Sandra was suddenly silent.

Had he killed them? I leapt from the bench and ran into

the kitchen, bumping into Dad as he stomped out. He shoved me aside and I banged into the closet door. He didn't even notice me.

"You clean that mess up," he yelled back at the kids.

As I entered the room, it was obvious what he'd done. The gallon he'd thrown had hit the wall a foot or so above Mark's head. Milk and splintered glass had rained down over both Sandra and Mark. The wall ran ghastly white. The kids were soaked with milk, as were the table, the benches, and the floor. Glass shards, large and minute, lay everywhere, especially on the kids. Several large splinters of glass were sticking in Sandra's arm. Mark's neck was also beginning to bleed from the shower of broken glass.

I wanted to cry out, "Mommy!" I wanted to scream for her to come and take care of these children, but she wasn't home. I wanted to run out the back door, run and run. I felt instantly guilty. They needed my help. I couldn't run away. I looked at Sandra. Her eyes were glazed in shock. Mark was screaming hysterically.

"It's okay." I tried to reassure them. "It's okay. Stop, Mark. I'll help you. Sandra, are you okay?" I picked one of the splinters from her arm and she began to cry. I tried not to be upset or cry. I needed to be calm. I didn't want to frighten them more.

Mark began to brush the glass from his hair. He had stopped screaming, but was crying incessantly.

"Don't move, Mark, or you'll make it worse. I'll get the glass." What could I do? They both needed help. I couldn't panic. There was no one else to help.

I picked the rest of the splinters from Sandra's arm and wiped her hair and shoulders of her dress with the kitchen towel. "Go upstairs and take this off. Be careful of the glass. Don't cut your face getting it over your head. Don't cry. You're okay. I'll get Band-Aids for you in just a minute."

Obediently she rose from the bench and walked slowly away toward the stairs. She was crying, still shocked.

I ran around the table to Mark. Huge pieces of the milk jug had hit him and fallen behind the bench. Fortunately none of them had cut him seriously. I didn't know what to do. My dish towel was already wet from the milk and probably full of glass from wiping off Sandra. I fought tears of helplessness.

"Okay, Mark." I tried to sound confident. "Slide out that way, where Sandra was. Watch the glass."

I went back around the table and met him at Sandra's spot. There I could pick the glass from his hair and neck easier. Milk ran down his face and I grabbed a paper towel to dry it. A glass splinter scratched his forehead when I wiped it and he began to bleed there, too.

"Ow! Watch it," Mark cried. He grabbed his head with both hands.

My fear and sorrow for him suddenly became anger, oscillating between Mark and Dad. Why did he have to say something to make Dad even madder? Why did Dad do something so stupid?

"I think I got most of the glass off you. Don't cry now. You're okay. Go up and get the wet things off, carefully, though. There's still some splinters on your shirt. I'll get some Band-Aids."

I looked at his pudgy little face, stained with tears and milk and drops of blood. I wanted to hug him and cry, but I was afraid of getting wet and cut from glass that might still be on his shirt. How I hated Dad. And there was still a big mess to clean up. . . .

I pulled myself out of bed, trying to shake off my revulsion of that memory. I tried to examine my thoughts and reactions as the therapist in *Scream Louder* had done. I felt that I had not been the victim here; Mark and Sandra were the victims. I had been playing a co-dependent role, invalidating my siblings' feelings of fear and pain. I felt guilty that I could not have reacted as I should, but I was a child from the same environment. I couldn't scream at my father, but what I should have done was calmly call the police to send help for the kids. That way, everyoney would have had a very realistic view of what had happened, but it never occurred to me back then.

As I thought of Sandra and Mark, I pictured their sizes. Yes, they must have been eight and ten. Dad had his crippled hand, which is why he "always" dropped the milk. Mark had been right, of course. Dad shouldn't have tried to carry so much. But Mark was also wrong to have pointed this out to the angry man, at least not with a snide attitude. Of course this last thought validated Dad's enforced premise that children were never to voice their opinions to their parents, especially if they were negative.

How should I have reacted? I had to be responsible for the kids. No one was there to care for them. Where was Mom anyway? Was she working? I figured she must have gone to one of her friend's homes and taken the rest of the kids with her.

Mark had made a remark many years ago, that if anything ever happened to Mom, the center of the family circle would just switch to be around me. I was pleased when he said it, but now I realized that it was because I had been forced into the mother role all my life. I know as I have struggled with my guilt over my own children that I also have fought with my guilt over my sibling children. Mom, where were you? And exactly where was I?

In the weeks that followed that memory, I discussed it with Sandra and Jack. Each reacted differently.

When I spoke with her, Sandra said, "It makes sense. Even as you tell me about it, I feel the same shocked feeling. The way I remembered this at all was related to Dad's accident. I was thinking about it when I was driving home one day. I pictured the wall covered with red blood. Then all at once it was white, instead of red. Little by little I remembered seeing milk on the wall, but it took me a long while to remember the milk was tied to an entirely different traumatic event in my life than the blood."

In my visit with Jack, he said, "Of course you were the victim, as well as Sandra and Mark. How can you say you weren't?"

"It isn't that I wasn't the victim. It's that I couldn't react to the horror of what had happened. I cleaned the kids up and sent them on their way, as if nothing terrible had really occurred. I helped to cover the bloody path for that unreasonable man."

Jack sat there and watched as I fought not to display my defensive smile as I said, "That man is stupid. Stupid! How could he do that?"

"And Mom?" Jack asked.

"I don't know. Did she even know this happened? Did anyone tell her? Did she find the mess? I didn't clean it up."

"You didn't?" Jack asked in his monotone voice.

I knew he didn't believe me.

"Oh, shoot, you know I did. He told the kids to clean it up and I knew they wouldn't or couldn't, so of course I did. I probably cleaned up the damn steps outside, too."

EIGHT

I ABANDONED MY STRUGGLE WITH JODY FOR A TIME TO BAT-
tle with day-to-day living. Hank had returned again and gotten himself a computer operating job for a hardware
company. He had worked the day shift and was home in the
evenings and night now. It made it hard on all of us. He had
no sympathy for my therapy process, though he expounded
on how evil people were to abuse their children physically.
He had always hated my father. Whether Hank was aware of
it or not, he was teaching his own children to hate their father.

"Okay, guys, time for dinner. Melissa, call your dad. He's
in the family room, watching TV."

Erin had been home from school for two days with an ear-
ache and sore throat. She crawled off the couch and slipped
into a chair. Melissa and Teresa sat on either side of her. We
said grace and started eating. When Hank's TV program
ended, he joined us.

At the dinner table, I saw Erin with her elbows resting on
the table as she ate her roll. Hank sat directly across from
her, next to me. Poor kid, I thought, I should have taken her

dinner to her. Even so, I knew Hank would never allow her to eat with her elbows on the table.

As I started to warn her, Hank glared at her and said, "Get your elbows off the table, Erin."

She quickly complied, and he replied in the same angry tone, "Thank you."

Erin glanced at me in fear.

"You roll your eyes like that one more time and you can leave the table!"

She dropped her roll onto her plate and started, "Dad—" but Hank interrupted her, "That's it—go from the table!"

"No, I didn't do anything."

"What do you call rolling your eyes every time I tell you to do something? And throwing your roll in your plate?"

"I didn't do anything rude. How can you know what I'm thinking? Can you read my mind?"

She began to cry.

"No, but I can read your actions."

"Hank?" He ignored me.

Glaring at Erin, he demanded, "I'll give you ten seconds to apologize to me or leave the table."

"Hank? Hank, are you going to talk to me or not?" I was almost yelling.

He turned to me angrily. "What?"

"What has she done that's so terrible that she has to leave?"

"She knows what she's done and you *should*, too! Would you let her keep her elbows on the table?"

"No—"

"Well, all right, then." He returned his glare to Erin, "Have you made up your mind yet?"

Erin began biting her knuckle, tears running down her cheek, and Teresa started crying too. Melissa looked into her lap, trying to avoid the confrontation.

I tried to intervene, but again he ignored me. "Hank?"

"Then go. Get up and leave the table."

"Erin," I asked softly, "are you finished eating?"

"No." She quickly wiped the tears from her cheeks.

Hank suddenly jumped up from the table. "Then I'll go. That's what you want, damn it! Okay, I'll go!"

He picked up his chair and threw it into the corner of the wall by the back door. The bottom brace broke off and flew across the room into the birdcage, shaking the cage violently. He stomped quickly to the stairway, but then turned and charged back to the table. As he grabbed his cigarettes, he shot one last hateful glare at Erin. As he ran off again, he kicked the birdcage with his foot, and the cage went tumbling off its stand onto the floor, the birds screeching in terror. The cage rolled a couple feet, clattering as bird food, gravel, and water showered the floor.

I grabbed the cage and set it back on the stand, and everyone started screaming at Hank, including the birds, who were hurling themselves against the cage sides in outraged frenzy.

Erin was livid. "You didn't have to hurt our pets! They didn't do anything to you!"

Teresa overcame her timidity and cried, "The birds! Why would you hit the birds?"

Even Melissa came to life. "Why don't you just leave us alone?"

"Yes, you go, you stupid bastard. You go. You think it's so terrible people abuse their children's bodies; well, you abuse their minds. You're stupid. Stupid. Stupid!" I went on yelling long after he slammed the door at the bottom of the stairs. I couldn't believe my own words, but I could keep calm no longer after he struck the birdcage.

I tried not to cry as I hugged the girls. "It will be okay."

"The birds won't ever trust us again," said Erin.

"Yes, they will. Just give them time to settle down." I put

the water and food dishes and the toys back on the sides of the cage. The birds were no longer flying all over it.

Erin sat on the floor next to the cage and continued to cry softly. Teresa went into the living room and began to make paper origami as though nothing had happened. I looked at her and wondered what was going on in that little head.

After I sent the girls to their beds, I crept quietly into my own, avoiding Hank.

What could he have been thinking? I knew when Erin glanced at me, the first time Hank addressed her, she was scared. She knew at that moment, no matter what she did, she was in for a battle. He was already glaring at her—nothing would avert a further attack on her. Why did she have to be afraid? Children had a right to react and a right to their own opinions. The fact that they complied with their parents' demands was enough. They should not be forced to agree or not react at all.

I slid over the edge of the bed and knelt, dropping my head to the blanket.

"Dear Lord, I know that you know what is happening here. Help me, please. You know how hard I've tried to make this marriage work, but I can't do this alone. I can't control Hank. How can I help my girls? He frightens them so much. He frightens me. Please show me what to do, Lord. Please guide me. I ask in Jesus' name. Amen."

I crawled back into bed. Sometime in the night Hank joined me.

I rose early in the morning, poured a glass of orange juice and sat at the table, staring down the hall at the bedroom door. Hank was still sleeping. I didn't know how to solve this. What would I do when he woke up? Would he act as if nothing had happened? I wanted to demand that he apologize to the girls for attacking their birds. He would undoubtedly feel justified. I believed he would also feel that because I didn't back him up when he was "disciplining" one of the girls, I was at fault for most of what happened. I wanted to kick something too, maybe a block of wood, but not the kids or their birds.

However, Hank slept until the girls were dressed and off to school. I left too, grateful that I didn't have to argue with him, but I still hadn't resolved the problem. What was I going to do?

It was late in the afternoon when I pulled into the parking lot of the strip mall. If Jean was not going to solve the problem, then I would, and I knew how.

The letters on the glass door read "Elaine Willis and Steve Hardly." As I pushed it open, the cute young thing behind an undersized desk was startled from her concentration. I thought she had been staring down at her empty desk.

"Hi, I mean, how do you do?" she said, flustered, nudging her nail file under her desk blotter with two fingertips. "What can we do for you?"

I smiled at the "we." It reminded me of hospital nurses. The front room of the small office was empty, except for this pixie with tiny bows clipped randomly in her brown, curly hair.

"Hi, I'm Jody Marshall. I'd like to see Elaine."

"Can I tell her what you want to see her about?"

Can she ask me that? I thought business with a lawyer was strictly private.

"Is Elaine in?"

"Yes. I'll see if she's busy."

With one of her long, manicured fingernails, the pixie tapped a button on her phone.

"Yes?" answered a disembodied woman's voice from the phone speaker.

"There's a—" the pixie started to answer, instead looked up at me, "what did you say your name was again?"

"Oh, Jean Marshall." Watch it, Jody, you have to do this legally.

"There's a Jean Marshall here to see you."

A Jean Marshall, as if there were fourteen of us. Well, there is more than one, but she wouldn't know, I chuckled to myself.

"Okay, send her in." The voice seemed happy to hear anything to disrupt the dreadful silence of the office.

But I was wrong. When I nodded good-bye to the pixie and opened the designated door, classical music poured out.

I was amazed. "Wow! This must be one insulated room," I said to the neatly dressed lady behind her organized desk.

"Yes, we purposely chose this office because you can't hear anything from the waiting room." She rose and extended her hand. "Hi, I'm Elaine Willis."

I took the hand in mine and shook it. A warm, firm squeeze greeted me. Just right. I hate the dead-fish handshake that so many women seem to have.

"Hi, I'm Jean Marshall."

"What can I do for you, Jean?" She gestured for me to take the chair next to hers, as she returned to her own.

Both seats were dark wooden captain chairs, the kind you'd find in someone's dining room, except the seats were padded in dark brown leather. They looked slightly out of place in the otherwise stark office.

"We need to get a divorce." I purposely chose the "we." I figured I'd have to tell her about Jean. I didn't think this would work unless I did.

"You and your husband want a divorce?" She heard the "we" and read it differently. It caught me off guard.

"Oh, no. I didn't mean that. I meant, well, I'll have to explain it to you." Already she thought I was a kook. She might want to call out the loony squad before I was finished.

"I understand. *You* want the divorce; he just *needs* the divorce."

"Yeah, yeah, that's it." I'd tell her later. Might as well get the divorce papers drawn up first, deal with the loony squad later.

"Okay, let's start with the family situation."

Elaine pulled a yellow tablet from under a file on her desk, and flipped a couple of handwritten pages over the back. She wrote "Jean Marshall" on the top line, skipped across the page and wrote the date in the right-hand corner. An hour later she had filled several of the legal-size pages.

"Now, I think that about covers it." Elaine sighed with finality. "I'll get back to you as soon as I can get all the papers drawn up. You'll need to sign them before I can file them in court."

What was I going to tell her? I needed to tell her. I couldn't let this thing go to court without her knowing about Jean.

"I don't think I've quite covered everything." I paused, waiting for a reaction.

Elaine cocked her head slightly and waited for me to continue. When I didn't, she leaned toward me. "What else do we need to cover?"

I looked into my lap and rubbed the ragged edge of my left index fingernail with my thumb. How was I going to explain this and not sound like a kook?

"Elaine," I started slowly, "do you know what multiple personality is?"

She sat up straighter, alert.

"Yes . . ." she said warily, waiting for the other shoe to drop.

"Well, I have two personalities, Jean and Jody. Actually, I'm Jody. I have been in therapy with a psychiatrist for a lot of years. The last few years I've been working with Dr. Reiter."

"Jack Reiter?"

"Yes." Oh, good; she knew him, or at least of him.

"I've seen him in criminal court—never worked with him, but I understand he's very good."

I looked into her eyes. They were a soft hazel with a bit more blue mixed in than most. They appeared thoughtful and clear. She wasn't disturbed by this at all. I could have been telling her I had two left feet and had been seeing a podiatrist.

"I'm sorry I interrupted you. Go on, please."

"The truth of the matter is this. Jean married Hank. I didn't. It's Jean that is going to have to divorce Hank. I don't know how the court would handle this at all."

"Why tell the court? They don't recognize a singular physical being as being married and not married at the same time. All you need to do is sign the papers."

"Maybe, but I do think you should talk to Jack about this. He may want you to talk with Jean. I wanted to make sure that the papers would be drawn up and filed. If Jean backs out, there's not much I can do about it."

"I'd be happy to talk with Jack. I'll have to draw up a note for you to sign for me. I'll need to have your permission for Jack to tell me anything about you."

"Sure. In fact it's getting close to the hour. Jack takes calls from about ten minutes to the hour up to his next appointment. Why don't I just call him?" Oh, boy. Jean is going to flip over this. She never wanted to believe she was multiple herself, let alone have other people know.

"Fine," Elaine said, handing me the phone.

I got through to Jack and he was happy to talk with Elaine. They made an appointment to talk later and discuss more details.

As I left Elaine's office, I smiled. The papers were going to go. Hank was going to go. There was never going to be a repeat of last night. That was too much. I sat back in the car seat and stretched my arms over the steering wheel. *Yes!*

•   •   •

It was nearly four months later when I sat outside the court-room. The wooden benches lining the walls of the hall were polished, but worn. There were several small groups huddled, whispering their last-minute instructions before going into one of the courtrooms.

Down at the end of the hall was a semicircle of elevator doors. Beside one of the doors, a man stood arguing loudly with a woman, who answered him quietly. His fists pressed on his hips and his face was animated, angry. Her hands were folded in front, clutching her purse; her face stern and righteous. I wondered what their problem was. Was she getting a divorce like me, and he didn't want it? Maybe they were suing each other over two inches of neighboring yards. If so, the surveyor must have agreed with her.

The elevator door opened and Elaine stepped out. She was dressed in black and looked more like a grieving widow than a divorce lawyer. She brushed by the arguing couple and waved at me as she came down the hall. As she approached I decided that her black suit was very business-like. It was her little hat that grieved.

I started to rise, but she motioned for me to stay seated. She stood in front of me and looked down questioningly. "Let's see. Yup, it's Jody, isn't it?"

That's what it was. She'd been talking with Jack—how to identify Jean from Jody. I wondered if I could fool her.

I laughed. "Yes, it is. You must have had lessons."

"Shall we get this thing over with?"

"It can't happen soon enough for me."

Elaine sat next to me on the bench. "When we go into the court, the judge will ask you if you want the divorce, if you think it is reconcilable. I just want you to answer yes or no, unless he asks you to explain something."

What would he ask me? Shoot, I wished I had talked with Jack before I came here.

"Don't worry," Elaine said. "I'll be right there with you.

If you're not sure about anything, you can talk to me." She sat back and sighed. "He's not going to ask you anything."

She was right. I said *yes* to the first question and *no* to the second, and it was over.

Amazing.

"Now," Elaine whispered as we left the courtroom, "I want to talk with you for a minute."

She ushered me into a small library, two doors down from the courtroom.

"Sit down a minute," she said, easing into one of the chairs next to the tiny table. I sat in the other chair.

"What's up?" I asked her.

"Jack said I should talk to Jean. How do you feel about this divorce?"

"Are you kidding? I can't wait for Hank to be gone."

"Well, let me talk to Jean."

I nodded and stared into the grain of the rough table. I hoped Jean wouldn't be too upset. I hoped she'd remember seeing Elaine before. I called her out. Jean? Come on, Jean . . .

Oh, shoot. This was Jody's lawyer. Where was I? I crossed my ankles under the chair and drew my elbows in close to my body, dropping my hands into my lap.

"Jean?" Elaine asked me. "That is you, isn't it? God, Jack was right. You *do* look so different. Don't be frightened."

I lifted up my elbows and rested them on the table. I wasn't frightened. I pressed my hands over my mouth and nose, hooking my thumbs under my jawbone. Then I shook my head, thinking, *No, I'm not frightened. This was just too weird.*

"Jean, we've just gotten a divorce from Hank. I want to know what you think about it."

Divorced. What was I going to tell Hank? He went absolutely nuts when he got the papers. I said I would get them canceled, but then I didn't. I didn't do anything, and now I was divorced, and I was the one who would have to tell him. What was he going to do? Shoot, he could break everything in the house, including me. What was to stop him? Could I take the girls and run away? I'd have to get another job. Maybe I could go to California.

"Jean, please talk to me."

I forced my hands down, drew in a breath. "I'm sorry. I don't know what I'm going to do."

"How do you feel about this divorce?"

"I think it's the right thing to do, but I don't know how I'm going to handle it."

First I had to go home and tell the girls, but I needed to have a plan before that. I scolded inwardly, *Think, Jean!*

"You have a good job. You can support your kids. You're going to be so much better off with him gone."

She didn't understand. It wasn't the rest of my life that concerned me; it was *today*.

"I'm not afraid of that. I can always support my kids. I've never had any trouble getting a job anywhere. No, I mean I have to get Hank to leave and he'll be mad as hell."

Elaine's joyful face looked a bit worried suddenly. "Are you going to be in danger? Will you need the police to help get him out?"

"No, that'd make things worse. You don't know Hank. He's like a little kid. He needs me to mother him. He'll throw a temper tantrum, maybe break some furniture. Then he'll probably run home to his *other* mommy. I need to find somewhere for the kids to go while he's doing it. I'll handle it somehow."

"Good." Elaine's smile returned. "Now, can I have Jody back?"

Jody? Not in your dreams. *I* had to work this.

"No. I need to be in control. I have to take care of my kids. I have to straighten this out with Hank."

Elaine regained the concerned look. "I told Jack I would talk to you, but then I'd get you to give control back to Jody."

"That's okay. Jack won't care. And really, Jody won't either. She doesn't like to deal with Hank, but I have to."

"Okay, then. I've got to run. I wanted to see that everything was okay with you and Jody." She pushed her chair back and gathered up her papers. Picking up a thin attaché, she shoved the papers into an outside pocket. I wondered if anything ever fazed this woman. I stayed seated as she exited out the door to my left, giving me a slight flutter of her free hand.

It was over. I was divorced. After fifteen years of being Mrs. Marshall, I was just Jean Marshall, no Mrs. It seemed too strange.

I stood up and walked to the door. My mind was disconnected; every thought and movement was an effort. I hardly noticed the corridor, the elevator, or the lobby as I passed through them. My mind was absorbed with how I was going to tell Hank, what I would tell him. However, I became suddenly alert as I stepped out of the revolving door onto the sidewalk.

Damn it, Jody! Where's my car?

NINE

It had been weeks since my day in court and Hank had left. He'd reacted to the divorce just as Jean had predicted. He broke the glass-top coffee table and threw a few loose things around the living room. But then he threw his clothes into a suitcase and ran off to his mama in Indiana.

Good riddance!

I'd been having a field day without him. I called up George, a fellow Jean used to work with and he'd been coming to see me and the girls. He couldn't tell the difference between Jean and me, but I told him to call me Jody. Then I had to tell him not to call me that in front of the girls.

What a game.

Jean hadn't done what I thought she would. Instead of celebrating the newfound freedom, she'd withdrawn into her shell, depressed. I couldn't give her back control when she was so depressed. It was hard for me to play Jean for too many days in a row. She needed to go see Jack, but I couldn't get her attention even to try.

It hadn't been too bad with the girls. They seemed to

enjoy their freedom from Hank. They got a lot of pizza, though; Jean was a much better cook than I was.

Work was another story. Jean was a leader on a new computer development project. Playing Jean at work was the hardest role I ever played. Today was one of the worst and one of the best. It began in the morning. Jean's boss walked up and leaned over the edge of her desk as I was looking up Chinese restaurants in the phone book.

"Eating out tonight, Jean?" John asked.

My finger scanned down the page as I answered, not looking up, "No, looking for take-out. I can't cook and the girls are sick of pizza."

"You can't cook? I thought you were an excellent cook."

I looked up quickly. No, Jody, no, I thought. Remember, he thinks you're Jean.

"Oh, no, I meant . . . well, what with working so much overtime, I haven't had time to cook." I threw out my hands despairingly, and hoped he had bought it.

He did. "I just stopped by to see if you were all ready for the presentation this afternoon."

"Sure, looking forward to it." What the hell is he talking about?

"Have you got your view foils ready? Or do you need any help?"

View foils. Oh, crap. Is this Jean's presentation?

I looked around the desk. In the corner was a flat box. A sticky-tab note on the cover said "New System Foils." I lifted the cover to reveal a pile of view foils. On top of them was a stack of three-by-five cards, neatly printed out with Jean's notes.

"Yup. Yup. All right here."

"Good. I'll see you this afternoon. I have to run up to corporate headquarters, but I'll be back after lunch. Do you need to do a dry run? The conference room up front should be empty this morning, if you need to practice, but I think the managers have a meeting there right before your presentation."

I said, "Okay, John. Thanks."

He waved over his shoulder as he left.

I looked over at Jean's cube mate, Penny. She was digging through a program listing, marking red lines through coding on the listing and pasting little yellow sticky-tabs on each page she marked. I was lucky Jean wasn't programming. I'd have had a harder time figuring out how to do that than fake what Jean did. But now I had to either get Jean back or wing a presentation.

Jean? Jean, where are you? You have to do this presentation. I can't do this. I don't know squat about programming or your new system. Jean, where the hell are you?

I hated it when she was depressed and I couldn't get her back. She wasn't going to take over. I was going to have to do this. I might have to become ill suddenly at lunch.

I pulled the box of foils over to the center of the desk and opened the lid. The stack of three-by-fives had everything I needed. Thank you, Jean, at least for being thorough. Her notes were not notes. She had printed the whole presentation neatly in tiny letters on the cards. I closed and picked up the box, and headed for the conference room. I'd lick this thing yet.

That afternoon, I returned to the conference room. The long table was packed with men in business suits and ties. The only other woman in the room sat at the far end of the table, also wearing a lady's business suit and a formal blouse with a bow. I looked down at my clothes. Why couldn't I have worn something a bit more formal? Oh, well, if the presentation goes smoothly, it won't matter what I'm wearing. If it doesn't . . . what the heck, it still won't matter what I'm wearing, will it?

The viewer for the foils had been placed at the head of the

table. I sat down next to it and berated Jean. *Why are you doing this to me? Jean, they're going to eat me alive.*

As John walked in, he closed the door behind him and said, "Okay, Jean, I think everyone's here. I'll say a few words and then you can get on with it."

He turned to face most of the crowd. "Jean and her crew have been working for the last three months on the new contract coverage. They have put together an excellent plan, and I thought it was about time we got a review by all the upper management."

Upper management? Holy cow! *Jean, are you sure you can't come do this? You really, really don't want me to blow this one. Jean?*

John was wrapping up his few words, "So now I'll let Jean tell you all about it. Jean?"

I stood up next to the viewer and opened the box of foils. *Here goes, Jean. Don't blame me if I blow your whole career.* As I took the first view foil out and placed it on the viewer, I admonished myself for my fears. *Don't shake, hand.*

Flipping on the viewer switch, I cleared my throat. Although I had placed the note cards next to the viewer, I had tried to memorize them all morning and through lunch hour, so I could avoid reading them here. My stomach growled slightly, remembering its lack of lunch. *Hush.*

"Before I cover the new system," I began, trying to look confident, "I need to give you a few points of reference from the old system. The current system was built twenty-two years ago. It is written in Assembler, which makes it hard to maintain or enhance. Most of the logical decisions are embedded in the coding. This means that every time we want to add a new company or a new feature, we have to change about half the programs in the system."

"Excuse me," a man named Bob interrupted. I could just barely read his name tag without my glasses. I couldn't wear my glasses and read Jean's notes.

"Yes?" I answered. *Don't ask a question. Please don't ask a question.*

"How many modules are there in the current system?"

Oh, no! Jean, Jean, what's a module? Is a module a program? Think fast, Jody.

"I'm not sure, Bob. I'll have to get back to you on that one." I tried to get out of it.

"I mean, just ballpark. I'm just trying to understand the magnitude of the maintenance problem," he insisted.

I'm dead. I looked up at the ceiling. *Okay, don't panic. Think. There's at least five rows of program binders. If a module is a program, let's see . . . there's about twenty binders in a row. . . .*

"I think we've got about eighty or a hundred modules, Bob."

I scanned the heads along the table to John. His was nodding slightly. *Oh, God, thank you, thank you, but please don't let there be any more questions.*

The rest of the presentation went okay, until I got to the next-to-the-last foil.

"Excuse me, Jean." It was Bob again. *Shut up, Bob. I can't handle your questions.*

"Can you tell us what the estimated manpower requirements are for your project?"

Thank you, God! Thank you, again. I could handle this.

"Give that man a quarter!" I said cheerfully, as I boldly placed the last view foil on the viewer. The bottom line figures were all there—head count, timelines, and everything they could want. I went through the figures and sat down.

Now, please, no more questions. I don't have any more information. I've read all Jean's notes.

John rose and thanked me. Then, to my great joy, he added, "I think you can go now. We need to discuss the funding issues and I know you have a lot to do."

Maybe Jean had a lot to do, but I was out of there. I called the Chinese place and left to see the girls.

Yes. Yes! I made it! I fooled them all and I didn't lose Jean's job.

TEN

THE PHONE RANG NEXT TO ME AND I PICKED IT UP.

"Hi, babe." Hank's softest voice nearly jolted me out of the kitchen chair.

My mind flew in circles. It had been nearly two months since he left. His last words, "I'll see you in hell," still rang in my ears. During his absence, I had spoken to his mother, Polly, several times a week. She had offered no sympathy for my situation, but had stressed how depressed Hank was and how much he loved me. However, her accusations of my un-Christian behavior hurt most. I had tried to make it work. I had prayed daily over us. But it took two, and he wouldn't even try. In his mother's eyes, I was supposed to bear up no matter what the situation became. Divorce was unacceptable. After all, she stayed married to an alcoholic for thirty-some years.

"Jean? Look, I'm sorry for the things I said when I left," Hank apologized. "Can I talk with you? I'm in town. Can I come over for supper?"

In town? In town! How can I see him now? What will I say to the girls? *Hank, you make everything so hard for me.*

"Yes, I suppose that'll be all right," I lied.

"Good, I'll be over in a couple hours." He didn't wait for another word, but hung up before I could sort out my thoughts.

I stared at the dead receiver. How could he be here, in town, with no warning? Why didn't Polly call me? What was I going to do?

I set the receiver back in its cradle and stared at the table. The Saturday lunch dishes were still spread over it. On the counter and in the sink were last night's supper and this morning's breakfast mess. Nothing had changed since he left. I still couldn't keep house.

I forced myself out of the chair and hurried to the front door to call in the girls, who were playing across the road. I watched for a minute and then came back into the house. As I went into the kitchen, I grabbed up an empty potato chip bag and part of the newspaper to shove into the trash. Those girls had to get the living room straightened up. I had to tackle the kitchen. The girls knew something was up as soon as they came in through the door.

Erin spoke first. "Why the hurricane cleanup? Is George coming over?"

"No, your father is, so get busy."

"Dad?" Erin asked. Was there fear in the voice?

"Yes, he called me a couple minutes ago and he'll be here for supper. He wants to talk to me." I snatched my dishrag off the faucet and starting running water in the sink.

The three girls were standing still in the living room, looking stunned. I suppose they had been enjoying their freedom without him. I had to admit things were tougher on them when he was here. He had to know where they were and what they were doing every minute of the day, whether it was out in the yard or somewhere in the house. His constant surveillance drove them to play almost exclusively in their bedrooms.

Poor Hank, though. He had lived fifteen years with me and had expected to go on that way forever. He was lonely; he needed a family, a home to be part of his life.

I went into the living room.

"Sit down a minute, girls," I said, tossing my dishrag back into the kitchen toward the sink.

They lined up on the couch. I sighed as I sat on the edge of the broken coffee table.

"Your father has had a really hard life. I know he doesn't want to be gone from us. You know how upset he was when he left. I know he loves us and feels terribly alone. He's coming over to talk with me tonight. Have a little sympathy for him. Be nice, now, okay?"

Convincing them or convincing yourself? Jody was asking me. I shook her thoughts away from me.

"Now, please help me. Let's get this place cleaned up in a hurry. Erin, get the dirty clothes out of the bathroom and down to the laundry room. Teresa and Melissa, pick up all the papers and crayons and stuff in this room. Don't worry about the family room. He's not going down there anyway. But let's get the upstairs neat, okay? I'll get the dishes and then I need to run up to the store. I don't know what I'll cook if I don't go shopping."

The girls nodded compliance and began to work as I slipped back into the kitchen and scooped my dishrag off the floor.

It was less than two hours later when Hank's car pulled into the drive. Teresa and Melissa were downstairs. Erin quickly joined them, so that I answered the door alone.

In his hand Hank held a dozen bright red roses. As he stepped inside, he handed them to me. He leaned forward and kissed me on the cheek as I took them.

"Gosh, it's good to see you," he said sincerely.

"And you," I answered.

He was a handsome man. His thick, black hair was graying a bit, but it was fashionable. Smiling broadly, he reminded me of Arnold Palmer, and he could have his winning ways when he tried.

"Can I sit here?" he asked, pointing to the couch. He was still being conciliatory.

"Sure. Let me put these in a vase." I turned as I stepped into the kitchen. "Thanks, Hank. They're beautiful."

When I returned, Hank was fingering the edge of the broken table. As I put the vase on the piano, he said, "I'm sorry about the table. We'll get a new glass for it. It shouldn't be too hard to fix."

"Don't worry about it. I'll get around to it one of these days." I waved it off.

"Come here," Hank requested, patting the couch next to him. "I need to talk to you."

I sat down next to him, but not too close. He noticed the distance.

"I've been in town a couple of days. . . ."

I didn't hear the next sentences. All I could think was *A couple of days?* Had he come by the house? He had a key. I wondered if he had seen Jody out with George? Oh, no, Jody hadn't been out; I was home the last couple of nights. I sighed with relief.

"Anyway," Hank continued, "I got a little apartment down in Federal Way and the hardware place is letting me come back to work. I guess things have been a real mess there since I left."

"I can imagine." I tried to step back into the active conversation. I fought hard to deny Jody's feeling of despair that Hank was back in town and living so close by.

"Yes," Hank said, more enthused. I knew he liked this job. I was sure he had missed it. "They were lost without me. I didn't have to ask twice; they couldn't wait for me to come back. The computer room and the orders are all screwed up. I'm going in tomorrow to see how to straighten it out."

"Tomorrow?"

"Yeah. With a little luck and a lot of work, I may at least get the orders straightened out before we run again Monday night."

"That will be good." I tried to be enthusiastic too, but I couldn't get into it.

"But I didn't come here to talk about work." Had he noticed my lack of interest? "I came here to talk about *us*."

He emphasized "*us*" and smiled expectantly as he said it. I didn't respond and he looked disappointed. He narrowed the distance between us on the couch.

"Look, babe," he said, taking my hand, "I can live down in Federal Way, but my heart will always be here. You know that. I don't want to end up some lonely old man wandering the streets in my last days. I need you."

"And the girls?" I questioned.

Hank jerked slightly, but smiled as he answered, "Yes, of course, the girls." He looked around suddenly. He'd only then thought about them. It angered me.

"Where are they, anyway?"

"Downstairs. I'll get them." I grabbed the opportunity to escape from the couch and went through the kitchen to call them.

Supper was a near disaster. Although the food came out great, the conversation was entirely one-sided. Hank talked about his folks, returning to his job, fixing up his car, and anything else that came to his mind. The girls hardly said a word through the whole meal. Hank didn't seem to notice, but the tension was thick. It wasn't going to work having him around, unless he could get in touch with his kids; they couldn't go through life being afraid of him.

After dinner, I sent the girls back downstairs and Hank and I played cribbage. Hank continued to talk randomly about any subject, but avoided the closeness. Maybe he had decided he was moving too fast.

In the next few weeks, I only saw Hank on the weekends. He had gone back to working second shift, so our conflicting workdays precluded his presence during the week. I struggled to keep control from Jody. I couldn't deal with her and Hank at the same time. However, Easter was coming up and Jody had invited George and my cube-mate Penny for Easter dinner. Hank would have no problem with Penny, but I would have a hard time explaining George. I didn't know how to disinvite George. In the end, I decided to see that Hank wouldn't come.

Wednesday before Easter, Hank called me at work. "Jean? I just realized that Sunday is Easter. Are we doing anything special?"

Shoot. What was I going to tell him?

"Well, Hank, I do have a little dinner party planned, but I think it would be awkward if you were there. I hope you don't mind if I don't have you join us." Please, please don't come.

"Oh." His disappointment came through as he commented, "I thought maybe I could bring the girls some huge chocolate bunnies or something."

"Maybe you could come over in the evening. I could call you when everybody leaves." I had to keep this under my control.

"I guess so." He sighed. "I really thought you would have me over for dinner, though. I can't believe you wouldn't."

"Humor me," I pleaded. "I would rather the girls and I see you alone, okay?"

"All right, but I'll see you Saturday, won't I?"

"Yeah. We're planning to go to Seattle to the zoo. I hope that's okay with you." I knew he would rather stay home and play cards, but I wanted to take the girls out.

"Oh," he said slowly. I knew he wasn't pleased. "Well . . . I guess I'll meet you there after lunch. Where do you want to meet? In front of the monkey house about two?"

"That'll be fine. I'll see you then. I've got to get back to work now, okay?"

"Okay, bye."

I thought maybe it would work out after all. If Hank didn't come Sunday, I might be able to keep control and get rid of George once and for all. Then I wouldn't have this problem.

Saturday came, but Hank was not at the monkey house at two. At three, I located a phone.

"Hank?" I questioned the hello at his house. "What are you doing at home? Did you oversleep?" I fought back the anger, expecting a reasonable explanation.

"I'm sorry, babe. I didn't get hold of you before you left this morning, and then I didn't have any way to get in touch. I'm sick. I can't meet you today. I hope you're not mad."

"What's wrong?" My anger turned to concern.

"Uh," Hank hesitated long enough for me to wonder if he might have been out drinking the night before. "I'm having a digestive problem. I'm a little embarrassed to tell you, but I've been constipated for a couple of days."

A little guilt ping hit me.

"I'm sorry, Hank. Is there anything I can do?"

"No, I just need to stay here. I don't feel like going anywhere."

When I got off the phone, I joined the girls, who were eating ice cream outside the nocturnal animal house. My concern for Hank was outweighed by my sense of relief. If he was home ill, he wouldn't be popping in unexpectedly at Easter dinner.

•   •   •

On Easter morning I dragged the girls out for sunrise services. I didn't know how it affected them, but I was always overwhelmed. My whole existence relied on the truth that Christ died for me and rose again, that somehow I would struggle through this life and find Jesus at the end. Easter celebration was an affirmation of my highest hope. I floated home, the scent of Easter lilies filling my heart.

George came early and helped me prepare dinner. Penny arrived as we set the table. After we ate, George and Penny helped hide Easter eggs all over the yard. We had to corral the girls in the basement to keep them from peeking.

The weather was perfect. Blue skies and warm air surrounded us. The red tulips and yellow daffodils had bloomed on cue in the yard. Everything seemed green and fresh and alive.

As we summoned the girls to hunt the hidden treasures, the phone rang.

"Jean?" Hank sounded desperate. "I need your help. I know you've got company, but I waited until I thought dinner was through before I called."

"What do you need?" I shook my head. I had hoped I wouldn't hear from him until George and Penny were gone.

"Look, I've been so constipated, I can't move. Can you bring me something?"

"What?" I was beginning to be irritated and I struggled with my responsibility to him.

"Anything. Just bring me something to help this."

"No, Hank, we're only now starting to hunt eggs. Oh, never mind. I'll be down in a little bit. Where's your apartment?"

George walked into the kitchen as I hung up, and questioned, "You're leaving?"

I sighed and looked out the window. "I've got to go. I need to take Hank some medicine."

"You're not his mommy anymore, you know."

"I know, but I still have to go help him. He doesn't have anyone else."

"He doesn't have you." It was more of a question than a comment. I didn't answer it.

I left George to supervise the hunt and Penny came with me. We picked up some Milk of Magnesia and a Fleet enema, and located the apartment complex.

"You better wait in the car," I told Penny. "Hank will be embarrassed enough as it is."

I walked alone across the parking lot and up the steps to his apartment. I wished I didn't need to come, but what could I do? I couldn't refuse the man I'd lived with for fifteen years, not when I knew he was suffering.

"Come on in," Hank answered my knock.

He was lying on the couch in his robe. I glanced around the apartment. It was a new complex and the rooms were all painted a clean, bright white. There was little furniture for a furnished apartment. The place reeked of cigarette smoke. I was glad the smell had subsided in our house since he left.

"I brought you some medicine. If I were you, I would take the Phillips and wait an hour or three before trying the enema."

"Thanks." Hank struggled up from the couch to take the bag from me. "Why don't you sit down and stay with me for a while?"

"No, I can't," I replied, shaking my head. "I have Penny in the car, and the kids and company are waiting for me back at the house." The smell of smoke was making me ill.

"Penny's in the car?" Hank suddenly looked angry. "You told her? Did you tell everyone?" His sudden anger frightened me.

"Hank," I said, "I didn't tell everyone why I was coming, but they knew I was leaving. I only told them you were sick and needed some medicine."

"Oh." Hank relaxed a bit. "Okay, I guess I should let you go, then. I'm sorry. Thanks for bringing the stuff."

As I started out the door, he called "I'll let you know how it worked."

Please don't bother, I thought, but didn't say.

On the way back, I drove without talking.

Penny noticed my silence. "You still love the guy, don't you?" she asked suddenly.

"Do I? Why, Penny, why? I seem to be happier when he's gone, except at night. Then I feel so very alone, and I feel sorry for him. I guess I'm one of those people who needs to be married. I need him like a security blanket, I guess."

"What about George?"

"George is a nice enough guy, but he's not right. He wants a fun relationship, but he's on the rebound from a divorce himself. He doesn't want another commitment. He is awfully good with the girls, though."

George. George—Jody's playmate. He wasn't like any of the others; he was strange. At least she wasn't sleeping with him. Of course, that might not have been by choice. George had had prostate surgery recently. I supposed that kind of activity would have been painful for him.

"So what are you going to do about all this?"

"I don't know, Penny. I suppose I'll get rid of George and remarry Hank. That's what he wants, anyway." I ignored Jody's protests in the back of my mind, as I wondered how the girls would react. Maybe if Hank got some counseling, he wouldn't be so hard on them.

"Well, whatever you decide, I'll back you," Penny said, patting my arm.

Later that day as the festivities ended, Penny had gone, and George was saying his good-byes, Hank called again. He graphically described his relief.

"Hank, that's gross!" I couldn't hide my disgust. Why did he have to call now?

George lifted an eyebrow and gave me a curious smile.

"I thought you'd want to know your errand of mercy was successful," Hank continued.

"Yes, yes, well, I have to go. Everyone's leaving right now, so I'll talk to you later, okay?" I couldn't get off the phone fast enough.

George had news for me too. "Listen, can we go out Friday night? I'm going to be leaving for California in a couple weeks and I'd like to spend a little more time with you before I go. My brother is in town this week, playing for a little bar down by Sea-Tac."

"California?" It was the only thing I had tuned in on.

George looked sadly at the floor. "I should have told you, but I didn't know how. I took a contract job down there. I don't know how long I'll be gone. It could be a year or two."

"I'm sorry." I tried to look sad, but as much as I liked George, having him gone would be one less complication in my crazy life. Jody was frantically trying to take control.

Too bad, Jody; I'm not giving it to you.

"Sure," I answered. "I'm not doing anything Friday. I'll be glad to go."

Friday, George showed up bearing two huge pizzas. I knew he thought he was bringing a treat for the girls, but since Jody didn't cook, they had eaten a lot of pizza lately.

I fought to retain control, but Jody took over swiftly.

"George, come in, come in. Here, let me take that. Aren't you sweet, bringing supper?"

"Wow! You look great," he said with appreciation. I was wearing a dark purple nylon dress, almost see-through. It tended to make me look thinner than I was. I had spent great effort to make my hair and face as pretty as the dress.

The girls, always happy to see George, wolfed the pizza as though they hadn't eaten the stuff for weeks, or at least not the day before. We played Tripoli with them until bedtime, and once they were down, George and I took off for Sea-Tac. I left Erin in charge. Twelve was the age Jean had started baby-sitting, so I figured Erin could handle it. She had no babies to care for, because Teresa was ten and Melissa was eight.

As we pulled into the parking lot of the tavern, George surprised me. "My parents are here tonight. I'd like them to meet you."

Was he looking for a commitment?

George's parents and his brother were friendly and out-going. We might get along great in the future if anything came of this. Especially if I could prevent Jean from getting back with Hank. However, I was not into country-western, and was relieved when George said he had a bit of a headache and wanted to leave.

As we drove home, George told me how happy he was that I had come along to meet his parents. They had worried about him since his divorce. Somehow seeing him out with another woman soothed their concerns.

"Do you mind if I spend tonight at your place?" he asked as we neared home.

My, he was getting serious.

But then he disagreed with my thought. "I don't think I can drive all the way back home with my head pounding this way. I can sleep on the couch downstairs, if that's okay."

"Sure. No problem. I'm sorry you're doing so poorly."

As we pulled into the drive, there was Hank's car, parked under the carport.

"What the hell is he doing here?" I said, vocalizing my anger. "Why can't he only come when he's invited? What the hell does he want now? Why isn't he working?"

"What are you going to do?" George asked, ignoring my profanity.

"I don't know!" I bit my words as I slammed the car door and stomped up the porch steps.

As I opened the front door, Hank sat forward on the couch.

"Where have you been?" he asked angrily. Then, as George followed me into the room, he continued, "Oh, I see. Out drinking, while the girls are left here to fend for themselves. What if the house caught on fire? Is this the 'company' that was here Easter?"

He didn't give a crap about the girls' safety. He was pissed because I was out with George, I thought. "Get the hell out of here!" I said, stomping into the kitchen.

Hank jumped to his feet as I told George, "Go on downstairs. I'll get rid of him and talk to you in a minute."

"Gonna be all right?" George asked as he descended to the family room. "Need any help?"

"No, I'm okay. See you soon."

I waited until George closed the door at the bottom before turning to face Hank. This was going to take all my power to keep Jean out. Profanity helped—Jean was intimidated by it.

"What the hell do you want?" I demanded.

Hank had crossed the room and was within spitting distance, glaring at me. He pointed his finger at me as he seethed, "I want to know how you can go out drinking and leave these girls here alone?"

He knew I couldn't drink. Alcohol made me ill. He was only looking for a way to make Jean feel guilty about going out. I could feel her struggle for control. However, I told her firmly, I'm staying in control this time, Jean. I turned my anger to Hank. "You don't have any right to come here uninvited, so get the hell out. What I do is my business."

"These are my kids too." Hank continued his feigned concern. He knew Erin was old enough to take care of herself and her sisters.

I drew in a huge breath and let it fly. "I said get out and I mean get out. I don't give a damn about your opinions and

I'll do what I damn well please. I'm not married to you any-more, and you have no right to be here. If you have a prob-lem with how I'm raising *my* kids, then take it up with the courts. But right now, just leave!"

Hank backed slowly toward the door. He wasn't sure what to say next. Suddenly he decided. His whole demeanor changed, and he said, "Look, I'm sorry. I'm sorry. I was so worried when I called and found out that the girls were here alone. I know they get scared by themselves."

I still wasn't buying it. "Get out," I said again.

Hank shifted again. "Look, I'm sorry. It makes me nuts to see you with someone else. You don't know. Don't blame the girls. They tried not to tell me where you were. I talked it out of them."

Blame the girls? I thought. *For what? You're nuts, Hank. You use people and then say don't blame them?* I tried my most contained voice, "Please . . . go . . . now."

"Okay, okay. I'm going, but please let me talk to you to-morrow. I'll come over and we'll talk, please?"

Anything, I answered silently, *only get out of here.* "Okay. I'll talk to you tomorrow."

Hank threw up his hands in a gesture of hopelessness as he stepped through the door. I hurried to close and bolt it be-hind him. I had to get that lock changed. Damn! I should have asked him for the key.

As I came down the stairwell, George opened the door. "Gone?"

"Yes. He'll be back tomorrow, but he's gone for tonight. What a jerk."

"I made myself at home," George directed my attention to the couch, which he'd made up into a bed. "I hope you don't mind. I swiped the blanket out of the laundry room."

I hoped it was clean.

"No, I'm happy you found what you needed. Is there any-thing else I can get you?"

"No. I'm fine. I need to get some sleep and knock out this headache. I took some painkillers at the bar, but they don't seem to be working." He gave me a quick squeeze. "Good night, Jean. Thanks."

"Good night, George."

Erin and Teresa were both sound asleep. I went back up-stairs and checked on Melissa. She had apparently slept through my screaming match with her dad. Then I went to my bed.

Violent knocking startled me out of my sound sleep. I rolled over and checked the clock. Six-thirty! That had to be Hank at the front door. What did Jody say to him last night? She was struggling to take control now. *Oh, no, you don't, Jody. I have to deal with Hank. You're not messing this up.*

I drew my robe around me and hurried to the door. I men-tally yelled, *Stop it, Hank! Don't wake up Melissa!*

Hank was fuming. He pushed open the door as soon as I turned the dead bolt.

"Where is he?" He stomped into the kitchen. "Is he in our bed?"

He headed down the hall. I hurried to get between him and the bedroom door. "No, he's not in there."

"Then why are you preventing me from going to see?"

"Because it's a mess, see?" I pushed the door open slightly so he could see the bed, but not the clothes piled on the chair and dresser. Hank stretched to peer in at the bed.

"So, where is he?"

"George is sleeping downstairs. He had a headache and couldn't drive home last night." I fought to recall last night. Jody had given me some of the details, but she was block-ing some too.

"A likely story," Hank replied indignantly. "That's one of the oldest in the book. Let me sleep downstairs and join you in the middle of the night."

"I wouldn't know, Hank. I only know that nothing happened between George and me."

Why are you being defensive? You're not married to the jerk anymore.

Shut up, Jody.

Hank marched back into the living room and I followed. He stared at me for a minute, then he collapsed onto the couch and began to cry, putting his head down on his hands.

"I'm sorry. I'm sorry," he sobbed. "I know I'm being jealous. I can't help it. I need you. You know I can't live without you. I've been up all night, driving around, waiting for it to get late enough to come see you. When I drove by and saw his car out there, I went nuts. I couldn't think about you being here with someone else. Not in our bed."

It's my bed, not our bed.

Shut up, Jody. Somehow I had to block her from my thoughts.

I stood in the doorway in shock. I had expected his anger, not this. I went over and sat beside him.

He lifted his head and looked at me through teary eyes. "I want to come back. I want to be here with you. I'll do anything. Just let me come home."

I was too tired to think this fast. He couldn't simply come home. Nothing had changed. It would be worse than before.

"No, Hank, not before you get some help." I struggled to control my feelings and what I needed to tell him.

"What do you want me to do?"

"Get some counseling. I don't care if you go to Jack or anybody you choose, but you need to get some help. The girls can't live with your temper. I can't live with it."

"I promise I'll go to counseling. Please let me move back here. We can get married again. Things will be better, I promise."

He was so desperate, he would promise me anything, but would he follow through?

"Hank," I said, looking into his pleading face, "I want you to try for a while first, before you come back here. Go for several weeks to someone and then we'll talk about getting back together. George is leaving for California for a year or more. He won't be around and there isn't anyone else in my life."

Hank looked relieved. He took my hands in his and sniffed as he said, "Look, babe, I'll do anything you ask. Anything. If I only have a hope of coming back with you."

"You're tired. Why don't you go back to your apartment and get some sleep. We can talk about this later when you and I are both rested and thinking clearer, okay?"

Hank drew in a long breath and let it out slowly. He wiped the tears from his face with his palms like a six-year-old.

He got up and walked to the door. As he reached for the handle, he turned and said again, "I'm sorry I came bursting in here like that. It's not because I think you've done anything wrong. It's that I love you and I want you so much."

"Yeah. I know." I tried not to see the little-boy look on his face. "Bye, Hank."

When his car pulled out of the drive, George came up from the basement. I was heading back into my bedroom.

"Jean?"

"Oh, I'm sorry that woke you. Are you feeling better?" I wrapped my robe in a little tighter.

"I couldn't hear what you were saying, but I know you handled him. I'm very proud of you."

George left for California the next week and Hank found a counselor. It looked as though things would work out for me after all.

It was barely two months before Hank and I stood together in the church, repeating our vows. Jody hid far inside my head.

"How could you let Jean do this?" I nearly screamed at Jack.

The honeymoon was over and Hank was back to his old tricks. He had gone to his counselor long enough to satisfy

Jean's initial requirement, but then was back to accusing that it was she, not he, who needed help. And she did. If I could have shot her, I would, but I was sharing this body and I didn't have a death wish. Not yet.

"Jody," Jack preached, "I cannot tell Jean or you or anyone else what they should or should not do. They have to work it out themselves. Jean has to work out her relationship with Hank, as you have to work out your relationship with Jean."

"Oh—bullshit! All you had to do is tell her she might think about it a little longer, or maybe she shouldn't remarry so fast, or anything to slow this down. Why didn't you give me control so I could stop it somehow?"

"Jody," Jack remained his calm self, "I think you would do better trying to work out your differences with Jean rather than fight her relationship with Hank."

"How can I?" I sighed and looked at the floor in defeat. My anger at Jack subsided. I was mad at Jean, not Jack. "She has successfully kept me blocked for months. *Months!* Do you understand? Ever since the blowup the night of my last date with George, I've been struggling even to talk to her. She ignores everything I say."

"Well, let me talk to her." Jack requested.

"No! This is the first day I've had control. I'm not even sure why she gave it up."

"All the more reason for me to talk with her. I'll give you back control when I'm done."

"Sure, sure you will. Like Jean will let you."

"I promise I'll try. Please?"

Crap. I threw my head back and looked at the ceiling. Okay, Jean. This one's on me, but you better give me back control, so help me. I bent my head down and stared into the carpet.

I felt a little chill as I looked up at Jack. He was repositioning himself, sitting forward on his chair, the way he did when he discussed something serious.

"Jean?" he asked, although he could see it was me.

I rubbed my neck and then my arms. I wondered if I should pull my coat around me.

"You want to tell me what's been going on?" Jack asked, putting on his best poker face.

What's been going on? I was so happy when Hank and I got married again. It was going to be different this time. Hank was going to get help. He was going to change. We bought a house. We put in a garden.

It was becoming a nightmare. Hank had stopped going for help. He had been put on day shift at work. Now he was home every evening with the same demands, accusations, and constant, sickening cigarettes.

I sighed. Jody wasn't far away.

Where are your rose-colored glasses, Jean? Jack is waiting for an answer.

"I don't know where to start. I thought things would be better. I can't push Hank into getting help. I don't have a bargaining chit anymore."

"Yes, you do." Jack said, "The same one you always had."

Did he mean my love for Hank? Maybe. Did I love Hank or pity him? I tried to think about Hank's life of growing up with an alcoholic father and an illiterate mother. I knew why he didn't have any self-esteem. If he did anything great, it was okay; if he did anything okay, it was okay; and if he did anything terrible, it was okay. You couldn't grow up knowing that it didn't matter how or what you did and develop any self-esteem. It probably accounted for his jealousy over his own children's accomplishments, or at least the attention they got for doing them. I might have even been able to live with that, but the paranoia was getting worse. Someone was always out to cause him grief, even his own children. I found him listening at their bedroom doors when they played inside. And then there was work. Something was definitely going on at his work. I didn't want to think about it.

"Jody came today. You want to tell me why?"

"I'm getting fat. Did you notice?" I wanted to draw away from my worry.

Jack smiled. "What's going on, Jean?"

"I think Hank is seeing another woman."

"What?" Jack sat back in genuine surprise.

"Oh, I don't know what I'm talking about. I'm working so much. I'm so tired. Everything seems so difficult. I don't know what to do." I rested my elbow on the chair arm and leaned my forehead into my hand.

"Is that why Jody has control today? Is it because you suspect Hank is unfaithful?"

"No, I was just kidding. I know Hank needs me."

Sure, Jean, keep lying to yourself.

Shut up, Jody.

"He's been working days, but he's been trying to get back on second shift. He seems so angry at his boss for shifting him to days. I don't know what's going on. He's so difficult to live with when he's angry at the world."

"What are you doing about it?" Jack always asked the most difficult questions.

What *could* I do?

"I guess I'll go talk to Pastor Dave. He'll give me some advice on how to direct my energy into some worthwhile activity instead of just being depressed all the time. And eating myself to death."

"Good, but why don't you talk with Jody too? She isn't all bad, you know. She may even have some good advice for you."

Jody again? He makes me mad.

"All Jody wants is out. If she had her way, I'd pack up the kids and move to California without Hank."

"You came here for help a long time ago. I almost gave up treating you for good because you seemed to go right back to being a depressed person. Do you want to get better?"

I nodded slowly.

"Then you need to talk with Jody. Work with her too. She's not so unreasonable. The first time I met her I thought she was totally selfish. Over time, though, I realized that she was looking out for you. It's time you acknowledged that care."

I give. Okay. I can't manage without your help, Jody. I've made all the wrong decisions. Maybe you're right about Hank, but we just can't pack up and run away. I have to resolve the situation with him. So what do you want, Jody?

I looked up at Jack. The strained look on my face grew into a large smile.

"Jody," Jack acknowledged. "What do you think?"

"I think I may have a bit more to say about what goes on around here now. It's about time. I've gotta find a way to get Jean to see Hank the way he really is. I'm not sure how it's going to work out, but it is definitely going to change."

Please, God, help Jean and me make it change together. You know the best way.

And *only* God could have foreseen the way Jean could be broken from Hank so completely. I thought about my prayer in Jack's office. God really did have a way of answering.

I was convinced that Hank was seeing Gloria, a girl in his office. He had managed to finagle a second-shift position, getting off at eleven at night. It was Gloria's shift. I was sure it allowed him time with Gloria that he wouldn't have to account for to Jean. She would be sleeping. And if she woke up when he came in at three or four in the morning, he was working overtime, wasn't he? I just couldn't get Jean to see it, or at least to admit it. However, Hank did something that made it impossible for her to deny. He left. By the third morning of Hank's absence, Jean was in a panic. I gave her control.

•   •   •

Where is he? I couldn't call the police; I had a nagging fear that he had planned to disappear, somewhat verified by his missing pairs of shoes. He wouldn't be wearing more than one pair. I called his workplace.

"Hello, is this the computer room?" I asked in desperation.

"Yes, who do you want?" A strange woman's voice answered.

"Is Hank Marshall working there tonight?"

"No, he isn't. Who is this?"

"Oh, this is his wife, Jean. I'm sorry to bother you. Is Gloria there?"

"No, she isn't here either. Didn't Hank tell you where he was going?"

"No. Do you know?"

There was a long pause at the other end of the line. Then Hank's co-worker, Al, came on.

"Jean?" he asked with softness.

"Al, is that you?"

"Yes."

"Look, Al, I'm sorry to bother you guys. I know you're working, but Hank hasn't been home in three days and I don't know what to do. I figured if he had been in an accident or something, I would have heard. I didn't want to call the police."

"Oh, Jean! I didn't want to be the one to tell you anything, but I don't want you to sit around worrying. I don't really know anything for sure, but both Gloria and Hank quit Monday. I just figured . . . well . . . with them being so buddy-buddy, you know what I mean."

I froze. Maybe Jody had been right all along. It couldn't be true, though. It couldn't.

"Al, can you give me Gloria's home phone number? I know you're not supposed to, but you know what it is. I have to call her. I won't tell anyone how I got it. Please help me, Al."

Al gave me the number.

I sat at the kitchen table staring at the phone. How could he leave me? He needed me. He loved me. I had always loved him. At least I'd always tried to do what he wanted.

It was the fat. I got too fat. Polly had warned me. Hank hated fat women. I had tried to lose weight.

Oh, Hank, this can't be true. Where are you?

I called. Gloria's sister answered the phone. She was more angry than I was afraid.

"You're Hank's wife? That old bastard. He's taken Gloria to Canada with him. I'm sorry if you still love him. What a jerk. She had a good-paying job and he talked her into leaving it."

"I'm sorry."

"You're sorry? I feel sorry for you. How old is Hank anyway? Did you know Gloria just turned nineteen? There ought to be a law against old farts like him taking teenagers off, and him married. Gloria didn't even tell me that. Shit. Well, I can tell you one thing, if I ever see him, you won't have to worry about it. You'll be a widow. Sorry."

I got off as quickly as I could.

Dear God, he left me, and with another woman. How could he? I put a record on the stereo and sat down on the fireplace hearth. As the words filtered into my brain, "Through the years our love will grow, like a river it will flow," the tears began to run down my cheeks. Hank, I thought you loved me. I tried everything to make it work. I gave you everything, everything. What am I going to do?

For three days, I sat on the hearth crying. The girls were bewildered. They wandered in and out, fixing what food they could find and trying unsuccessfully to comfort me.

On Sunday, Sandra's ex-husband, Carl, came to visit.

"What the hell is going on here?" Carl asked.

"Oh, Carl," I sobbed, "Hank has run off to Canada with a nineteen-year-old girl."

"It's about time he got his butt out of here," he snarled

with conviction, confirming my belief that Carl had always hated Hank, but how could he be so heartless? I began to sob uncontrollably.

"How long has your mother been doing this?" he asked Erin who had crept quietly into the living room.

"Since Thursday night, I think," Erin whispered. "She was crying when we got up and went to school on Friday, and she still was when we got back."

Suddenly he turned and slapped me across the face, "Stop that! Get up! You have these girls to take care of. You can't just sit around crying. He's gone. Let him go. Good riddance."

I jerked back and held my face with my hands. I was stunned, and then so tired and thirsty, I didn't know what to do. I wiped my face on my sleeve as he pulled me up from the hearth.

"That's better," he said, the anger slipping away from his voice. "Now, let's make some tea and figure out what to do."

Carl helped me get through the next few weeks, but then he and his new bride moved to Eastern Washington. I was on my own. Jody took over.

Now, Jean, what is it going to take you to divorce the guy once and for all? The final thread of the relationship is broken. You know Hank used you. He needed you all right, but he has his real mommy and now some young thing too. Maybe he even loved you once, if he was capable beyond his needs, but that's over. Listen to me, Jean!

It was barely two months before Hank's money ran out and then the girl ran out. Hank appeared at the door again, begging forgiveness and professing love. Jean took over for a while and let him stay, but it would never be the same. She was never going to let him get close enough to hurt her again. I was going to get him out permanently, and Jean was going to let me.

As I drove home from work the second week that Hank

was back, I plotted how to get him to leave. I had to separate him from Jean. He wasn't working and he wasn't likely to get another job in this area. He must have quit thirty-five of them here now. How could he get one job after another in computer operations, walk out on it, and get another? There couldn't be another job in his field left in this city.

It was time for a change. Hank would jump at the chance to travel. I'd suggest that he look in other cities for a good job and we'd move there later. Not very nice of me, I admit, but I had to get him away from Jean long enough to convince her that she was better off without him.

I slipped into Godfather's and picked up a pizza. Good thing Hank liked pizza as well as the girls. I didn't want Jean back to cook supper, not just yet.

After supper, I stopped Hank from going to watch TV.

"There's a Disney show on tonight. Why don't you girls go in the family room and watch it. Your dad and I are going to play cards in here and talk."

"We are?" Hank was surprised.

I put on my sweetest smile, not too much, though, and nodded.

As the girls closed the family room door, I turned to Hank and said, "What do you think about leaving Seattle?"

The question startled Hank. I saw the wheels grinding—did I mean him or us? His paranoia was in full swing. I had to head it off quick.

"What I mean is, we're not very happy here and maybe we should move." Even if you're paranoid, Hank, it doesn't mean I'm not out to get you. Ha.

Hank relaxed a bit and shifted in the breakfast nook.

"You'd do that? You'd give up your job and move somewhere else?"

"Well, there's not much out here to keep me, is there? Sandra's in Alaska. My poor sister Ailene and her husband,

Allen, would be here without family, but what the heck. You need to get back to work somewhere."

Guilt, guilt, stay away. Sorry, God, I know I shouldn't pull this crap, but I need to get him out of here.

"What if I went back to Indiana? I think I could go back to work for the bank there." Hank brightened with the expectation of a different lifestyle. "I could stay with Mom until I got enough money together to get a house. Then you and the girls could come out."

"Sure," I said, but Jean was fighting for control.

You can't just lie to him like that. It's not fair. He trusts me. I don't lie like that, Jody. Stop this.

I'm sorry, Jean. It's for your own good. It really is. Look, for most of your life people have manipulated you and your emotions, especially Hank. Now he's due a taste of his own medicine.

Hank was getting excited with the prospects. He would go out and make a new life for us. We would stay home and be a good little family for him once again. Almost the only time he was happy was when Jean wasn't working in Florida years before. I was sure he pictured that happy, totally dependent home, restructured in Indiana. I let him go on thinking that.

In the weeks that followed, Hank got ambitious. He wouldn't go out and get another job, but he needed money. So instead, he went to flea markets and had garage sales, selling off anything and everything he could take from the house or the storage shed.

One day I came home to find he had sold my new washer and dryer for less than half what I had recently finished paying for them. Then he sold off our living and dining room furniture. I could get new ones in Indiana, he told me. Nothing we had was sacred to him. The last straw hit when I found he'd sold the gold necklace Sandra had given me for Christmas years ago, but there was nothing I could do. He was determined to take anything that would bring a buck.

I took the girls aside and told them, "Let's let him take whatever he wants. This is the last time he's leaving us and he's not coming back. After he's gone, we'll buy what we need and it will be all ours." I protected their desk, TV, bedroom furniture, books, and toys, though. Those were not his to sell.

Finally he put together his traveling money and packed to go. In one last desperate move to raise cash, he sold his old car and arranged to drive someone's new pickup truck into Chicago for a car delivery service. He brought the truck to the house and loaded up anything else he thought he could sell to take with him. Then he was gone.

It took me nearly four months to get Jean to consider divorce again. I had gotten Hank out physically, but he had to go from Jean's conscience. This time I enlisted Pastor Dave's help. If there was one thing I knew about Jean, she would do what God allowed. I set up and went to Dave's appointment. Then I gave Jean control.

"Jean," Pastor Dave greeted, smiling, "how have you been?"

"Pretty good since Hank left." I settled into a chair in Dave's office. He picked the one next to me. "Really, Dave, that's what I came to see you about. I just don't know what to do."

"Tell me about it."

"You know it was Jody that divorced Hank the last time, and I remarried him." I paused and glanced out the window past Dave. He was nodding his head slightly in agreement. "I haven't told you, or anyone for that matter, except my sister's ex-husband, that Hank ran off with another woman the last time he was gone."

Pastor Dave took in a breath audibly and scratched his head.

I continued, "I let him come back and I tried to forgive him. The truth of the matter is that I just don't love him anymore, but I don't know what to do. I think he needs me, but I don't believe he loves me."

Dave shook his head. "Where is he now?"

"He's gone back to Indiana. He's living with his mom and working at the bank where he used to work before we moved. He thinks he's putting money together to buy a house where we'll all live happily ever after. But I can tell you, the girls don't want him back, except maybe Melissa. I worry about her. Hank always treated her as the favorite."

"Why don't you just let him go?" Dave asked.

"Let him go? You mean divorce him again?"

"Yes."

"But everything I've ever been taught is that you make it work. Divorce just isn't part of my upbringing."

"Even the Bible allows for divorce," he said with finality.

I was surprised. I hadn't read it in the Bible. I read for all sorts of comfort, but not for divorce.

"Let me show you," Dave said, taking a stack of Bibles off the shelf beside him. "Let's look at First Corinthians seven:fifteen. Here, read this."

I read it aloud: " 'But if the unbeliever leaves, let him do so. A believing man or woman is not bound in such circumstances; God has called us to live in peace.' "

"Look at this King James Version," he said, handing me the other Bible.

" 'But if the unbelieving depart, let him depart. A brother or sister is not under bondage in such cases: but God hath called us to peace.' "

"Listen," Dave said, "Hank doesn't want to stay. That's why he keeps running off. Sure, he came back when he needed comfort and money, but weren't you finally convinced when he chose another woman to run away with? He's not a Christian. Let him go."

So it was, armed with the knowledge that I was not divorcing but releasing Hank, I finally bonded with Jody and put in a call to Elaine's office.

ELEVEN

FINALLY JEAN AND JODY WERE ONE PERSON. NEITHER OF US had "disappeared" in the process of integrating as feared. I had the shared memories of Jean and Jody. I was celebrating my new strength from the union of Jean and Jody. I was now going to be a whole person, in control of my life, free from the fears and pain of my past. I knew what the individual women had valued and I profited from the interweaving of these two sets of values. In spite of what Jean had thought of Jody, or Jody had thought of Jean, I hadn't been very different in areas such as faith and morals, as either Jean or Jody. But, for example, from being Jean I gained computer expertise and well-grounded steadfastness, and from being Jody I gained more humor and assurance that life was really worth living. The combination seemed unbeatable and I rejoiced.

However, on this day I had a particularly bad appointment with Jack. Jack was not convinced that I was so complete, so free. My dreams were still filled with violence, and small things in my life brought on flashes of terror. I remembered the pictures I had seen in my mind and the horrible scream as I looked at a handful of lint. They had nothing to do with either the Jean or Jody personalities. I shuddered wondering who else could be holding back the tide of hidden pain?

Jack thought it was another personality.

"Look at your dreams," Jack explained. "There are clues there that clearly show Jean and Jody. Think about the fire dream where one sister was burned and the other pretended to be her. Those types of dreams typify the Jean/Jody behavior. But what about other dreams, the ones where someone is getting stabbed or bleeding? What about your 'Alice in Wonderland' type dreams? Who's trying to warn you? Or who are you trying to warn? Who got stabbed?"

I didn't want to know. Getting the Jean/Jody personalities together had taken so much; I didn't see how I could deal with another. Yet it nagged at me. The Jody memory of a depressed, frightened Jean was not part of the Jean memory. Who was it? Another Jean?

That night after the girls went to sleep, I lay down on my own bed and picked up a magazine. As I flipped through the pages, I came upon a suntan lotion ad. There was a young girl jumping up to hit a volleyball. The suntan line at the top of her pink shorts was clearly displayed. Suddenly a memory from my childhood leapt into focus in great detail.

Where was everybody?

I was just into my teens and watching television in the living room. The kids and Mom and Dad had been in and out, but now it seemed I was home by myself. The house was getting cold.

"Dad? Are you here?" I called out. No answer.

I walked to the stairs and called up, "Is anyone home?" Still no answer.

Bother! It was getting too cold. I was going to have to go down and put some coal in the furnace. I hated the basement. There were always spiders in the furnace room and the coal bin stayed full of them. They crawled down the coal chute into the bin where the air was warmer and there was a plentiful supply of other crawling things seeking warmth.

I opened the stairway door and looked down. Dim illumination of dusk shone through the glass panes below the narrow window wells, but no light was on downstairs. I flipped the switch on at the top of the stairs and shivered as I descended into the basement.

Only a single bulb in the long main basement room was lit and it was next to the stairwell. The back of the room was dark. The heavy, wooden door to the furnace room was open. I wished Dad would put a lightbulb in the ceiling fixture on the far end of the main room. That way the light would stream into the furnace room and I wouldn't have to pull the cord in that dark, creepy hole.

I stepped slowly into the furnace room, checking overhead for spiders.

Jeesh, how I hated spiders.

I jerked the cord and as the light came on, I jumped back out of the room. Now, looking slowly over the ceiling, I stepped back into the room. As I turned and looked back, I spotted a big, ugly, brown one, busy in a corner web over and to the left of the doorway.

Yuck! It made my skin crawl. Mom always harassed me about why I was so afraid of spiders. I had answered her disdainful comments a million times, "I know, I know, I'm bigger than they are, but I still can't stand them."

I opened the furnace door and peered in. The coals were dying away. I shivered. Even the furnace room was getting cold. I would definitely have to put new coal in the furnace and I really hated to do that. It meant opening that dreadful coal bin.

I grabbed a newspaper off the stacks against the coal bin wall, wadded it up and shoved it into the furnace. It caught fire almost immediately and lit up the inside of the furnace. Good. The new coal would burn okay.

I picked up the shovel in one hand and slowly unlatched the coal bin door. As it opened, another big spider dropped a couple inches in the doorway where it had been working its web.

I shivered involuntarily.

I quickly shoveled up some coal. Resting the full load on the floor, I shut and relatched the coal bin door. I turned to the furnace, lifting the load and pushing it through the furnace door. Two pieces of coal dropped. One rolled behind the furnace.

I wasn't going after that one.

The other rolled over against the newspapers. I set down the shovel and picked up the escapee. I snatched up another newspaper and wrapped the piece of coal to stuff it into the furnace, but as I looked at the paper stack, I froze.

Underneath the newspaper was a magazine. It frightened me. I didn't know why. The name and the words on the cover were not in English. Maybe it was German. In the caption under the cover picture was the word *kinder;* that meant "child," I thought. The picture was of a girl about ten or so. Her lips were bright red with lipstick. She was dressed only in tight, pink shorts and she was lounging on a couch. Her thumbs were hooked into the top of the shorts on each side and the band was rolled down slightly as though she was just putting them on or taking them off.

Where had I seen this before? No, I couldn't have seen this before. Why did it disturb me?

I grabbed another newspaper and covered up the magazine.

I felt sick. No, I was getting cold. I had to get out of there.

I shoved the newspaper-wrapped coal into the furnace and leaned close to feel the warmth as the paper flared up and burnt.

That should do it.

I eyed the spider in the corner as I pulled the light cord and ran out of the room. As I went up the stairs, I heard the piano playing.

Was Dad home? No, it was Matthew.

"Where have you been?" I asked him, as I shut the basement door.

"Over at Mike's. Did you put some coal on the fire?"

"Yes, but I hate doing that."

"You and your spiders," he said, as he shook his head.

I wondered if I should tell him about the magazine.

"Matt, have you ever seen any of the magazines in the furnace room?"

"You better stay out of those," he warned, stopping his playing. "Those are *Dad's*."

"I know, but—"

Matt interrupted, "He's got all kinds of girlie magazines hidden in the newspapers down there. What do you think he does when he goes down there? You think he's just feeding his fish? But I tell you, he better not catch you looking at his magazines or you'll be sorry."

"I wasn't looking at his magazines. I was getting a newspaper to start the coal and saw one."

"Did you cover it back up?"

"Yeah, I threw another newspaper over it."

"That's good. Then he won't know you were looking at it."

"I wasn't looking at it."

"Shush! Here comes Mom. Don't say anything more about it."

I wondered if Matthew knew what I was talking about. I thought girlie magazines were like the *Playboy*s that Becky's brother, Philip, had. I had never seen any with little kids on the cover, or had I?

• • •

I threw my magazine toward the nightstand. What had the memory meant? Why was it coming back now with such clarity? Had Jack been right? Was there another Jean hiding in my head? Was this the "other Jean" Jack had thought was the superdepressed and frightened me?

I wanted desperately to call Jack, but I waited until the next day.

"Jack," I pleaded. "I really need to see you. I need to talk about this other Jean."

"I'll try to find a slot in the next couple of days. I'll call you."

"Thanks, Jack."

Two days later I was again sitting in Jack's office, trying to explain my fears.

"You know I didn't want to believe that there was another personality in my head. But I don't know what to think anymore. When I was Jody, I used to think there could have been another Jean, whenever the Jean part of me was superdepressed. Now I'm not so sure that other Jean wasn't really another personality, as you've suggested."

After I related my memory flash to Jack, he asked me to think about what frightened me in the memory. Had I remembered seeing the magazine before? There were child pornography magazines, but they were more easily found overseas than here in the States, where their production was outlawed. And why was I so afraid of spiders?

"I'm almost ashamed to tell anyone why spiders have always frightened me, but I do know," I told Jack, sighing and shaking my head. I looked into the corner above his desk and pursed my lips. Why did I feel guilty?

Jack sat patiently waiting for me to continue, as he usually did when I was dueling with my emotions. I traced the line of the ceiling with my eye until I was looking above him, and then passed quickly over his poker face, his brown and tan plaid shirt, his dark brown corduroys, down to his tan leather boots. As I stared at the swirls cut into the leather, he shifted in his chair, and I looked up suddenly.

"I guess," I thought aloud, "that it's tied in with my feelings for my mother and how she never accepted how frightened I was as a child."

"What happened?"

"It's a very young memory, so I'm not sure I have it all accurate." Already I was beginning to feel guilty about telling Jack. "That's probably one reason that I don't like to talk about it—I doubt if my mother remembers it, and she rarely believes that I recall anything accurately. However, I know essentially what happened because it's such a painful memory."

"What do you remember?"

"We were living in a housing project, built shortly after World War II. Some of the houses were still under construction, and there was a huge sandlot behind our yard that ran for nearly a block. Our backyard, like most of the yards along the street, was cyclone fenced, with a gate that opened into the sandlot. It might have been a nice place to live except there were so many big, mean boys that lived around there. I don't really know how old they were. I must have been about three and a half or four at the time, so almost everybody looked big.

"Matt was a year and a half older than I was and Mom was pregnant with Mark at the time. I'm sure of that, because I can picture her so clearly in her cotton flowered housedress with the middle buttons undone and her slip showing through where she bulged.

"Anyway, Mom had let me play out in the backyard by myself. She was busy in the house, cooking or sewing. I don't know where Matt was, he might have been at kindergarten. I wasn't supposed to go out of the yard, but a couple of the big boys were out in the sandlot and called to me. . . ." My mind drifted into my childhood as I relived the memory.

• • •

"Jean?" One of the boys yelled, "Come here and see what we have. It's something for you. Come on over here."

I walked to the gate and leaned against the fencing trying to see what he had, but he carefully hid it from my view.

"Bring it over here," I called back to him.

"Naw," he answered. "If you don't want it, I'll give it to someone else. If you want it, you have to come over here."

Without knowing what he had, I wanted it, or at least I wanted to see what it was. I reached up and pushed open the latch on the gate. As I stepped through, I glanced back to see if Mommy could see me; I knew I wasn't being good. I ran across the lot out to the boys.

"What have you got?" I asked as I ran up to them.

"This!" One of them yelled as he grabbed my arm with one hand. In his other hand was a large glass canning jar. The jar was full of black and brown garden spiders, the kind with big heads, long bodies, and long, spindly legs. They were crawling over each other, trying to get to the top of the jar where the boy was holding a paper with punched holes in it for air.

"We got these just for you," the other boy said.

"No," the first boy said, "we got you just for them."

The two boys laughed and pulled me down on the ground. Each of them put a knee on one of my arms so I couldn't get up or defend myself. I was too afraid to scream for my mommy.

"Do you know what we're going to do? We're going to feed you to our spiders. We're going to dump them in your face and they're going to eat your eyes out and crawl inside you and eat your guts out."

"Mommy! Mommy!" I began screaming, but immediately the boy started shaking the spiders onto my face and into my hair. I shut my eyes tightly and stopped screaming to keep from getting one of them in my mouth. Fuzzy little legs clambered down my cheek and over my ears, frantically escaping from their captors. I squeezed my mouth and eyes closed tightly and cried, *"Mmmm! Mmmm!"* as I rolled my head from side to side to shake the horrid creatures from me.

I tried to kick the boys and pull away from them. I was able to free one arm and I madly brushed the scrambling spiders from my face and hair.

The boys suddenly let go of me and ran off laughing. I opened my eyes as I stood up, wildly flinging my head around, swatting my face, and screaming, *"Mommy! Mommy!"* Spiders dropped off me in all directions. Some of them fell on my pink dress and I hit them off as I ran toward my house.

"Mommy! Mommy!"

I saw her open the side door and clumsily hurry down the steps and across the yard, calling to me, "Jean! What is it? What's the matter?"

I reached the gate seconds before she did.

"Mommy, those boys dumped spiders in my face! They said they were going to eat me! Get them out of my hair, Mommy! Get them out of my hair!"

"Oh, for crying out loud, Jean Darby," she replied angrily. "What were you doing out of the yard anyway? There aren't any spiders in your hair."

"But, Mommy—"

"But nothing. If you can't play out here without running out in the sandlot, you have to play in your room. Go on, now."

I continued to flail at my hair and she grabbed my hands.

"Stop that," she commanded. Then she brushed down my hair with her hands, and said more calmly, "There's no spiders in your hair. Now go on to your room. You wouldn't have trouble with those boys if you'd stay in your yard where you belong."

I ran away from her, up the steps and into the house. By

the time I reached my bedroom, tears were running down my face. She didn't care. I snatched the pillow off my bed and hugged it as I huddled in the corner of the room. My hair and the skin on my legs seemed to crawl. I kept jerking around, expecting to find that one of those spiders had hung on and come home with me. But the thing that I kept thinking most was that she didn't care. I was almost eaten alive by big, ugly spiders and she didn't care.

I shook my head and rolled my eyes up at Jack. He had lost his usually straight face and was shaking his head also, but said nothing.

"It wasn't until night came that the terror of those spiders came back," I continued. "I have no idea if it was that same night or whenever. I remember that Mom and Dad had company and after I went to bed I could hear them talking in the living room. Then I spied a huge spider crawling on the ceiling. I knew it had come back to eat me. I couldn't hide from it. If I went to sleep, he would drop down and bite me. I screamed for my mommy again. She came rushing in and was upset that the only thing wrong with me was a tiny, little spider on the ceiling. She had my daddy come in and kill it, but they both laughed about it.

"From then on it was a horror for me and a joke for everyone else. I had to check out the ceiling of every room for fear a spider would be up there, waiting to drop on me. I had nightmares that they were on the floor, waiting for my foot, and I was afraid to get up and go to the bathroom—which may have contributed to my bed-wetting. Even long after I was old enough to tell myself the fear was irrational, I couldn't shake it. To this day, I nearly become hysterical if something crawls on me."

As I spoke about the spiders, quick flashes of black-and-white pictures began to snap through my mind. I closed my eyes and shuddered. One flashed into view and I saw the coal bin looming before me and felt as though someone were pushing me into it. I looked up quickly at Jack. I didn't want him to know what I had seen and felt. I guessed he would think my shiver was due to my last statement.

We talked at length about the probability of the "Other Jean." Jack was convinced she existed. We began to call her "OJ" for short. She was the voice I heard screaming in my mind when I had seen snapshots of the basement flash through.

"I'll tell you something else strange that might be an OJ action," I told Jack. "Shortly after Erin was born, a vacuum cleaner salesman came to the house. I remember asking him in, but thinking at the time that I couldn't afford the Kirby he was carrying. The next thing I remember, the man was gone and I was holding the vacuum and the sales contract. I had to call him back the next day and tear up the contract. I lost the twenty-five-dollar deposit, which was a huge loss for me at the time. I assumed it was part of my insanity.

"Then again after I first got a house in the Seattle area, I found that I had purchased a new Rainbow vacuum for around two thousand dollars. It took me a while to get that straightened out, because apparently I had it for several weeks before discovering it—I couldn't just tear up the contract and lose a deposit. I thought I had really lost my mind then. I never did get my old cleaner back and I ended up having to charge another one at Sears. I guess it would all make sense if there was another person that bought them, but why would OJ want to buy an expensive vacuum?"

"I couldn't tell you, but I'm sure there's someone else in your head."

I was convinced Jack was right about OJ, but I wasn't sure I wanted to know what she held for me.

For the next few sessions, I tried to tell Jack what flashes of memory I had seen, especially what looked like the corners of black-and-white photos, not quite revealing enough for me to see. He felt they were clues to what had happened to me and why my mind had created this other personality, OJ.

"Jean," Jack said finally. "I want to try to talk with OJ, but I think I should have another woman present when I do. I don't know how she'll react. Would you object to me asking my wife to come in when I try?"

"No, I guess not, but why?

"I'm concerned about how OJ might react to being alone with an adult male. She may or may not recognize me. She might be afraid. Having a woman here, even if she doesn't know her, might make her less afraid."

Pictures flashed by quickly in my mind. It seemed so ominous, I suppressed a shudder. "I see. She might be afraid of you?"

"Maybe. I'd like to make her as comfortable as possible."

"Okay," I said. "I don't know if I can pass control to her, though. I remember how hard it was for me as Jean to give it up to Jody."

"I think you could try. If I could get her to talk to me, I might understand how to help her."

I nodded agreement, but a small knot was forming in my stomach. I wondered if it was OJ.

Then I thought, this is ridiculous. We can't call her OJ.

"Jack," I laughed. "I don't think we should call this other person OJ. Maybe we could call her JD for Jean Darby, instead. Somehow OJ sounds like orange juice or some athlete."

He laughed too and we changed the name.

It was two weeks later when I returned for our session with JD. Terrible nightmares had become a regular occurrence, as though to prepare me for the realities that JD would give me.

I had begun to try talking to this "third person." I wasn't sure whether she could hear me or not. I tried to think of any

time she might have spoken to me. However, all I could remember were screams from somewhere inside my head at
times when something bothered me and I didn't know why.
I hadn't looked forward to this meeting with Jack. Somehow
I thought it would open a door into a room I didn't want to
see.

"Jean, this is my wife, Pauline. Pauline, this is Jean."

I wondered how much Jack told her; probably everything.
He had spoken of her with affection, although I knew very
little about her. I smiled thinking about what he had told me
of her wry sense of humor.

I looked into her eyes. They were filled with gentle concern, but I was certain that they could easily change to those
of the amused, girlish prankster Jack had described. I knew
so little else about her, I worried how JD would react, if she
took control at all.

"I told Pauline why I wanted to have a woman here, in
case JD reacted badly to being alone with a man." Jack interrupted my thoughts.

I took a quick breath and tried to let it out slowly. I didn't
know if I could turn control over to JD. I wasn't sure I even
wanted to.

"Do you want to talk about anything first or would you
like to try to get JD to talk with us now?" Jack offered.

"I guess I'll try to find her." I looked down at the carpet
and tried to find her in my head. *JD, you have to come out
from wherever you are. I'm leaving. You'll have to talk to
Jack and Pauline. JD?*

*Oh, no! I can't be here. I can't talk to them. You know Shad-
owman can hear me! You know what he'll do to me. Jody!
Don't leave me here!*

Off to the left I could see a woman sitting in the chair
across the table staring at me. Jack was staring too. I know
Jody talks to him, but what did they want from me?

I can't talk to them. *He'll* hear me. Shadowman will hear me. Maybe I can get away. Maybe I can get out of here. If I don't say anything, he won't know I was here. The door is over there. I will have to go around the couch to get to it. Jack could stop me before I got to the door. *Jody, where are you?*

The lady's hand was touching my arm. "JD, it's all right. No one is going to hurt you."

I was trying not to move. Maybe I could just go away. *Jody!*

There was no other door. I couldn't see how I could leave. I had to go inside.

Jody, please come. You know he will hurt me.

No he won't. Talk to them.

No! I'm going. I don't want him to hear me.

Whoa—my arms ached.

"Jean?" Jack tilted his head in recognition of the change. "Yes?"

"How do you feel?"

"My arms ache like I've just been holding off a steam-roller, single-handed."

"I'm not surprised. It appeared as though JD was reliving some horrible experience."

I started to say no, but then her fear seemed to flood into my mind. I gripped my beads and tried to control the feelings.

"She was terrified," I explained. "She kept screaming that *he'll* hear me and trying to figure out how to get out of here. She called me Jody. She begged me to come back."

"Who will hear her?"

"Shadowman."

"And who is Shadowman?"

"I'm not sure, but she is frozen with fear about him."

I shook my head and looked at Pauline. A picture of a

huge shadow flashed through my mind. It was threatening and somehow reminded me of dust. "I don't know. I still have problems understanding what happened. Could you tell a difference?" I asked Pauline, in an attempt to escape the current line of thought and discussion.

"Yes!" Her eyes opened wider as she spoke. "It was really amazing. Your face turned into a frightened child's face. It was so different."

I wondered if anyone would believe this. I wondered if I believed what had happened. Why not? Hadn't there been Jean and Jody? But why was JD in my head? Had I known forever that she was there? I didn't want to know what memories she held for me.

Jack read my mind again. "You are going to have to face whatever happened to her."

"I'm not sure I can."

"Not now and not all at once. She protected you from having to deal with some horror as a child, but now that you're older, you're going to have to start dealing with it. Don't be surprised if you start having some pretty violent dreams in the next few days. You'll need to remember some of them."

In the months that followed, we were unable to get JD to appear again in Jack's office, but Jean and Jody had integrated. In my joy of having the combined strength now, I thought I could handle anything, maybe even JD.

Jack had tried unsuccessfully to bring JD out to talk with him. I had begun to listen to her voice, trying to determine what made her appear and retreat so rapidly. She seemed to know about me, as the Jody part of me had known about the Jean part of me. She had called for me when she had appeared, and she had answered when I tried to calm her. Yet I knew so little of why she existed. I sensed that she had feared Hank as well as her Shadowman.

It was August, nearly five months after I had asked Elaine to draw up my divorce papers again, when I finally went down to her office and signed them. She would have to get Hank served in Indiana. It was time to end this marriage once and for all time. I slipped off my wedding band and popped it into a tiny tin Tylenol box in my top dresser drawer. It was the only real gold I had left, since Hank had sold my gold chain necklace, along with almost everything else of value before he left. A white band of skin marked the ring's absence. I was sure it would tan over with the garden work.

This Seattle summer had been wonderful. The weekends had been clear and warm. The garden had grown tall in the cultivated space next to the house. Even the potatoes, partially hidden under the Italian plum tree, were in full bloom. As I left for work, I longed to spend the day weeding and digging the new carrots and radishes. My gardens had truly been my security blanket. Almost every year since I married Hank I had planted one. Sometimes the only food we had in the house had come from the garden. It reminded me of the scene from *Gone with the Wind*—none of my family would ever go hungry again.

On my way in to work I wondered if anyone would notice that my ring was gone. I felt a sense of freedom I hadn't felt since I came to Seattle from Florida. I was getting better and I was going to be free.

There wasn't much offered in the form of amenities at the company where I worked. Our small troupe of programmers and analysts took our breaks in the tiny lunchroom and drank orange juice over ice. We trekked back down at lunch and tried to outdo each other with gross stories, or to discuss the fate of Seattle's soccer team or how the Seahawks were playing.

After our morning break, Don, one of the analysts, came over to my desk.

"You told me last week you were filing for a divorce," he said, then hesitated slightly. "I, ah . . . have a pair of tickets for the Seahawks preseason game this Friday and I wondered if you'd like to share them with me."

"Sure," I answered quickly.

"Great." Don's smile widened. "How about we leave from here after work Friday and grab a bite to eat before the game?"

"Sounds good."

Our boss stepped into my office doorway and summoned Don.

"Oh, I'm sorry. I need to see what Kathy wants." He headed toward her office and grinned. "I'll talk to you later, okay?"

I nodded and turned back to my desk. Then it hit me. Oh, my, what had I done? I only filed my papers a few days ago and now I've agreed to go out? A date? I wasn't even single yet and I was dating? I had to call my sister Ailene. She had done some contract programming here a short while and she knew Don. I needed to see what she thought.

When I reached Ailene, she was pleased and surprised.

"Robbing the cradle, aren't you?" she asked jokingly.

"I don't think so, Ailene," I said with much more confidence than I felt.

"Well, I think Don is a nice guy, even if a little strange."

"Strange?" I wondered how he could be stranger than I was.

"Yeah. You know how he sweeps his lunch crumbs into a little pile and leaves them on the table." She laughed. "After Don's had lunch, you can always tell where he sat in the cafeteria."

"Ailene, I don't care about that. He told me he did that because there's no wastebaskets or napkins in the lunchroom. What I want to know is what you think about my going out before my divorce is even finalized?"

"I say go for it. Hank has been gone for six months and he isn't coming back now. You may as well make a life for yourself."

"Thanks, Ailene. I guess it's no big thing, but I haven't been out on a formal date for years." At least not as Jean, I hadn't.

I hung up the phone and looked at my computer terminal. I'd never thought about an age difference. I didn't usually think about people in terms of age. What if I was ten years older than Don? What was I going to do?

Don's employee profile would be in the human resources database. As I was building new on-line screens for the system, I would have access to those records. I knew I wasn't supposed to access the production employee files, but I needed to know. I looked around the office. Most of my fellow employees worked earlier hours than I did and had gone home for the day. I logged on to the system and keyed in "Cline." Two record selections came up; I picked "Don Xavier Cline." His header information flashed up on the screen. I looked closely at his date of birth.

Whew! He was younger, but only four years. I could live with that.

The girls were visiting with their grandmother. It made it easier for me to accept Don's invitation. After the initial surprise over my acceptance, I found I was looking forward to it.

That Saturday we sat on Don's couch and watched the sun fading over the Olympic Mountains across the Sound. His apartment was on the ground floor of a building in West Seattle. The sliding glass doors that separated us from the swimming pool and the beach beyond were open to let the summer breeze cool the apartment. The water on Puget Sound was fairly calm and only small waves glistened in the sun's last rays. The view was worthy of a Marshall Johnson painting.

As carefully as I could, I tried to describe my mental state. This was one man I didn't want to scare off right away. I had only been with him for a couple days, but I already thought he was special. After a year of working a desk away from each other, Don and I had a lot of respect for each other professionally and personally, but I had surprised myself by agreeing to go out with him.

We had gone to Omar's for dinner and to the Seahawks football game, and then come back to his apartment to talk. I surprised myself again by staying the night and all the next day, and now we were watching the second sunset together. My anxiety was heightened as I contemplated spending another night wrapped up with him.

"I don't know how to tell you this, but . . . well . . . don't be surprised if I suddenly act a little weird." I took a chance.

Don raised an eyebrow and looked suspicious. "What do you mean, 'weird'?"

"It's just that sometimes I get . . . well . . . I act different."

"Different? How?"

"I'd have to tell you a lot more than I think I can right now to explain the whole situation. It has to do with some problems that I'm working on with a psychiatrist."

"Well, you can tell me what you want or not. I just need to know what I should do if you start 'acting weird.' "

"I'd rather not get into all the details right now. But if I should start acting like someone else, what you need to do is ask to talk to Jody."

"Someone else?"

"It's hard to explain, but I can sort of change into someone called JD. She knows me as Jody, so if you just ask for Jody, I'll be okay. I felt I should tell you just in case, but I really don't want to talk about it right now, if you don't mind."

"No, I don't mind if you don't want to talk about it," Don said as he rose from the couch. "I think I'll close the door all the way. The breeze felt good, but it's getting a little chilly now."

I watched as he closed the sliding glass door. I wondered what he must think of me after that cryptic little discussion. I really didn't want to tell him about all this yet, but I couldn't take the chance of a surprise visit from JD. My neck was beginning to cramp and she seemed to show up often now when I was in pain.

When he came back to the couch, Don snuggled up to me, and said, "I know another thing we can do to warm up."

We moved into the bedroom and got thoroughly heated. Afterward, we showered and I cuddled up naked against his body for the night.

Where am I? I'm in bed with someone I don't know. Where are my clothes? I've got to get out of here. If I move very slowly maybe he won't wake up. I'll put one foot on the floor next to the bed and move over a little bit. No, he's trying to wrap around me. Don't touch me! Good, he's still asleep. I'll move his arm off me, carefully, and slide out of the bed.

Where are my clothes? It's too dark to find them. Here's the door. The hall is dark, too. There's another door—it's the bathroom. Is there a towel? Yes, good. I'll wrap up in it and try to get out of here.

"Jean?"

No! He's awake. Where can I hide? Into the living room. Behind the fireplace. Maybe if I hide in the corner he won't find me.

"Jean? Where are you?"

No, no! He's seen me.

"JD? Is that you. Don't be afraid. Just let me talk to Jody, okay? Can I talk to Jody?"

• • •

"Don?"

"Yes?"

"I'm sorry, really I am. I was afraid this would happen."

"Don't be sorry. C'mon back to bed. We can talk in the morning. It's late. You okay?"

"Yes, thank you, but I'm sorry I woke you."

"It's okay."

We snuggled back into bed.

Doggone it. I hadn't wanted this kind of thing to happen, not yet, anyway. I'd wanted for us to have a chance to get to know each other better before I had to explain this. He must think I'm a certifiable lunatic now. I probably brought it on myself, talking about JD this evening.

In the morning, Don made breakfast and we returned to the couch to talk.

"Want to tell me what happened last night?"

"It's difficult to explain. I've been under therapy for so many years that I've lost count. It's only been in the last three or four years that we've even known what the problem was." I looked at Don to see how he was reacting. I was relieved to see him absorbed but not shocked. I smiled, thinking, *He really is special.*

"When Jack—that's my doctor—and I got to talking about my father, I recalled several times when he was extremely abusive. Apparently Jack believes I was abused even worse by my dad, and I couldn't handle everything that happened. What Jack found was that I had split off my emotions into three parts or personalities to survive: Jean—who was good, obedient, hardworking, self-sacrificing; Jody—who was somewhat egotistical, protective, fun loving; and JD—who was and still is the injured child. JD is holding those abusive memories for me. Two of the three have been what Jack calls 'integrated,' that is they have become one person. You know me as Jean, but I am really the integration of Jean and Jody."

"And where is JD?" he asked with a casualness as though I had been talking about my children instead of my weirdness.

"Well, she's still in my head somewhere. That's really why I needed to explain this all to you. Last night, it was JD that came out."

"What do you mean, 'came out'?" He looked curious, but not terribly serious.

"Oh, boy," I said with a sigh. "It's even harder to explain, I'm afraid. Most of my life, I lived as three people, usually with Jean in control. When Jean got severely stressed or depressed, Jody took control from Jean. After Jack discovered that my problem was multiple personality, I learned that I was able to pass control back and forth between the two by concentrating. Eventually I integrated the two personalities into one Jean/Jody.

"As far as I can tell, JD hasn't had much control since I was a child," I continued. "I guess she was only around whenever I was being seriously abused. I've been able to pass control to her once in Jack's office, but she was so frightened that she wouldn't talk with anyone, not even to Jack. I heard her clearly in Jack's office as she screamed for me to take back control. However, when I'm really tired or in pain, she does get control sometimes. Since I got rear-ended in a car accident last year, I've had a lot of pain, so unfortunately she's been around more. Anyway, when she 'came out' last night, she didn't know where she was and was scared."

"I'm glad you told me last night before that happened. I don't know what I would have done. I probably would have thought you were in shock or something and called a hospital." He looked relieved. He also didn't look overly concerned about what I was telling him. I was amazed by his reasoning and acceptance.

• • •

It was early November when Elaine's office called to tell me that my divorce couldn't be finalized until January. The authorities in Indiana had taken nearly two months to find and serve Hank his papers. For nearly a month more Elaine's pixie of a secretary tried to get in touch with me. The girls and I were practically living with Don in his West Seattle condo. I didn't have an answering machine at the house, so the pixie finally reached me at work.

The girls seemed happy to have Hank gone, but they were uncomfortable with Don. They needed my attention, but I needed Don's. I hadn't had a man doting on me since Jean drove Brian out of my life in Chicago. It made me feel guilty and neglectful. I had a hard time giving the girls what they needed, and at the same time taking what I wanted from life. I needed Don's love and he gave it to me so freely.

One frosty morning after I had dropped off Teresa and Melissa at school, Erin had asked me to drive her back to the house to pick up a book. On the way back, as we waited at the busy cross street, a small van turned in and stopped in the street next to us. It was Hank. He quickly rolled down his window and I followed suit to hear him.

"I need to talk to you *now*," he called to me.

"Right now I have to take Erin to school," I called back. Why had he come? I had hoped never to see him again. I loved Don and was beginning to enjoy living again. "Wait for me at the house; I'll be right back."

He waved and continued down the street.

I found a break in traffic and pulled out. As I looked to my right to check traffic, I saw Erin. The color had drained from her face. Had the sight of her father frightened her so much?

By the time we approached the school she was shaking visibly. I had to end this nightmare for her.

"Erin, honey, your father is not coming back. I won't let him. I promise you that he will be gone long before you get out of school. You don't have to talk to him or even see him again. We're done with that kind of life. We're going to make a better life without him."

"You're sure?" Erin asked meekly.

"I'm positive. Look, I love Don. Hasn't our life been better since your dad left? I don't want to go back to wondering whether or not I should be wearing armor before I open the front door. I hated the yelling and the tension, more than you did. He's not coming back with us."

"I couldn't stand it. I couldn't live there if he moved back," Erin cried.

"That's not going to happen." I tried to assure her with a hug. "Now, you better scoot or you'll be late to class."

Reluctantly she opened the door and slid out. She walked about halfway to the building and I threw her a kiss when she looked over her shoulder.

I hadn't taken to heart how hard Hank had been on his children. When I had my divorce drawn up, Jack had recommended *no* visitation rights, but I had allowed for two weeks in summer to be put in the papers. As I watched Erin's fear surface physically, I was reminded of Hank's unreasonable treatment of her. One day in particular came to mind.

Erin had been in a bicycle accident. Her elbow had been badly skinned and a bit of bone exposed. Hank had refused her medical care for nearly an hour, because he believed she was lying to him; he thought that she had been struck by the car that brought her and Melissa home. Finally he called me at work, came and got me, and I took her to the hospital.

In the emergency room, Erin's elbow was cleaned, dressed, and bandaged. The hospital folks told her she would probably have a nasty scar on her arm. They had certainly been right about the injury—two years had passed and Erin was still wearing long sleeves to cover that scarred arm. I wondered how much better it would have been if more than an hour hadn't passed before it got treated. I also wondered what kind of emotional scars the girls would have.

No, Hank was not coming back. I had filed those divorce papers and he was not coming back. I prayed for the strength to handle him.

Hank was sitting in the living room when I came into the house. I rushed by him and on into the kitchen, saying, "I'll be with you in a minute. I just need to call work." Quickly I dialed Don's number. As soon as he answered I blurted out, "Hank is sitting in my living room."

"What's he doing there?"

"I don't know, but I'll get rid of him. Let the boss know I won't be in until later, will you?"

"Sure. Is it okay if I call you after a while?"

"Yes, please do," I answered gladly. I might need him. I was beginning to feel the pull of the Jean/Jody conflict again—part of me wanted to "make things right" for Hank, the rest of me was pushing away from him. The Jean part of me had been so manipulated by Hank for so many years, it was difficult to prevent Hank from separating her personality from the combined Jean/Jody again. I almost wished I had asked Don to come help. I felt desperate and alone.

Hank rounded the corner into the kitchen as I hung up. "Who were you talking to?"

"Someone at work. I needed to let them know I would be in late." It was true, but I also needed someone to know, someone who loved me, that I was alone with Hank. I didn't feel physically threatened, but did I have the mental strength to send him packing immediately?

Hank took my hand and drew me back to the couch.

"Jean, why are you doing this to me?" I knew he meant the divorce. "You know how much I love you. I need you. Is it just because I've been gone? You know I've been trying to earn enough money to have you and the girls come out there."

"Hank," I said firmly, "I have no intention of coming out

there. The girls don't want to live with you and neither do I."

He immediately broke into tears. "How could you say that when you know how much I love you? There's never been anyone but you. I drove day and night without any sleep to come out here and talk to you."

The Jean part of me was drawn out with pity. The Jody part of me was screaming in my head, *He's a liar! Don't listen to him. He ran off to Canada with that girl. Don't let him sucker you again.* I realized that I was Jean, only Jean, separated from Jody once again.

I hugged him, ignoring Jody's pleas, but I held on to her message. "I'm sorry, Hank. I don't mean to hurt you, really I don't. But you must understand, you wouldn't get the help you needed. I couldn't let the girls go on suffering with your treatment of them, or me either, for that matter."

He looked up through his tears. "Give me another chance. I told you things would be better. I'm working now. We'll get a house out there and—"

"No, Hank. I can't do that."

"Then there's nothing for me to live for. I might as well die. I don't want to end up a lonely old man, wandering the streets with no family."

I reached past him and picked up his car keys. In his mental condition, he could easily drive off a bridge or into a wall. I wasn't going to be the cause of his suicide.

Yeah, like he's really going to do that, Jody was scoffing.

"Jean, please let me stay with you," Hank begged, tears running off his face.

"Hank, you need to get some sleep and then we can talk. You're too tired to be reasonable."

He rubbed the tears off his face and sat quietly for a moment. I wondered what I could say. Just then the phone rang.

I jumped up and went into the kitchen. As I answered the

phone, I dropped Hank's keys into the recipe box on the counter.

Don's sweet, concerned voice was on the line. "Are you okay? I know it hasn't been very long, but I needed to call you."

"Yes, I'm okay, but thanks for calling. I love you. I'll call you back in a little while. I need to get Hank out of here first."

"If you don't call me in an hour, I'll call you back." He hung up.

I stepped into the doorway and leaned against the wall. Hank had given in to his tears and was sitting on the couch with his face in his hands. What was I going to do with him? He needed me, I was sure of that, but I didn't want to take care of him the rest of my life. I had three kids; I didn't need four. Besides, I did love Don.

"Have you had anything to eat?" I asked, trying not to acknowledge his pain.

"No," he said, his voice muffled through his hands. "Not since I left home, other than the sandwiches that Mom made for me the first day."

"I'll fix you something."

I opened the refrigerator. It was nearly empty, but Hank liked eggs and potatoes, and they were available. I managed to find a small jar of instant coffee and put together a meal. I drew up a folding chair as I handed Hank a cup. He sat in the breakfast nook eating in silence.

I felt totally stressed. I didn't know what to say to him. I was sorry for him, but I never wanted to live with him again. Still, somehow I felt responsible for him. He needed me.

You don't need him. Jody was continuing the battle for my emotions. *Tell him!*

Hank looked better after he finished eating. He surveyed the room slowly. I noticed a couple of Don's shirts lying on the floor in the laundry room. Hank spied them as well.

"Is there someone else?" His anxiety was apparent; he quickly retracted the question. "No, don't tell me. I don't care. I just want you to know I love you and I need you."

"Hank," I answered slowly, trying to think how to put it. "I have been seeing someone else, ever since I filed my papers. I love him very much. That was him on the phone a while ago."

"Don't tell me about it," Hank insisted. "I don't want to know. It doesn't matter. All that matters is whether or not you will give me another chance."

"Oh, Hank. I don't know what to do. I'll think about it. Why don't you get some sleep and we'll talk about it later."

"Can I stay here?" he asked, looking back at the bedroom door.

Thinking of my promise to Erin, I replied, "No, I don't think that would be a good idea. I think you should go down to the motel and get a room."

"Okay. But, promise me, you'll think about it. Where are my keys?"

I retrieved them and he left, saying he'd call me later. I telephoned Don and went to work.

At afternoon break, Don and I sat alone at a table in the lunchroom.

"Don," I whispered to him, "this has absolutely pulled me apart. I'm back to the Jean/Jody split again. I'm Jean. Without Jody, I don't know what to do."

"Have you called your doctor?" Don was concerned.

"No, I don't know what to tell him. I know I need to get Hank out of my life, but I also know he needs me."

"*I* need you," Don countered.

"I know, I know, but what am I going to do?"

"Tell Hank to go back to Indiana."

"You don't know Hank. He might kill himself or try to and I'm still married to him. I'd be responsible for him."

"He's not going to kill himself. You told me he used to threaten to do that all the time. Did he ever try?"

"No, not really."

Suddenly Don demanded, "Let me talk to Jody."

I let her take over.

"Well, isn't this a mess," I stated.

"I hardly know what to think," Don said earnestly. "I didn't know that Hank's coming here would cause Jean to split off again. You're going to have to handle this."

"I know. It's going to be a struggle, but I'm going to do something about it right now."

"What are you going to do?"

"I'm calling Hank's motel and telling him to leave. I'm going to remind him that his mother needs him back in Indiana and he better go back to her. He's not going to kill himself. He's played that game with Jean so often."

I was determined to keep control from Jean until Hank had left. I would deal with him now. I had more power than Jean. When I called, however, Hank did not have a telephone in his room. I left a message: "Please go home to your mother. She needs you."

It was nearly time to leave work when Hank called back. He was crying. "How could you be so cruel?"

"What do you mean?"

"Just leave a message that you don't need me and to go home."

"I'm sorry. That's not what I intended to say. I only meant that you shouldn't think about killing yourself because I decided that I didn't want to get back together. Your mother is getting so old and disabled, she really does need your help."

"I have to see the girls before I go. Can I come see them?"

I weighed my promise to Erin, but he was going to be out of their lives. I couldn't refuse to let the man see his children before he left.

"I'll bring them down to the motel to see you later."

All the way home I tried to think what I would say to the girls. Erin would have told them about their dad showing up this morning and her fear that he might be coming back. I needed to convince her and Teresa to see him one last time. Melissa still openly loved him and would be happy to see him. I decided to explain the situation and let each girl decide. It was especially difficult for Erin, but she finally agreed with the other two girls to go with me to see their dad.

It was early evening when we pulled into the parking lot of the motel.

I stood in the kitchen area of the small apartment Hank had rented as he talked to the three girls. Although I wanted to jump in several times, I decided to let Hank say whatever he wanted, unchallenged. I would have time to straighten the girls out on a few points later. I wouldn't let Jean have any say, and I wouldn't let Hank's tears weaken my resolve.

And there were a lot of tears. First Hank cried and then the girls cried as Hank told them, "I don't want this divorce. This is your mother's fault. I never wanted to leave. I wanted us to all be together. What did I ever do to you? I don't know how I'm going to live without all of you. I won't have anyone. I won't have any family. I'll be alone for the rest of my life."

Finally, I thought the girls had suffered enough of his emotion-draining drivel. "We have to go now, Hank."

He hugged and kissed each of the girls before I sent them out to the car. Still seated on the couch and shaking, tears streaming down his face, Hank grabbed my hand and begged one last time. "Please don't say it's over. Tell me you'll give me another chance. At least think about it."

I pulled my hand from his and said flatly, "I'm going to marry Don." Then I turned on my heel and walked out without looking back.

On the way home, everyone was quiet. I wanted to go over what Hank had told the girls, but they looked as emotionally overwrought as I was. I decided to feed them and send them off to bed instead. We'd sort it out later.

Thinking about what I had said to Hank, I wondered if I would actually marry Don. I hoped so. I loved him so much.

My first concern was how I was going to get Jean back together with me again. I tried calling Jack, but he was out of town.

During this time my mother was in town visiting with my sister Tina. My folks knew very little of my life in Seattle, except that I was divorcing Hank and had begun a new relationship with Don. I hadn't mentioned anything of the Jean/Jody/JD struggle; I needed to sort all that out myself first.

Hank had tried to call me two days after he left. Unable to reach me at home, he had called Tina. When Mom answered Tina's telephone, she had been surprised to hear Hank's voice. Mom told me about it when she and Tina came over to Don's apartment to have dinner with us.

"I think Hank was a bit shocked that I answered, but he was very pleasant to me. He said to tell you he was sorry for all the trouble he had caused and he wouldn't bother you again. That's about it."

"That's about it." I repeated the words joyfully. He's gone, Jean, are you listening? It's over!

Don fixed a roast leg of lamb in his own ginger sauce for dinner, and Tina cracked open a bottle of Asti Spumanti afterward. Neither Don nor I drank, but Don got glasses of water for the two of us to toast with the others, to the end of a bad marriage and the beginning of a new life.

After everyone left and the girls were asleep, I lay wrapped up with Don and talked quietly.

"I'm looking forward to a whole different way of living.

I almost feel like it should be spring and I could be planting new flowers in my garden."

Then it struck me. I was so excited I sat up in bed.

"Don, did you hear what I said—*my* garden? Do you know what that means?"

"No, what?"

"It means I'm whole. Don't you see? Jean and Jody are one again!"

TWELVE

"JEAN?" I HEARD THE EDGE OF PANIC IN DON'S VOICE.

"Yes, I'm awake."

"I thought I heard you whine in your sleep."

"I guess I did. I don't know. I woke up again and thought I'd check the time."

"It's a little after three in the morning again, isn't it?" His voice changed to concern.

"Yes, about five after."

"That's the third time this week. You want to tell me about it?"

"I can't right now. In the morning we'll talk about it. It has to do with the rape in Florida. I thought I was over it, but it seems to be back to haunt me again."

"What happened?"

"Can we wait until morning? I'm really tired now."

"Okay. Scoot over here and I'll cuddle around you and we can both sleep."

"Thank you."

As I edged over to him, he enveloped me in warmth and love. I was so tired and I loved Don, but I still couldn't sleep. My eyes didn't want to shut. The clock with its digital numbers was staring at me as the minutes ticked slowly by. Why was this still haunting me now?

Don was already beginning to breathe evenly in deep slumber. We usually slept well curled up together. Since our first weekend-long date four months ago, Don and I had practically been inseparable. But now something from my past was waking me again.

Think of something else, I told myself. Go to sleep.

Three-zero-five. I remembered the sight of those numbers much too well. I thought I had worked with Jack through all that mess from my Florida ordeal. It didn't have the same horrible impact it once had, but now I kept waking up at the same dreadful hour every night, as though to remind me again. Why? Was this another symptom of my madness? A morbid sort of play-it-again trick of my mind? When was it going to end?

I brought it up with Jack the next time I saw him. Jack was certain the memories from Florida were somehow tied up with experiences of JD.

"You were sexually abused as a child."

The words were too harsh for me. I didn't know what had happened to JD. Jack didn't know either. But I finally knew about both the Jean/Jody parts of me. When Jody had separated from Jean, I was only three years old. As Jean I had loved my daddy, who had fondled me lovingly, but the guilt was there. I had wanted to be his little princess, but if we couldn't tell Mommy, then it was bad. Jean didn't want to be bad, so Jody would be the good me.

Now the dreams of good and bad sisters became clearer—sisters Ann and Tanya of my dreams were in real life Jean and Jody. My subconscious mind had been telling me for years what my conscious mind refused to accept. I felt guilty and defensive when Jack diagnosed sexual abuse. Logically I knew he was right, but emotionally I was still hanging on to a dream of what my relationship could have been with my father, that I was his little darling. I couldn't look directly at Jack, but studied the edge of his rolltop desk instead, noting that his bottom two drawers were actually one, probably for files.

Finally I voiced a halfhearted agreement, "Yes, but not violently. My father played with me when we were both naked in his bed. He had me play with him and he fondled me, but he didn't hurt me physically."

"Mentally and emotionally you were unprepared for that kind of activity. That's what caused Jean and Jody to become separate entities. You don't think that's violent?"

"I . . . I suppose so . . . maybe emotionally violent enough to draw Jean and Jody apart. But the violence in my dreams and flashes of memory are so terribly physical. For example, I recall a strictly Freudian dream I related to the doctor in Chicago. In it I was riding a huge white horse. All at once I was surrounded by fire and my father was there. Instead of trying to help me, he started throwing a big snake up at me. The horse bolted up in fear and nearly threw me off into the fire. I don't remember more of the dream."

Jack leaned forward, nodding his head for emphasis. "And you still don't consider that your father sexually abused you?"

"I don't know what to think anymore. My father was a physically violent person when he got angry, but he wasn't angry with me when we played together. I know what he did with me was wrong, but sexual abuse sounds so violent. I don't know. I only wish the nightmares would stop and I could start getting enough sleep to be alert at work. My job is eating me alive and I don't have the energy to fight back."

"Why don't you let me try to talk to JD again?"

"You can try, but I tell you she simply screams that Shadowman will hear her and she can't speak to anyone except me."

"I want to try something," Jack said, getting up and reaching toward me. "Let's go outside. Maybe JD will be more comfortable out there. There's lots of noise and no one else can hear us there. What do you think?"

"I think it's worth a shot." I followed him out the office door.

Jack had moved from the cozy little house on Capital Hill to new offices across from Swedish Hospital in Seattle. We went out to the front of the building. There were brick steps that led up to the outer door.

Jack and I sat down on the steps.

"Now," he said, "let me talk to JD."

I didn't have to look far for her.

Jack leaned forward to look into my face. "JD? I can see you're here. Can you talk to me now? We're outside. Shadowman can't hear you here. Nobody can hear you but me."

I bent my head down and looked out of the corner of my eyes at him. I bit my lower lip and was afraid to talk.

"JD, you can talk to me. I'm not going to tell anyone that you are here. Can you talk to me?"

I watched him for a minute and slowly I spoke, "He said he could hear me wherever I was."

"Well, he lied to you, JD. He can't hear you anywhere. He just said that to make you afraid."

"But he did hear me."

"No, JD. He may have found out something you said, or he may have found out that you talked to someone, but he can't hear you unless he's with you. Do you want to talk to me?"

"Yes, but I don't want him to hear me."

"I promise you that he cannot hear you, no matter where you are. My office is safe. He can't hear you in there, because he's not in there."

His office was safe. Shadowman couldn't hear me.

"Can we go inside, JD? I promise you'll be safe."

I shook my head. No, I couldn't go inside. He'd hear me.

"No? Well, that's okay. We can talk here. Can you tell me something?"

I nodded.

"How old are you, JD?"

How old was I? I didn't know. I shook my head.

"Can you let me speak to Jean again?" he asked.

Jean? I was Jean.

"That's me," I told him.

"Oh, I'm sorry. I've been calling you JD. Is that okay?"

I nodded.

"Okay, then let me speak to Jody."

Jody, you can come back now.

I shook my shoulders to loosen some of the tension JD had generated. "Well, what do you think?" I asked Jack.

"I was going to ask you the same question. Let's go inside."

I got up and followed him slowly back into his office.

"So JD is really called Jean. She thinks of you as Jody."

"I wonder if she ever recognized there were three of us or now that there's only two."

"I don't know. I think we'll have to continue to call her JD, but I'll have to refer to you as Jody when I'm working with her. For a while I was afraid she was too young to talk. How old do you think JD is?"

"I'm not sure." I tried to visualize JD, the way she curled her fingers and gnawed at her knuckle in fear. "If I ventured a guess, I'd have to say about eight or nine."

"Okay, then you've got to figure that whatever happened to you with Shadowman started at that age at least. Who do you think Shadowman is?"

"My father, I assume."

"I just wanted to hear you acknowledge it."

• • •

In the weeks that followed, I talked with Don about JD. He was certain that he could convince her that Shadowman could never hear her and she was safe, both with him and Jack. I tried to talk with her, but she seemed to disappear from my mind when I encouraged her to talk with Don.

One night as we were lying in bed talking, Don asked if he could speak to JD. I tried to give her control.

"JD?" Don recognized the difference right away.

I pulled myself away from the man Jody called Don and curled up, pulling the pillow down between us.

"JD, I'm not going to hurt you. I love you. You don't have to be afraid of me. There's nothing to fear anymore."

I wanted to run away, but I was wearing a nightgown and I didn't know where to go. Shadowman would know I was here. I couldn't say anything. He would hear me.

"JD, I wanted you to know I was here and I love you. I won't let anything happen to you. Shadowman can't hear you. Jack's right. Remember what he told you? Shadowman's not here so he can't hear you. And, JD, I will *never* let him hurt you again. I love you. Please talk to me."

I bit on my left thumb. Through my bangs I could see Don. He was sitting up on his left elbow, holding out his right hand to take mine. I drew farther back and shook my head.

"Okay, JD. Let me talk to Jody then."

As I took back control from JD, I congratulated Don, "Hey, not bad for a first try." I was encouraged that Don had been able to draw her out enough to get a response, albeit marginal, but it was a beginning.

For several nights, Don tried again and again to talk with JD, assuring her that she was safe—Shadowman was thousands of miles away and couldn't hear or hurt her. Eventually, she began to answer, but was very timid. I became aware that she was terribly uncomfortable being in bed with Don and in any state of undress, so Don was careful to call her out in the living room, in the car, or in some public place where there weren't a lot of people close by.

When I met with Jack, he was amazed at what Don had accomplished in getting JD to surface, even if she wasn't saying much. After that, JD became more and more aware of my visits to Jack. He called her out nearly every time, if only to acknowledge her presence and to assure her she was safe in his office. She hesitated to provide much information yet, but Jack reminded me that it had taken months before I was sufficiently comfortable with him to relate my rape in Florida. It would take a while for JD to be enough at ease with us to share her experiences.

During this time, my parents were cleaning out their garage in the Midwest. They found my old high school yearbooks and sent them to me. As I looked through my junior yearbook, I was shocked to find a picture of JD. It was clearly JD. I knew that both Jean and Jody had been at the high school at various times. I couldn't imagine JD being there. The picture had been taken in the instrument room where she was putting away my string bass. Her eyes were downcast, her body wrapped weakly around the big bass limply, as though it were too heavy, and she looked almost in pain.

I took the yearbook to Jack on the next appointment.

"Why would JD be at the high school?" he asked.

"I don't know. I didn't think she was ever around by that time."

Jack called out JD and asked her. I was with JD almost all the time when she was in control, aware of what was said and of both JD's answers and her thoughts. However, when Jack asked her why she was at school in that picture, there was a small blip of a blackout. JD had blocked something from me.

When I left Jack's office, I didn't even get to the I-90 floating bridge before I knew. JD was simply too embarrassed to tell Jack. She said it was okay for me to tell him, but she couldn't.

I had turned sixteen a couple of weeks before the picture was taken. I had gotten a bladder infection and went to our family doctor the day before the picture. I had been going to my pediatrician who kept seeing "his kids" up to sixteen, but after that he referred them to someone else. My mother had made an appointment for me with her doctor. He had insisted on doing a gynecological exam, the first I ever remembered having. There was no nurse in the room, just the doctor and me.

The first thing he said to me during the exam was, "I see you're already sexually active."

I was mortified. I answered indignantly, "I am not!"

He answered quickly, "I can see that you are."

"No, I'm not," I insisted again.

This time he stood up and leaned over me slightly. He looked very irritated as he said, "Look, you can lie to your parents, but I'm a doctor and I can tell."

JD took over immediately. . . .

He could tell. Would he tell? The last time Shadowman knew I had been talking to someone, it was horrible. I lived in fear for days after the doctor's comment, afraid that he would tell. So I had to go to school for Jody. I couldn't do her work and I couldn't play the bass very well, but I tried. Finally she came back and did the work and I went back to hiding.

So there it was. I listened to her telling me and tried to think how it must be to be that frightened child. I knew that I was that child, but at the same time, I couldn't seem to bridge the gap. The doctor hadn't meant he would "tell anyone," only that he could see from my physical condition that sexual activity had occurred, but I could see how easily his words were misunderstood by JD.

Now my worst fears were confirmed. I had never been "sexually active" as a teenager. If the doctor thought I had been, then I must have been sexually abused. JD was still holding back the answers and the pain.

Some weeks later I went to my appointment with Jack. As I opened the door into his waiting room, his receptionist looked up and smiled.

"Good afternoon," she said with more enthusiasm than appeared on her face. Her forced smile faded quickly as she returned to her keyboard. The stack of papers next to it needed more attention than I did.

I was early, something that rarely happened to me. I laid claim to what Jack called a "left-brain deficiency," an inability to organize my time to be on time. It wasn't that I didn't know when I had to be somewhere, or how long it took to get there. Inevitably there was always one more little thing to do before I left, and it invariably took me a little too long to do it. Years ago I set my watch five minutes fast to help compensate, and even though I knew it was fast, it had helped somewhat.

Traffic flowed on Broadway outside Jack's office. I watched it through the entry courtyard. Nurses and orderlies were hurrying down the block, disappearing from my narrow view. Shift change at Swedish Hospital, I figured.

I turned back to look at Jack's office door. Why had I come early? JD wanted to talk with Jack. My arms tensed. I hated it when she talked to him, hinting but never revealing. I always ended up with such horrible nightmares.

I have a right to talk to Jack. It sounded as if JD was pouting.

I looked over at the receptionist, but of course she couldn't hear JD in my head.

What do you want, JD?

I just want to talk to Jack. I brought him something.

You brought him something? I was angry. I didn't realize that JD could have brought him something without my knowing. I grabbed up my purse and began to look through it.

No. It's not for you. It's for Jack.

I had just opened the zippered pouch compartment when Jack opened the waiting room door.

"I'll be with you in a minute, Jean," Jack called to me as the door closed behind his patient.

A man walked through the waiting room and hurried out the outer door. I watched his back as he took long strides through the courtyard and disappeared around the corner of the building. I wondered if he was angry. He never looked back or to either side.

Now, what was I doing? Oh, yes, my purse. I dug into the compartment, but there was only my checkbook, makeup bag, and wallet. I flipped to the other compartment. My address book was so stuffed with papers I often had trouble finding the addresses. I thumbed through the loose papers. What did you bring?

It's not for you, JD repeated quietly.

I lifted the address book carefully from the compartment and stared into the collection of objects in the bottom. Let's see, my missing black earring, my keys, a couple of pens, nail clipper, a dime, a handful of pennies. I should get those pennies out of there; they make my purse too heavy. Nothing unusual in the bottom of the bag. What did you bring?

It's not for you.

I stuffed the address book back into the purse and zipped up the other compartment. I patted my hips, but the pockets in my dress were empty. Where else would I have anything?

I felt defeated as I watched Jack open his office door and walk out to the reception area. JD was going to give Jack whatever she had. I couldn't find it.

Jack opened the door to the waiting room.

"Come on in," Jack said, leaning slightly on the door.

I struggled to get out of the love seat with some semblance of grace. It was impossible, but Jack didn't seem to notice.

"Would you like some tea or anything?" Jack asked, as I marched on past him into his office.

"No, I'm fine," I answered, biting on the word "fine." I wasn't fine; I was mad. I didn't know what JD had brought him.

I chose the single chair between the end table and the office love seat. There was a grouping of two chairs on the other side of the table, but I preferred to sit directly opposite Jack.

"So, how've you been?" Jack asked as he settled into his leather chair.

"Okay," though I wondered what being okay meant—that I had survived another two weeks?

My eyes flitted around the room, not willing to choose something to stare at. I took in the painting of Oriental children playing, the ceramic frogs on Jack's desk around an old-fashioned green-shaded brass desk lamp, the wicker desk chair, the volumes behind glass doors in the built-in bookcases, the end table, my purse. Darn that purse.

Jack was waiting for me to say something. I looked up at him suddenly.

"Well, what's been happening?" Jack asked cheerfully.

I couldn't let go of that purse. I knew whatever JD had was in it. Crap.

I sighed. "JD wants to talk to you."

"Oh?" Jack sat forward in his chair and leaned toward me.

"Yes, so I guess I'll have to let you." I was pouting now.

I hated to give her control, but I knew Jack would see that I got it back again. JD couldn't drive.

I looked down at the blue carpet and drifted into my mind. I thought about my childhood vacations in Florida. The blue reminded me of the evening tide at Saint John's Pass. My bare feet relished the warmth of the sand and the coolness as I dipped my toes into the blue.

"JD?" Jack called to me.

I smiled and rolled my eyes to the purse on the floor. It's still there. Jean didn't find it.

"Um-um." I bit softly on my lower lip. I shifted my eyes to stare at Jack through my bangs.

"JD? Is that you?"

I sat back in my chair and crossed my arms, holding each elbow with the other hand. Didn't he know me? He always had.

"Jean said you wanted to talk with me."

"Uh-huh."

"What did you want to tell me?"

"I brought something for you." I bit my lip and smiled more broadly. I leaned forward on my arms.

"You brought something?"

"Yes. Jean is mad at me 'cause she couldn't find it, but she looked right at it." So there, Jean.

"What is it?"

I pulled the purse up by the shoulder strap and dug into the papers in the address book. There in plain sight was a piece of paper folded into fourths.

"It's a drawing I made." I unfolded it as I handed it to Jack.

As he took the picture from me, he moved to the couch next to my chair. He turned the picture and his head so that we could both look at it right side up.

"Is this the basement?"

"It's the laundry room," I said, picking up the strand of black beads hanging around my neck and biting on one bead behind my curled knuckle.

"And this is the washer and dryer. What's this?" Jack asked, pointing to me in the picture.

"Me." He didn't know me. I was disappointed.

"You're a flower?"

"Yes, I'm growing in the floor. I can't run away."

"Oh, I see." Jack stared at the picture for a couple of minutes. We didn't talk.

Then he pointed at the flower, and asked, "What are all these little lines around you?"

The little lines looked like rays from a drawing of the sun, encircling the flower growing from the floor.

"That's God." I smiled. I was never alone in the basement. God was there, taking me from Shadowman and holding me until he was gone.

"Jean?" Jack's voice penetrated my fog.

I looked up as the room came into focus. Jack was returning my control from JD. I wondered how long she had spent with him. In his hand was a piece of paper, probably what JD gave him. Bad enough when Jean or Jody dumped out the other's secret thoughts, but now JD?

Jack placed the paper into my lap.

"Do you know what this is?"

God, it's the basement. I flipped the paper over as black-and-white snapshots of JD's memory poured through my mind. I tried to shake them away.

Jack grabbed the paper and turned it over in front of me. This time he retained his hold.

"What are you thinking? What does this remind you of?"

I glanced off into the bookcases and tried to read some of the titles.

"Look at it!" Jack insisted. "What is it that disturbs you about JD's picture?"

Slowly I brought my eyes back to stare at the drawing. I shuddered.

"It's a drawing of the laundry room in the old Webster Street house. I'm sure most of the things that happened to JD happened there."

"Happened to you," Jack corrected me.

"Okay, to me." JD is me and I am JD. I am JD and JD is me. How can I accept that? I could do this mental exercise, but I didn't want to be JD, so it was just words.

"Go on," Jack said.

I pinched the bridge of my nose with my left hand and leaned forward on my elbow. I had an almost overwhelming urge to cry, but not in front of Jack. I did my crying alone.

Slowly I began, "When I look at the drawing, I get a lot of pictures of what happened there. Sort of like looking very rapidly through a stack of old black-and-white photos. It's not that I feel anything," I lied.

I paused, shook my head, and took two quick breaths to fight back the tears and the overwhelming sadness. "It's that I know intellectually that her memories are mine, but emotionally I don't want to be her or see her memories."

I pressed my hands together, interlacing the fingers so tightly two knuckles crackled.

"Can you tell me about any of them?" Jack's tone had softened.

I tried to bring up one picture in my mind. They didn't want to be held still. They fanned through quickly, barely letting me glance. I lifted the drawing from Jack's hand and held it up in front of me. Slowly one picture came into focus.

"I can see the laundry room, as it is in the drawing. On one side, toward the basement windows, there are two machines, the dryer and a broken washer or dryer nobody's bothered to haul away. On the other side there's the washing machine. In the corner there's an old wringer washer." JD shuddered with the last sentence, shaking my whole body. Why, JD?

"Back against the wall is an old footstool with a brocade design on it. I think it was purple, although it looks black in the picture. Everything is covered with lint and dust. The light's coming in the doorway from the main basement room. The light in the laundry room isn't working. It's a bare bulb with a string pull, but it's burned out. I can see a huge shadow across the doorway. It must be Shadowman." My throat tightened and the picture blinked away.

Silently I sat for a minute staring at JD's picture. It was the drawing of a young child, but the essence of the room in my memory was captured on it. Back in my head I could hear screaming. I knew it was tied to this drawing. I'd heard it so many times before, but then I had attributed it to my insanity. So had other doctors.

"What are you feeling?"

"Fear mostly. I know that is the first snapshot of Shadowman. I know most of what happened after that snapshot. I just don't want to remember it. I don't want to feel it."

I handed Jack the picture and he moved back to his chair. He sat on the edge and set the picture on his ottoman. Then he slid his clipboard out from under the picture and began making some notes.

"You still don't think I'm insane?" I was grateful he didn't, although sometimes I thought it might be simpler.

Jack sighed a little half laugh and shook his head as he replied, "No, I don't think you're insane." Then he looked seriously at me, and added, "But I think you've got a lot to deal with. You're going to have to accept that what happened to JD happened to you."

"Being insane would be easier," I jested. I knew it wouldn't be, but this was too painful.

"No, it wouldn't," Jack said flatly.

"I know. I know. I've been in the wards. I wouldn't want to spend my life there."

"Look," Jack said forcibly, "JD has protected you from an awful lot so that you could continue living a relatively normal life. But it's time for you to deal with what she has. You can handle it. Understand? You've survived. Now you need to acknowledge the pain she went through and deal with your anger over it."

"How can I?" I asked in despair. My mind ran through the questions over and over. Why must I? Why can't it be over and done with? Why do I have to know everything that happened? How can I deal with it?

"By listening to JD. By realizing that JD is you, and that you were injured. By letting your anger over what happened to you come out."

"I'm not angry."

"You should be. Listen to JD. Look at her pictures. Think about what happened and who did these things to you. If you're not angry, you're not accepting that these things happened to you."

"I don't want them to be mine. I want it to be over. I've been through hell for years and years. Why do I have to go back and live it all again?"

"So it can be over." Jack slumped back into his chair. He started to put his feet up on the ottoman, but realized the picture was still there. He grabbed it up before his feet landed on it and slipped it into the back of the pad on the clipboard.

My mind was beginning to spin. I knew that Shadowman was my father. I loved both my parents. I knew my dad was a violent person and a "social retard," but he was my father. Even thinking about how he hit us when he was mad made me feel physically ill. My stomach was beginning to squeeze tight.

No, remember instead what redeeming qualities he had. Remember what I said to Sandra, to think of all the good things we could about Dad. Didn't Dad take all us kids out to the tree farm each Christmas? Didn't we march through knee-high snow for miles to get the *perfect* tree for him to saw down and drag back to the car? Remember the Christmas caroling in the car on the way out and the sweet wonderful scent of the pine on the way back? Dad had a rich, deep bass voice. Remember the barbershop quartet rehearsals at our house? Singing was so much of the good memories of Dad. Remember raking leaves into the huge piles in the vacant lot attached to our house, and then sitting around the bonfire in a circle and serenading the neighbors with "I Got a Home in Glory Land" and all our other favorites? People used to come out and sit on their porches to listen to us. Remember . . . ?

"What are you thinking?" Jack interrupted my thoughts.

"I guess I was trying to recall the good things about my father. You know Sandra and I had a discussion about them some time ago. I don't want to hate him."

"But you need to acknowledge what happened to JD too."

"But it's so hard." I gripped each thumb with the other fist, stretching them over my knees. As I sat back in my chair, I let my clasped fists slide into my lap. My gaze scanned the wall edge where it met the ceiling above Jack's head and on over to the door. I sighed, wanting so much to keep the fond memories of my daddy intact, wanting so little of JD.

Jack sat still in his chair and watched me silently. Finally he said, "We need to wrap this up now, but you think about JD. Remember your dreams the next few days; write them down."

It was over for today. I put Jack's next appointment card into my purse as I started down the brick steps. But what was I in for tonight? What would JD bring me now?

"All right, JD, bring on your worst. I can't go on being crazy all my life." I tried to sound confident as I talked aloud in the car on the way home. I didn't really want to know what she held from me, but the cryptic nightmares needed to stop so I could get on with my life. The little flashes of still photos in my mind were enough to frighten me away from anything more JD had to offer. Nevertheless, if I was ever going to be well, I needed to know.

THIRTEEN

IT DIDN'T TAKE LONG BEFORE JD FILLED IN THE TERRIFYING details of the first episode, the one behind the memory brought on by JD's picture. I was alone in my bed remembering that first day; JD brought me the recollection of the horrible man she called Shadowman and the rest in caustic detail.

It was Friday. I could hardly wait to get home. Daddy had promised to take me to the barbershop meet. I left the school-yard and ran down the two blocks to our patrol lady's crossing. Miss Cullen was our crossing guard on Middleton Avenue. She always wore her blue uniform that seemed a little too tight with lots of metal buttons and a big smile for all "her kids." She knew everyone's name and when they came to cross.

"Hello, Jean."

"Oh, Miss Cullen! I've got to get home in a hurry today. My daddy is going to take me, just me, to the barbershop meet tonight."

"The barbershop meet?" Her eyes squinted narrowly.

"You know. The guys that get together and sing all the pretty songs. Four guys make up a quartet and lots of them will be at the meet tonight. My daddy sings with three other guys. They always come practice at our house 'cause we've got the piano."

"Oh, you mean barbershop quartets." Her face broadened into a huge smile. "Yes, I like their singing too. You sure are a lucky girl to get to go."

My brother Matthew caught up with me as there was a break in the traffic and Miss Cullen moved to the middle of the street, held out her little red flags on sticks, and said, "Come along, now, kids. You have a nice weekend and I'll see you on Monday."

We said good-bye as we crossed in front of her.

Matthew hit me in the arm as soon as Miss Cullen had turned to watch for other kids coming down from the school.

"Why didn't you wait for me?" he asked angrily.

"I wanted to get home fast. You better not hit me again or I'll tell Dad. I want Mom to roll up my hair so it looks real pretty when Daddy takes me to the barbershop meet tonight."

"Why do you always get to go?" Matthew was annoyed, but not really with me. "I'll have to watch Mark and Sandra by myself if you're not going with us to Grandma's. And maybe even Luke," he added. "That baby cries all the time. I never know what to do with him."

"I don't either, but I know he doesn't like to lie down. With his asthma, he can't breathe very well when you lay him down. If you do have to watch him, just prop him up where he can see what's going on and he'll be a lot better."

When we got home, Matthew headed for the backyard and I went into the house. Mom was busy changing Luke's diapers on the couch. A striped baby blanket was underneath him and he was trying to pull on one corner of it. He hadn't really learned that his hands were part of him yet or that he could put them into his mouth. When he bumped his hand on his face he tried to suck on it, thinking it was Mom, and then was surprised when it pulled away from him.

"Mom? Will you roll up my hair so I can look really nice when Dad takes me to the barbershop meet tonight?"

"Oh, Jean," Mom said, and sighed wearily. "I have so much to do before your father gets home. You know the rest of us are going down to Grandma's for the weekend. I have to pack. I don't have time to do your hair. Look at it. I'd need to wash it before I could roll it up."

"Please, Mom?" I persisted. "I'll help you get ready. Please?"

She shook her head as she held a diaper pin in her teeth, but as she took it out to use it, she relented. "Well, if you can help me get packed, I'll see if I can wash and roll your hair."

"All right!" I rejoiced.

After we finished the packing, I leaned backward from a chair while Mom washed my long, blond hair in the sink. She always got soap and water in my eyes and it seemed forever before she was done, but I tried not to complain. I was afraid Dad would get home and want to leave before I was ready. However, he didn't get home until long after Mom finished rolling my hair and pulling the hair dryer bag over the curlers.

I was still sitting upstairs with the dryer bag when Dad finished helping Mom, Matthew, Mark, Sandra, and Luke into the car, along with their baggage, and said good-bye. We were alone.

"Well, princess," Dad said with a smile as he came into the bedroom, "Are you ready for a big night?"

"Yes, Daddy," I said, feeling very much the princess. "I have my pink dress all washed and pressed to wear--you know, the one with the red-and-white striped ribbons you like."

"Yeah," he replied, sitting down on the edge of the bed. "How long are you going to be in that bag?"

"I don't know how long it takes to dry my hair."

"Well, I'm going to go down and fix us a couple of hot dogs, okay? Do you want mustard or catsup on yours?"

"Catsup, please." Yuck, I thought, how could anyone stand the taste of mustard?

I tested my hair. It felt dry so I took off the bag and hopped into my bedroom. I got my pink dress out of the closet and slipped off the one I wore to school.

I was buttoning it up when Dad called, "Jean, come on down, the hot dogs are ready."

I started out of the room when I looked down at my shoes. I called down the stairway, "Just a minute Daddy, I have to change my shoes."

I checked under my bed. Where were they? I found them in the closet. I pulled out my black, patent leather shoes, slipped off my saddle shoes, and buckled on the others. Now I would look like a princess—well, when I got the curlers out.

I hurried downstairs. I hoped he would notice how nice I looked.

"Well, well," he said, fulfilling my wish, "Don't you look wonderful. Be careful you don't spill catsup on that pretty dress." He flashed his most charming smile.

After we ate, he came upstairs with me. While I took the curlers out of my hair, he changed his tie. He put on one that was striped red-and-white, exactly like my dress ribbons. Then he brushed the curls in my hair, and reminded me to get a sweater as he pulled on his jacket. I couldn't find my white one that would have matched my dress, and I felt funny as I put on a green one that I didn't like. I never liked green clothes of any kind.

"Now you really do look like my princess," Dad said, ignoring my ugly green sweater. "Come on, I want to show you off to all the guys. Nobody will be there with a gorgeous gal like mine." He gave me a big hug before we went out to the car.

The whole evening was a dream come true. I got to watch all the quartets perform and my daddy's quartet sang best of all. After all the groups performed, they went off to different areas in the big hall and gathered around pianos, singing different versions of songs until late into the night. I got to sing with Daddy's group some of the time. He said I could sing like a little angel. When I got thirsty, he bought me a Coca-Cola. I *loved* my daddy.

It was very dark out when we left the big hall. The moon was up, but not very bright. I fell asleep in the car on the way home. I remembered my daddy carrying me up from the car, but not getting me out of it. He laid me on my bed and pulled off my shoes. He pulled a blanket over me and gave me a kiss.

"Good night, princess," he said quietly.

"Good night, Daddy," I answered. I wished I could wake up enough to put my dress back in the closet, it would get all wrinkled, but I was too sleepy.

In the morning, I changed into my slacks and a shirt. Daddy made pancakes for us and we played cribbage for a while. He always beat me at it, but we had fun. Later we went out to the grocery store. He usually went late on Saturdays to buy up all the bread or bananas they had left on sale, because the stores were never open on Sunday. However, this time he only wanted to pick up a few things and lots of milk. We did guzzle milk.

When we got home and unloaded the groceries, Dad said, "Mom needs some help with the laundry. Go on up and get the dirty clothes out of all the bedrooms and bring them down. I'll set up the washer, okay?"

I did as he asked, even hunting under the beds for dirty socks and underwear. Mom couldn't do that very well. I hauled everything down to the basement. I didn't see Dad, but the washer was prepared so I started a load washing. I went back upstairs and looked around for him. I didn't find him anywhere, so I played at the piano for a while and then began reading a new mystery novel that had arrived in the mail a couple days earlier.

As it got late and I still didn't see Dad, I turned on a couple lights in the living room. I wondered if he was going to fix supper or if I should just go ahead and find something to eat. I didn't know what to do. If I ate and then he came to fix supper, he might get mad at me, but if I waited and he wasn't planning to fix supper, he might send me to bed without eating.

Well, the laundry I washed would have been done a long time ago and I needed to put it into the dryer. I opened the basement door but was reluctant to go down. The basement was dark and I stepped back to switch on the light. Only the light nearest the stairs worked and half the largest room was left dark. At the bottom of the stairs, I turned sharply and went into the laundry room. I pulled the string on the single bare lightbulb, but the light didn't come on. I noticed that the shutters were closed on the windows and no light filtered in from the window wells.

Suddenly a panic struck me. The windows weren't boarded when I was down here earlier. Why were they now? As I turned toward the door, a shadow filled the doorway and stretched across the floor in front of me from the single basement light.

The huge Shadowman blocked the doorway. He stood looking at me. He had no face, but in his huge hands he held a magazine, the pages open toward me. As he stepped into the room, he held it up to my face.

"This is you, isn't it?" His voice boomed into the room. "Look at this. It's you, isn't it?"

I tried to focus on the magazine in the dark. There was a

girl in the picture sitting in a chair and another of her lying
on a floor. She didn't have any clothes on in either picture.
Her hair was tied up in French braids as my hair often was.
I couldn't see much else. He hit me in the face with the magazine.

"Well, tell me! This is you, isn't it?"

"No— " I couldn't say more; the magazine struck my
mouth.

"We'll just see about this!" Shadowman said, hitting me
in the face again.

"Stay here," he ordered, throwing the magazine onto the
floor in front of me. He went up the stairs two and three at a
time.

I was nearly frozen to the floor. I looked down at the
magazine. It had fallen open at the very page he had shown
me. There were lots of words under the pictures, but not in
English. I didn't know what they said. The girl was smiling.

Suddenly Shadowman was coming back down the stairs.
Hung over one arm he carried one of our dining room chairs.

"Take off your clothes," Shadowman ordered as he shut
the door behind him. He pulled on the light string but it
didn't respond with light for him either.

"Damn!" he said as he fumbled to open the door again.

He turned and shouted at me, "I told you to take your
clothes off! I'm going up and get a lightbulb and you better
be naked as a jaybird before I get back down here, do you
hear me?" His huge hand punctuated the order on the side of
my face. He bounded back up the stairs and into the kitchen
directly above me.

My face stung; my head began to spin. Who was he?
What did he want? That wasn't me in the pictures. As I
heard him rummaging through the kitchen drawers for a
lightbulb, I shuddered and pulled my shirt over my head. I
knelt down and untied my sneakers. I pulled off my socks
and shoes and slipped my slacks off on the floor. I was

standing there in my panties when he bounded back down the stairs and into the room.

He changed the lightbulb and turned it on. He closed the door and turned to me.

"Get those panties off now!" he yelled.

I saw for the first time that his own pants were unzipped and his penis was sticking out from the flap. I was frozen to the floor. He bent down and almost ripped my panties down my legs. I had to fight to keep my balance as he pulled them off my feet.

He pushed me toward the chair.

"Sit in it, just like you did here," he demanded, picking up the magazine from the floor.

I sat back into the chair and tried again to tell him, "It's not me. That's not me!"

"Shut up," he said, hitting me in the face with his huge hand again. "It *is* you. Get your leg up here." He grabbed my left leg and shoved it forcibly over the arm of the chair and pushed my right leg to the right, pulling me down slightly on the chair.

"There," he said more calmly. "Now, you look just like your picture. No, smile."

I couldn't smile. I was too frightened.

"Smile, I said!" He swung his hand close to my face but didn't strike.

I tried to smile.

"Now, see, you'll get what you want. You want this, don't you?" As he asked, he knelt and pushed one of his huge fingers into me slowly.

"No!" I said as I tried to pull my leg back over the chair arm, but he pressed it down with his other hand.

"Yes, you want this. You're just another dirty little girl and this is what you want." As he pressed his knee against my leg so I couldn't move, he grabbed my hands with his free hand.

"You're hurting me!"

"Oh, no, this is a good hurt. You like it, don't you? You want it. Say 'I want it.' Say it!" He pushed his second finger into me.

I cried out as the pain increased.

"See, it's good, isn't it? Say 'I want it.' Say it!"

"No!" I struggled to free my leg from over the arm chair. It was becoming numb. "It hurts! You're hurting my leg!"

"Okay," he said pulling out his fingers and releasing me. "Get on the floor. It will be better on the floor. No, wait a minute." And he spread a sheet on the cement floor.

I hadn't moved from the chair and he yanked my arm to pull me down to the floor.

"Now, you dirty little girl. Take your other pose." He bent over me to retrieve the magazine. He pushed his pants down slightly to let his penis stick out more. I didn't know what to do, but he propped me up on my right elbow and spread my legs, bending my right leg up to my chest.

"Yes, that's it," he said calmly again, and he got up and sat in the chair.

I opened my mouth to ask why he was doing this, but before I could get a word out, he said, "Don't say anything. Just stay there."

He began to rub his penis hard as he stared at me, looking up my legs from my feet to my chest slowly. After a short while, he began to breathe harder. Slowly he stood and slid his pants and underwear down. His held one shoe with the other foot and pulled his foot out without untying it. He repeated the removal for the other shoe. Then he stepped out of his pants and knelt down beside me.

Once again he said, "You do want this. This feels so good," as he pushed his finger into me.

"No!" I cried again.

"Yes, you do; you want this. You wouldn't have made those pictures if you didn't. I know what they're for. It makes guys want this too. See this?" He pulled my arm out from under my head and wrapped my fingers around his penis.

"Squeeze it. Squeeze it hard." He pushed another finger into me as he said it.

"Stop!"

"No," he said through his teeth. "You want this. You know you do. That's what you filthy little girls want. Good pain. This feels good."

He began to push harder into me. My stomach hurt.

"Let me go!" I begged him, but he rolled me over onto my back and balanced much of his weight against me.

"Say 'I want it.' Say it!"

"Will you let me go?"

"*Say it!*"

"Okay, I want it," I said through my gritted teeth.

As soon as I said it, he pulled his fingers out, pressing them apart as far as he could as he did. Then he climbed onto me, pushing his penis into me fast. It felt as if I was on fire. I urinated and it burned worse than anything I could remember. He pulled his penis out slowly, but not all the way.

"Yes. Yes!" he said. "This is so good. Isn't this good? Say 'it's good!'"

I cried with pain. I couldn't form any words.

"Yes! See, I knew you wanted it." He pushed back in hard and drew out slowly again.

"Okay, now say 'please.' Say '*ple-e-ase*.'"

I could only groan and cry out. It still hurt so bad I couldn't form words.

"Okay, don't say 'please.'" He began to push in and out much faster.

Pain shot through to my back.

I can't stand it! Oh, God, be my rock!

Suddenly I was in a bright red room. I felt as though God had made it for me. The walls were made of silk scarves blowing in the wind. I leaned against the wall and fell through it into a bright blue room. Somewhere in the distance I could hear someone screaming and screaming. The blue scarves were mixed with green ones on one side. I rolled over and through that wall into the bright green room and through the next wall into a bright yellow one. I couldn't get away from the screaming. Everything was soft here. It was getting darker and darker. Then all was black. The screaming had stopped.

"Wake up." Shadowman was shaking me. Then he slapped me. "We're not done yet. Wake Up!"

I opened my eyes. I was still lying on the sheet on the laundry room floor. He was on his knees beside me. My hands were full of soft lint from the floor.

"Clean yourself up. Here, take a towel." He threw a towel into my face from the top of the washer. It was still wet.

The burning between my legs was raging and as I looked, I saw blood running over the side of my leg. My stomach hurt so bad I could hardly move and my back hurt as well. I brushed the lint from my hands, picked up the towel, and I wiped the blood from my leg and underneath me. Just touching myself hurt so bad, I didn't know if I could get all the blood wiped off.

"Get up," he commanded.

I sat up slowly, but when I tried to bend my leg to rise, it hurt so bad, I didn't want to move.

"Get up!" He grabbed my arm and jerked me to a standing position. It was easier than getting up myself, although now my arm also hurt.

"Boy, are you a little slut," he said angrily. "You are going to hell for sure."

"No . . ." I tried again to speak, but once again his hand smacked my face.

"Yes, to hell. *To hell!*" he said, slapping me again. He turned me with my sore arm and began to spank my bottom, which already hurt. "But we'll give you a little bit of it here!"

He dragged me over to the chair where he pulled me onto his lap and continued to spank me.

I cried and screamed, but he wouldn't stop.

His penis was still hard underneath me. He pushed it up into my stomach with each blow.

I begged him to stop, but he leaned right to my ear and yelled, "Shut up, filth. I'll stop when I'm done with you and that may be tomorrow!"

He whacked my bottom a couple more times. Then he shoved me back onto the floor and pushed into me with his penis again.

"Yes. You want this. You want it. You want it!" he kept saying with each push and draw.

I didn't think the pain could be any worse, but I was wrong. *Please, where is my rock?*

As the colored rooms began to appear again, the pain slipped away. All I could hear was that girl off somewhere screaming again. I wished someone would stop her screaming. I fell gently through the walls. The wind was blowing down the halls harder and hotter than before. I wanted to stay there. I didn't want to go back with Shadowman.

But there he was—shaking me again.

"Oh . . . Wasn't that nice now?" His penis was hanging over my stomach and white gook was dripping down on me.

My mouth struggled with the words, "Are we done yet?"

"No! But I am for now. You got what you wanted. But we have lessons to learn another day. And you *will* learn them. Oh, yes."

He got off me and cleaned himself with another towel. As he got dressed, I lay back on the floor trying to catch my breath. I couldn't swallow. My throat was burning almost as bad as between my legs. My back and shoulders felt as if I had been run over by a truck and left on the pavement to die. I wondered if I would die now and go to hell.

"Get up," he said at last, as he tied his shoe.

I didn't think I could move.

"Get up." He said it louder. "Or didn't you have enough yet?" He raised his eyebrow slightly as though proposing that he would come down and hurt me again that way.

Oh, God, help me!

I pulled myself off the floor, bringing the towel with me. I tried to wipe some more of the blood off me, but it ran in a small trickle down my legs and onto the sheet.

"Now, go upstairs and take a bath. You're a mess."

Then he gripped my shoulder hard and, leaning down into my face, he said, "And don't you say one word about this, do you hear? I can hear you wherever you are and whoever you talk to. And if you ever do, you'll wish you had died first, because we'll do this all night next time. Am I making myself clear? *Nobody*, you hear?"

He let me go and I tried to wrap the towel around me and pick up my clothes. Before I could get to the door, he was squeezing my shoulder again, "You know, you are the worst little dirty girl in the world. If you say anything, everyone will find out. I'll show them your pictures. You better pray to God. You're going to go to hell."

I hung my head and cried. I didn't want to go to hell, but now I was dirty and ruined. I went slowly upstairs. Every part of my body hurt. When I got to the bathroom, I ran some water in the bathtub. Getting over the high side of the tub was difficult. It made me bleed some more. I sat in the warm running water and wondered if I would die. My head was hurting. My eyes wouldn't focus anymore.

"Jean! What are you doing? You're going to run the water over on the floor."

I opened my eyes. The bathtub was totally full and the

water was still running. I scooted quickly down to the faucet and shut off the water.

"I'm sorry, Daddy. I must have drifted off to sleep."

"Well, watch it," he said angrily. "You don't need to use so much hot water." I listened as he walked across the hallway and went downstairs.

I washed myself slowly. Boy, was I aching. I wondered if I was getting the flu or something. I crawled out of the tub. As I swung my leg over the side, a stinging pain shot up between my legs. What was wrong with me?

I'm just tired. Daddy and I stayed out so late last night, I need to go to bed early tonight, I said to myself.

I wrapped myself in a towel and looked at my clothes. There was blood dripped across them and lots of blood on a towel next to the tub. A panic rose up in my head. What happened? I shook my head. Something inside said, *Don't think*. I left them where they lay and went into my bedroom.

I pulled a nightgown out of my dresser drawer. It was the only thing in the drawer.

I have to get the laundry put away. The laundry. Did I put those clothes into the dryer? I couldn't remember. Again there was something telling me not to think.

I'm hungry. Did we have supper? I still couldn't think. Boy, I thought, I must be tired. I wondered what time it was. Walking to Daddy's bedroom was hard; my legs and insides hurt. I pushed open the door and checked the clock. It's after ten. I'm going to bed.

I went back into my room. As I climbed into bed, I could hear the rustle of Daddy's paper as he was reading downstairs.

I called, "Good night, Daddy."

"Good night, Jean." His voice sounded strange.

I closed my eyes. Somewhere in my head I could hear a girl screaming.

I hope I'm not going to have nightmares.

• • •

I opened my eyes. It was morning. I could hear Dad down-stairs in the kitchen directly below me. I wondered what time it was. I slid out of bed and headed for Daddy's bed-room, but I went into the bathroom instead. Walking was painful.

As soon as I started to urinate, it burned so bad I cried out, "What am I going to do? I am too sore to go to the bath-room!" I got up and opened the medicine cabinet. There were all kinds of jars and bottles of stuff in there. I took down a jar of Vaseline and rubbed some of it all over be-tween my legs. Then I tried again. It still burned, but not so bad. "Gosh, I hope I don't have an infection."

I finished up, washed my hands, and checked the clock in Daddy's room. I still had time to get ready for church. Good. I hoped Daddy was going to church. I went to the top of the stairs.

"Daddy? Are you going to church this morning? Should I get ready?"

He came out of the kitchen and to the bottom of the stairs. I couldn't see him, because the stairway turned ninety de-grees, five steps down, but I could hear him.

"Yes, Jean. I'm planning to go. If you want to go, hurry up and get ready and I'll take you with me."

I would have liked to wear my pink dress, but after I slept in it, it was too wrinkled and I didn't think I could get Daddy to press it for me. I looked in my closet. The dress I wore Friday to school was draped over the side of a box. It would be okay. I picked up my slip off the floor next to the box and hurried to get dressed.

Daddy was finishing some cereal as I came into the kitchen.

"You better have some cereal too, Jean. We don't have much time."

I got a bowl out of the cupboard and had some Cheerios

with milk. We had lots of milk. None of the kids were here to drink any of the milk we bought yesterday.

I had barely finished my last bite when Dad called to me, "Come on, Jean. We need to go now. I want to go a little early. The choir is singing a new song this morning and I want to go over it before church."

I ran out and grabbed my green sweater off the end of the couch as I got to the door. The sun was barely up and frost covered the ground. My sweater was hardly warm enough and I wished I had my jacket, but I wouldn't have time to go back. Maybe I was coming down sick. I was so awfully cold and aching; even going down the front steps hurt.

I got into the car and scooted close next to my daddy. He put his arm around me and gave me a little hug. Then we went off to church. We parked on the street across from the church. I took his hand and we walked together to the old, gray stone building.

I had slept too late for Sunday school, so we went around to the front and up the big steps into the church. I loved this church. Daddy left me and went down to the front and through the door that lead back to the choir rooms. I went down the aisle and picked a row near the front where I could see him sing, but far enough away that he couldn't see me drawing on the program during the sermon.

As I sat down, one of the ushers came up and handed me a program. I read through it as I waited for church to start. Then I looked around the church as a few people came in and found seats. I looked up at the cathedral ceiling, all done in bluish gray stone, with big arches making a flower design in the middle.

The pews were polished wood, dark brown with a curved top on the back. I always thought they were so pretty, but this morning they seemed terribly hard. I was so sore.

The church service began. I was glad no one sat very close to me. I liked to be alone in the church. The choir came in and sang. Daddy smiled at me. Then we came to prayers. I bowed my head and went to sleep, but JD stayed awake to pray.

Please God! Please don't let me go to hell. I want to be a good girl. I don't mean to be dirty. I don't think it was me in those pictures. I don't think Jody would do anything like that. Please make me good. Please let me be pure again. And please don't let Shadowman hear my prayers either.

I looked up from my nap. Everyone was standing and singing one of the hymns. I jumped up, grabbing a hymnal and my program. What song was it, and what verse were they singing? I found it and started singing. As I looked up, Daddy gave me an angry look with one raised eyebrow.

I tried to convey my thoughts with an apologetic smile, *I'm sorry. I'm just so tired.*

Then came the sermon. I tried to listen, but the pastor went on and on, and so I began drawing patterns on the back of my program. I glanced up at Daddy. He was sound asleep. Well, he couldn't be angry at me when he was sleeping in church, too.

The sermon ended and someone nudged my daddy with his elbow. There was another prayer and we all stood up to sing the closing hymn. I loved church, but I did love its ending too.

After church, someone stopped Daddy and started talking. I wandered down to them as they kept on for a while.

"Yes, well they did do surgery on her leg," Dad was saying as I got there, "But they aren't sure that it will help. It might make it worse. Cancer's like that. You operate on it and it travels all through your body. We just keep hoping that isn't what's going on with her."

Grandma. They were talking about my grandma. I loved her so much.

"Well, I've got to run. Betty will be getting home from there in a little while and I want to get dinner on for her. She hasn't been too well since Luke was born either," Dad said as he took my hand and moved us slowly away.

"Really? I didn't know," the other man was saying. "I'm sorry to hear that. I hope she'll be doing better soon. You're a good man, Fred. Take care."

We walked out to the car without talking. I wondered what he was thinking about.

As we got into the car, he said, "Mom will be home this afternoon. Let's try to surprise her. I'll cook dinner and you wash the dishes. We've got to get the laundry done, and the living room cleaned up a bit, okay?"

"Okay, Daddy. We'll work together and surprise her."

He gave me a big hug before he started the car.

As I lay in my bed remembering JD's experience, having felt the horror and pain, I cried until early morning. I loved my father. As I was growing up I had feared him, but he couldn't be Shadowman. I knew that he was capable of terrible violence when he was angry. There was no reason for his anger here. I was not the girl in those pictures. And my father could not be the man in that memory. I was insane. I had always believed it. There was no other explanation. Jack was wrong. JD *was* my illness, not my answer.

Even the Jody part of me couldn't accept this. My father had played indecent games with me as a toddler, and yes, he was an insufferable social failure, but this was sick.

I called my work and said I was ill. It wasn't a lie. Then I waited until the girls were off to school before I called Jack. Miraculously, he found a slot for me that day and I stumbled into his office that afternoon.

"Jean," Jack said when I had explained what I had recalled, "you remember how you couldn't believe there was Jody? You didn't want to acknowledge her memories as yours, either, but they were. JD is you. What she is relating happened to you. Whether you want to accept it now or not, JD is you and her experiences are your experiences. She has had to deal with this and hold it from you all these years until you could handle it. Now you can."

"No, I can't." I stiffened my lip. I would not cry in front of him.

"Yes, you can. This wouldn't be happening now if you couldn't. It's not going to be easy and I'm not sure what else JD has to share, but you need to try to accept her and her memories."

"Oh, Jack," I pleaded, not so much with Jack as with JD, "I don't want to remember this. Why can't it end now?"

"You're getting better. You need to remember that. Every time you deal with JD's memories, you are getting closer to dissolving the wall between the two of you. You're going to make it."

He gave me a hug as I left.

As I walked away from Jack's office, I fought inside my head. Maybe JD's memory was true. Maybe I wasn't insane. But how could this happen to me? My father loved me. I loved him. He couldn't be Shadowman of JD's memory. He just couldn't be.

FOURTEEN

Don and I had become inseparable.

During the Christmas season we decided to announce our wedding plans to Don's best friend, John Farr, and ask him to be the best man. We met at the home of John's parents. The elder Mr. and Mrs. Farr had been like second parents to Don from his high school years. They had helped Don deal with his alcoholic father, and Don and John had remained best friends for over two decades.

John and his wife were delighted.

The elder Mrs. Farr interviewed me at length about my beliefs, activities, and goals in life. When she had finished, she announced, "She's too good for you, Don."

I laughed. "No, you're wrong. As I've told my friends, he must really love me, to marry me with three teenage daughters."

Later that same evening, John took me off to a corner of the large living room, presumably to tell me some important secret. "Jean," he whispered. "I feel that as the best man, it is my duty to warn you."

"Warn me?"

"Yes. I think you should know that Don is very *weird*."

I responded immediately, "Oh, good. Then we should get along famously."

He turned quickly and loudly proclaimed, "I think you found the right one, Don!"

So John thought Don was weird? I couldn't help chuckling to myself. How would he react if he knew about me?

Less than six months since our first date, on the day of our wedding, Don wrapped me in a loving hug. Over those months, he had worked with me on transferring control back and forth to JD, and becoming closer to her than I thought would ever be possible.

"Let me talk to JD," Don said, holding me tightly.

I smiled and hugged him back as I gave JD control.

"JD?" Don asked quietly. "I wanted to know what you thought about getting married."

"Well . . ." I didn't know what to say to him. "I thought you were marrying Jody."

"But, JD, you and Jody are the same person. Don't you want to marry me?"

"You're marrying me?" I felt lighter and happier than I ever felt in my life. I was getting married. I was marrying Don, who loved me and was so nice to me.

"Yes, JD. I'm marrying all of you—Jean, Jody, and JD. I just wanted to let you know how much I love you."

I hugged him tighter and he kissed me.

"You need to let me talk to Jody now. We're due over at the church in less than an hour. Okay?"

I let go of him as I said, "Okay."

"Well, JD seemed pleased," Don said in recognition of my return.

"Pleased is too mild a word for what she's feeling."

"I feel a little guilty now, though. I should have asked her instead of told her."

"I wouldn't worry about it now. She's happy. Listen, we've got to hurry. Will you check on the girls? I know it only takes a few minutes to get to the church, but we need to leave soon."

"Okay." He hurried off to the other end of the house.

JD took over immediately.

I gripped the long skirt of my burgundy wedding gown with one hand and danced around the room, humming. I'm getting married. I'm getting married.

Don walked back in time to see. "JD. What are you doing?"

"I'm so happy, I just have to dance."

"Oh, JD. I'm glad you're happy. I wanted so much for both you and Jody to marry me. I think it would be a shame if only one of you wanted to. I wouldn't want to end up in a relationship like Hank did, with one married and another that wasn't. Now come on, we've got to get over to the church. I'm going to call the girls and go start the car."

The telephone rang, and Jean took over to answer it. Don waited to see who it was.

Polly's voice cut through my euphoria like a sledgehammer through my wedding cake. "Hi, Jean. How are the girls?" Hank's mother was the last person I wanted to talk to on my way to my wedding.

"Polly, I can't talk right now. I'm leaving this very moment for the church to get married."

"You're getting married?"

"Yes, right now." I tried to quell my irritation.

"Oh, I'm so glad. I just hate it when people shack up together."

"Good-bye, Polly. I've got to go." I hung up quickly and turned to Don. "We've got to change our phone number."

"Well," Don hesitated, and then replied in his usual reasonable way, "she is the girls' grandmother, and she does love them." He was right, of course. Hank was out of my world, but Polly would be there for the rest of her life.

As Don and I headed out to the car, he chuckled softly.

"Are you still laughing about Polly's call?"

"No. Forget her. I was thinking that I'm probably the only man in this state who can commit legal bigamy."

On our honeymoon, I came to appreciate the depth of Don's patience. We took the three girls with us for the first week of our two-week trip. I arranged for a church friend to come in and cook for them at home the second week, so Don and I could be alone.

We went to bed early on our wedding night to get up for a seven o'clock flight. On the first morning in Honolulu, we had to get up early to straighten out a car rental problem. All that week as we stayed at a hotel on Waikiki Beach, with the girls in a separate room, Melissa prevented us from sleeping in. On the third morning of our marriage, Melissa telephoned us at seven to seek permission to go down to breakfast alone. The next day she called about the same time to go to the beach, and the next to go shopping at the International Market, and finally to go to the zoo. On the last day in Honolulu, we again rose early to put the girls on the flight home.

As we boarded our interisland flight to Maui for our real honeymoon, Don joked with me. "We've been married a full week now. Every day of our honeymoon we've been up before seven thirty in the morning. Tomorrow we might sleep in all day without our seven o'clock wake-up call."

A year later we returned to Maui. Since our first date, Don had taken an interest in my mental health and how to deal with JD. He was so good to her. I felt strange giving over control to her, but I never feared that I wouldn't get control back. JD couldn't stand to be naked with Don. Eventually when we would shower or sleep together, JD would quickly relinquish control.

From the beginning Don had tried to be understanding and supportive of JD, but it was on this second trip to Hawaii that JD was free to appear.

"Can I talk to JD?" Don asked me, as we walked along Kihei beach.

I took a quick look up and down the wide beach. We were in the remote area where the two big sections of Maui met. There were no hotels or homes close by and the closest sun-bathers and surfers were far from earshot.

"Sure." JD? She wasn't far.

"Hi," I said, biting my lower lip as I smiled and looked down slightly.

"How do you like it here?" Don asked.

"I like it anywhere with you."

"Do you like Hawaii? Have you been here enough to see?"

"I've been here most the time."

I liked the feel of the sand between my toes as we walked.

"Do you want to go in swimming?"

"No," I said, shaking my head. I didn't know how to swim, but I wouldn't tell him.

Don walked down to the water's edge. The sand was firm where the water had been washing over it. I dragged my big toe through it into a huge heart shape. I carved "JD loves Don" in the middle of the heart. Don waded a bit and walked back toward me. He smiled as he saw the heart.

"And Don loves JD," he said as he hugged me. He took my hand and we walked up the beach to some rocks that had once been a retaining wall. "Are you with Jean a lot?" he asked as he sat on one of the rocks and pulled me close to him. He had tried to make me call Jody "Jean," but that was *my* name.

"Well . . ." I tried to think of how much I was with Jody. "Not a lot. I can't be with her when she's working or driving or anything like that. And she doesn't like it if I have control and anyone else is around. She thinks I might embarrass her. But I like to be with you."

The frown that had passed over Don's face quickly disappeared. He stood and hugged me tightly against him. "I love you, JD."

I wondered why. I had never done anything for Don. It was Jody that cooked for him and made love with him. Did he just love me because I loved him? He was there to hug me when I was afraid at night or began remembering something awful. And like today, he sought me out to talk to, but why? Could I ask him?

I hugged him back. I drew in a breath. I might have to hide quickly. "Why do you love me, Don?"

I tried to hold tightly to him, but he pushed me back slightly so that he could see my face. "JD, you're very sweet and you love me. Why shouldn't I love you? You're part of Jean, and I love Jean, too."

I searched for a sign of disappointment in his face. Would he be upset that I asked? But there was only the clear, honest expression of Don's love in his eyes.

Suddenly I felt warm and secure, more than any other time in my life. Here was someone who really loved me. I fought back tears as I hugged him again. As he put his lips to mine I gave control back to Jody.

"Ummm," I murmured as I kissed Don. I pressed up closer against him.

"Jean?" Don asked as we parted lips.

"Yes, it's me again."

"Why did JD leave?"

"I don't know. Maybe she just wanted to let me have this kiss."

"Happy?"

"Oh, Don, I love you. Sometimes I'm amazed at what you've taken on. Not many men would knowingly have married a crazy woman like me."

"Jean, you're not crazy. I saw an interview of a woman who had been in a concentration camp as a child. She had been raped by the guards. In the interview, they talked about the problems that person was having now. She was basically a very strong, stable person who had been traumatized. That's how I see you, as a basically strong and stable woman who was traumatized as a child. I couldn't have gone through what you went through, and come out as sane, as well, and as strong as you did. So how can I be critical?"

FIFTEEN

IN THE COUPLE OF YEARS PRIOR TO JD'S APPEARANCE, I HAD made friends with an extraordinary woman named Amy. She and I had seemed to have so much in common in our attitudes about life—our work, Christianity, closeness of family. One day I sat back on Amy's soft couch and she sat in the arm chair opposite. Normally I felt relaxed in her brick tudor, but I had been talking about my childhood abuse. I needed the softness of the cushions. I picked up a pillow and hugged it over my stomach.

"I don't understand why you want to get into all that old stuff now." Amy questioned, "Why can't you just forget it and get on with your life?"

Amy meant well, and to her it must make a certain degree of sense to "move on," but it couldn't happen that way. My blood pressure was rising and I was fighting for some control. This question always threw me into a spin. Be calm, be calm, I told myself, and took a deep breath. Amy was my friend. I needed her to understand and be supportive. I needed to avoid alienating her with my inner anger which she had not caused nor could she control.

"I can't forget it. That's the problem. It has affected everything I've done all my life—how I've interacted with everyone I've met, worked with, loved, hated, feared, revered. It's affected my decisions, my reactions, my emotional state of mind, my achievements, my failures, my self-esteem, everything that makes me *me* has been altered by the abuses of my childhood."

"But it's over. How can you change what happened?"

"Amy, you know that I am a Christian first, last, and always. I wish I could forgive and forget. I even wish I could just forget. For years I prayed that I could be spared the agonizing dreams and the insanity that seemed to pop into my life at the worst possible times. I didn't know what was going on with me. Even now, knowing much of what happened, I can't forget, because the ordeal hasn't ended. When I talk to Jack about forgiveness, he reminds me that I have to work through all the anger and fear and other emotions that lie buried, before I know what or how to forgive. I have to relive the experiences."

"How do you relive them?" Amy asked.

"Mostly, I don't have a choice. It usually happens in Jack's office. Well, in reality, I remember a lot more in a day or two after meeting with Jack. Sometimes it comes in a flood of memories and I'm ready to start screaming that I never want to deal with another thing." I explained the multiple personalities to Amy as clearly as I could. At first she seemed dismayed, but slowly she understood and accepted.

"When you learn everything that JD knows, can you be cured?"

"How can I know? I had to work to bring Jean and Jody together. I'm assuming I'll also have to bring Jean/Jody and JD together to be *cured*. I believe that when I knew what was happening with Jean and Jody, the differences could be reconciled. But it's so different with JD. She's stayed a child and a frightened one at that. How do I reconcile our differences?"

Amy gave me one of her "chin-up" smiles. "If anyone can, you can. I don't know anyone else who would have survived as intact as you did."

"Thanks. I do give God the credit, though. I find it amazing that He made our minds so powerful that I could spin off the horror and go on living as a fairly normal person. However, I could tell you some bizarre tales about Jean-versus-Jody experiences."

"I can imagine," she said, nodding her head and rolling her eyes slightly.

I wondered what she would think of me if I told her about Edward?

Sometime later, when Sandra and I met with Jack, I related my encounter with Amy and my reaction to her initial opinion. Jack sat quietly as we talked for a short time.

Sandra agreed angrily. "It's hard for anyone who wasn't abused so severely to understand you can't simply *put it behind you*. I was abused; I'm working with Jack to recover and deal with it. I can't put it behind me until I *see it before me*! I get so mad when someone tells me that."

"But," I tried to soften her a bit, "Amy's my friend. I think she appreciated the problem, once we talked about it for a while. Amy thinks we have to treat this as a kind of loss, that we have to go through the stages of grief until we can finally accept what happened. I suppose she's right."

"It's good that you recognized that. However," Jack pointed out, "I think you need to work with JD, and accept that what happened to her happened to you, before you can start grieving. I'm not sure you've shown any anger yet about your mom's neglect, for instance."

He was right, of course. My first thought was, don't start in about my mom again. I loved my mother. Ever since I first knew about JD, my emotions had set my father apart from me. I wanted to love his memory, but the real person had become a nonentity. If I saw him, I couldn't react either with love or anger. I wanted to work on that first. My mother I had already forgiven, as it was, without giving her any blame. Somehow I rationalized that she was unable to deal with my father's violence and was ignorant of his sexual abuse.

My face must have revealed a bit of my disgust, because Jack answered the look. "Okay, we don't need to get into that yet."

"What I want to know," Sandra asked, "is what made Dad act that way?"

I offered my opinion. "I think he had psychotic episodes—that he went temporarily insane. When I think about how he acted, so cruel and inhuman, I'm sure he was off the deep end."

"No," Jack disagreed. "I would say that your father had a personality disorder. Many sexual abusers do. If he came to me, I wouldn't take him on as a patient; I think he's untreatable."

"Do you think he could have multiple personalities, himself?" Sandra asked. "Could that be how he could do these things and still live with himself?"

I hadn't thought of that before. I liked the idea. It would allow me to keep the Daddy personality I loved and hate the Shadowman personality.

"No, I don't," he replied emphatically. "I haven't seen him myself, but from what you've told me, he fits the typical sexual abuser who rationalizes his behavior and then forgets it. He didn't do anything wrong at the time, so why remember? Why feel any guilt?"

"I don't know," Sandra countered, skeptical. "I have some sketchy but scary memories. I have one foggy memory of coming upon him unexpectedly. I think he was doing something to someone, probably Jean. Anyway, I clearly remember his turning and glaring at me with red eyes. I was so frightened that I ran away and hid. I'm not sure when that was, but I believe he was crazy at the time."

"That's the one thing that makes me think he must have had psychotic episodes, his eyes. You had to have seen them, Jack. I don't remember them as being red, but they were certainly wild looking when he got angry or abusive. They really did change."

As much as I wanted to believe what Sandra and I had said, I couldn't discount Jack's opinion. He was the professional; he had the experience. I could foresee a long period of emotional conflict for me.

On my next appointment, I was in Jack's office alone. I told him I was having a lot of trouble reading a recovery book called *The Courage to Heal*. Some of the excerpts by the interviewed victims brought back such vivid memories. I had been through a terrible recollection of one of JD's experiences a few nights before coming, but I wasn't sure I could share it with him in detail.

Jack pulled his copy from the bookshelf.

"Show me," he said, handing me the book. I sensed that he knew I was more disturbed than I was telling.

I flipped through it, looking for something that would not upset me.

"Better yet, let me talk with JD."

"Why?" I felt a little panic rise.

"I want to see what she thinks about the book."

"Okay," I agreed warily. JD? She was close to the surface.

"JD?" Jack asked me. "What do you think about this book?"

"It's kind of scary," I said. "There are parts of it Jody won't read at all."

"Parts, like what?" He handed me the book. "Show me."

I turned the pages slowly, looking for the section at the top of one certain page. When I found it, I handed him the open book.

"She especially doesn't like this. It's too much like what really happened."

"Okay. Thanks, JD," Jack said. "Now let me talk to Jody, okay?"

I nodded my head and released control to Jody.

"I want you to read this to me." Jack handed the open book back to me.

I looked at the page. Grasping the book, I slammed it closed. Jack quickly flipped it back open and held it in front of me. It was an instance of a young girl who had been forced into oral sex with her grandfather.

"Oh, Jack." I almost burst into tears, "JD has shared with me why it is she couldn't speak to you in this office. It's the most terrifying thing that ever happened to her."

"Correction: to *you*," Jack said. But I couldn't accept that.

"It was like I was there watching a horror movie, but it was real, and suddenly it became real for me. If Don hadn't been there to hold me through the rest of the night, I think I would have died. It happened when I was eleven. . . ." I began relating JD's experience as I had relived it only a few nights before.

I shivered with anticipation and fear as I stood before the State Children's Home. I was so tired of crying in the park by myself. I felt so terribly alone. I wanted someone to listen. I didn't even know what I was going to talk about.

The Children's Home sprawled several blocks from the corner of two main streets. It was made up of many old, brown brick buildings with white tuck-pointing at the corners and sweeping cement steps. The one closest to the street was the main office. I timidly entered the front gate, went along the chipped cement walkway, up the dozen steps, and through the front door.

A very large lady dominated the desk in the entrance hall. Her face was pinched up in deep thought over the papers spread before her. Her mouth was twisting around as though she were talking angrily to some unseen companion, though no sound came from her. I almost backed out again, when she looked up and a deep loving smile swept away any trace of anger.

"How can I help you?" she asked, as though I were an adult customer in a clothing store.

"Well, I . . . I need someone to talk to . . . I just need to talk to someone." I floundered, looking down at my shoes. My socks were rolling down badly and I longed to pull them back up, but not in front of her.

"Of course," she said, as though she heard this every day. "I'll see if Mrs. Miller is available now." She disappeared around the corner as she finished her sentence. I wondered why she moved so quickly, moreover, how she moved so quickly and quietly—she seemed too big to be so agile.

Suddenly I wanted to escape back out the front door. It was as though something in her speed had set off an alarm in my head. Maybe they wouldn't let me leave after I talked to them. Before I could turn to exit, she appeared from around the corner. I hadn't even heard her. I looked at her shoes. The soles were a kind of rubber that made no noise at all on the green marble floor.

"Yes, Mrs. Miller is in her office and she can see you right now. Come along with me." She pointed around the corner. As she spoke, she reached out her other hand, not to take mine, but almost as if she were about to grab hold of me. I stepped back sharply. She knew instantly that she had frightened me.

"No one is going to harm you, my dear," she said softly, her smile changing to concern. "Mrs. Miller is one of the

nicest counselors you could ever visit with. You said you
wanted to talk. She wants to hear whatever it is you want to
say. Please come along."

I followed her around the corner and down the hall to the
corner office, staying a few steps behind. I could always turn
and run.

Mrs. Miller had the office of a school principal with a big
wooden desk in the middle. Stacks of paper littered several
in/out boxes and there were three or four ledger-type books
open, one on top of the other in the center where she had
been working. A pencil cup with one very dull pencil sat
next to the telephone, while scores of pens and pencils lay
scattered in among the papers and books all over her desk.

Even Mrs. Miller looked as though she belonged in a
school. Her hair was pulled back from her face in wide
combs that made her look older than she probably was. As I
looked at her long gray dress and gray shoes with clunky,
short heels, I wondered if everything in this place was required to be gray.

"Come in, come in!" Mrs. Miller greeted me like an old
friend she hadn't seen for a long time. The lady from the hall
desk had disappeared as quickly as before, pulling the door
closed behind her. "Miss Carson tells me you've come to
talk with me. I'm so glad. What's your name?"

"Well, I don't know . . . I . . . it's Jean, but . . ." I didn't
want to tell her. I wasn't sure why; I just didn't want to.

She didn't seem to notice my reluctance at all. "I'm glad
to meet you, Jean. Won't you sit down?" She gestured to a
chair in front of the desk as she sat down next to me.

I slid into the designated chair with a growing sense of
guilt. I felt as if I was doing something wrong. What if it
cost money to come talk with Mrs. Miller? How should I ask
her? Why did I come here?

"You look frightened," Mrs. Miller said. "Are you afraid
of me?"

"No, ma'am," I said quietly. "I just don't know if I should be here."

"Why?"

"Well, I . . . I don't have any money."

"Oh, is that it?" Smiling with relief, she continued, "You don't need any. Everyone here works for the state. You can come anytime, free. Now tell me, what's bothering you?"

I looked down at my shoes again. I didn't know exactly what to say. She waited while I sorted out my words carefully.

"It's . . . that I don't have anyone. I mean, I have a family, a mom and dad and lots of kids, but there's no one to talk to. I know a lot of the kids who live here and they come and talk to you. I just go to the park and . . . and . . . I'm just alone."

"How many brothers and sisters do you have?" she asked.

"Six, three of each. I mean, there's six of us, three boys and three girls. I'm the oldest girl. My brother Matthew is the only one that's older than me."

"So you help take care of the younger ones?" she asked as though she knew.

"Yes. I even do some of the cooking. I'm learning a whole lot about cooking. And I do the laundry sometimes."

I stopped. She was reaching over the corner of her desk and pulling a tablet out of the drawer. I was afraid. What was she going to do? "What are you going to write?"

She flashed another kind smile, "Nothing too complicated—your name and anything you want me to remember whenever you come back to see me again."

"Oh, am I supposed to go now?" I suddenly feared she wasn't going to let me talk with her.

"No, no. I meant that I wasn't planning to take notes or anything. I like to have a tablet and pencil handy. Sometimes the kids who come here want me to check on something for them or remember to ask them something the next time they come. Things like that. Now, please tell me some more about yourself, like where do you go to school? What grade are you in? How old are you? What do you like to do? And that sort of thing, okay?"

I told her all those things and lots more. My grandmother was dying of cancer, and my mother was gone a lot to take care of her. I couldn't actually talk to my mother much, because she worked too. I didn't really have any close friends except Becky. I couldn't talk a lot to Becky; she was always talking. She was pretty fat and kids teased her all the time, so she liked me and wanted me around all the time. I was the only close friend she had too, but Becky was gone visiting her grandparents now, so I didn't have anywhere to go except the park. And I had been at the park most of today until I had decided to come here.

"So, with your mother working, and taking care of all these kids, and driving down to take care of your grandmother, she doesn't have much time left to talk with you?" Mrs. Miller said finally.

"No, I guess not." I was beginning to get tired.

"Well, I want you to know that I am here most days during the week and you can come by and talk to me. When would you like to come back?"

"Tomorrow, I guess." I felt sleepy and hot, but I wanted to stay now or come back soon.

"Okay," she consented slowly, "but I need to schedule in some time for you. Tomorrow's sort of busy for me."

She got up and leaned over her desk to flip a page on her calendar. Taking her pencil into her left hand, she started to write on the calendar, "Jean . . . what did you say your last name was?"

My throat tensed again. "I didn't say, I didn't want to tell you. Well, I didn't want them to know that I came here, you know?"

"It's all right, Jean, you can tell me. We're going to be good friends from now on."

So I told her.

In the next two weeks, I saw Mrs. Miller every couple days. I brought her my notebook with my school notes and poems and doodles all over the sides. She seemed particularly interested in a scribbled mess on the bottom of one page. In the middle of the mess, I had written "ME" in big letters, and then disguised the word with little curls wrapping off the letters, but she still could read the word.

I told her about the fights that I had with my older brother, Matthew, who had lots of friends at school. I had only Becky. Most of the other girls were in a local girls organization, the Sunshine Girls.

Then I told her about not being able to join the Sunshine Girls, since they had to have a committee come visit your home to see if you "fit in" to their organization. My house was always a giant mess. There was never any time they would be able to visit, and if they ever had, they would have known that I would never fit in. I didn't tell her the other reason—I couldn't tell her—that not only could the Sunshine people not come, but no one else could either. I was too embarrassed to tell her. On warm evenings my father sat around naked, reading the paper in his chair in the living room. Who could even bring a friend there?

Then came Friday night of the second week that I had seen Mrs. Miller. Mom had cooked dinner and gone to work in the living room on her typewriter, leaving us kids, as she often did, to the terrible fate of eating with Dad.

As we gathered around the square table in the kitchen, Dad dished up the plates. I sat on the end of one of the benches, around the corner from Dad, closest to his right hand. As he took up my plate to serve my food, without turning to look directly at me, he asked almost nonchalantly, "What did you do today Jean?"

I started to say nothing much, but then I caught a quick side glance of anger in his eye. I gasped quietly. He knows.

How can he know? I fumbled for words and then began to panic, "I went out and about, to the park and places. You know, I had to see if Becky was back. She was supposed to be back today. . . ."

I would have kept rambling frantically except he interrupted me to yell at Mark, "Close your mouth when you're chewing! Nobody else wants to watch you eat!"

I began eating to be busy and so did Dad. I carefully watched the side of his face. He seemed to have let it drop. Maybe I was wrong. But then, without turning again, he shifted that one angry-looking eye back at me. No, I wasn't wrong. He knew. Why should he care? Why couldn't I just tell him? Because he doesn't want his kids going to talk with someone, especially from the state, I answered myself. I had to get out of there.

Suddenly Dad exploded again, "Luke, don't put so much meat in your mouth at one time!"

Luke huddled down, frightened. Tears wet his little eyes.

"He's just a baby, Dad. Matthew didn't cut his food up small enough." I tried to make him not scream at Luke, who was nearing his third birthday.

"It doesn't matter," Dad shouted angrily at me. "He's still got to learn to eat right."

Luke curled down further onto the bench. Dad turned back to him and shook his head. Then he said less loudly, "Luke, sit up and eat your supper. Matthew, cut up his meat better."

Matthew shot a grimace of blame over the table at me, and started cutting up Luke's food into tiny pieces.

I didn't mind Matthew's look, but there again was that evil, angry-looking eye, glancing out of the side of Dad's face at me as he chewed rapidly. As he turned the back of his head toward me to berate Mark's eating again, I said, in almost one word, "I have to go to the bathroom."

I bolted from the table and down the hall into the living

room, giving the kitchen door a push as I flew past it. That would cover my escape later if no one else got up first. I ran up the stairs and into the bathroom. I couldn't swallow my mouthful of meat, so I spit it into my hand, threw it into the toilet, and flushed it.

As I tiptoed back across the upstairs hall, I realized that Dad had undoubtedly heard the toilet flush and would expect me to be down soon. Instead, I ran down the stairs and across the living room to where Mom was typing in the corner.

"Please, Mom, I need to go over to Becky's house, *right away*. She's supposed to be back today. I want to spend the night there, okay? I'll be back in the morning, I promise. Please?"

"Well," Mom said. She could hardly be distracted from the page she was finishing. "I guess so, but don't stay up too late. . . ."

I didn't hear her other words of advice. I was practically running before I reached the front door. I looked to see if the kitchen door was still in place. It was. No one would see my escape.

I ran down the steps, across the street, into the neighbors' yard, and between their garages into the alley beyond. When I made the corner, I knew I was out of sight of the house. He hadn't called me back, so, for tonight at least, I was safe.

When I got to Becky's house, it was dark and deserted. In despair, I sat down on the porch swing. No screens had been put up along the porch walls. Except for the swing, the porch was empty. Oak trees towered over the front yard blocking out the last reflections of sunset and screening the streetlights. As I sat there, it seemed the porch got darker and darker. Somewhere in the distance I could hear the bass from someone's record player booming softly. Down on Miami Avenue, there were a few passing cars, but the neighborhood was getting quieter with the dark.

I didn't know how long I'd been sitting there. It must have gotten quite late. I silently cried out in despair, *Oh, Becky, where are you?*

Suddenly, beside me, inside the house, the telephone began to ring. It rang three times.

"Nobody's home," I tried to tell it, when a voice in the dark room answered it, "Hello?"

It was Philip, Becky's older brother. He was home. He would let me wait inside for Becky.

"No, no, I haven't seen her. Becky and Elizabeth aren't home yet, so she may have come by and seen they weren't here," his voice was answering. It was my mother on the other end, I was almost certain. Did Dad have her call to have me sent back?

"Okay, I'll tell her, if I see her. 'Bye." Philip hung up.

I jumped up and knocked at the door. The end table light turned on.

"I'm coming," Philip's voice called from inside.

As he opened the door, I blurted out, "Don't tell me, Philip. Then I can honestly say that you didn't tell me."

He laughed as he let me into the house. "Okay, I won't tell you. How long have you been on the porch anyway?"

"I don't know. What time is it?"

"About eight o'clock."

"Then I guess I've been out there about an hour and a half. Have you heard from Becky and Elizabeth? Are they going to be home tonight? They just have to be home tonight."

"Whoa!" Philip was laughing at me again. "I'm sure they'll be along any time now. Elizabeth took Becky shopping. I've been sleeping on the couch here until my friend Bill comes to pick me up. What are you up to?"

"I'm escaping again. Mom knows I came here, but she'll think I went out with Becky and Elizabeth, so don't tell me what she said."

I always found it strange that Becky and Philip called their mother Elizabeth, never Mom. She was Elizabeth to me too, although I could never hope for a better second Mom. As an editor and publisher, she was always full of funny stories and sometimes sad ones. She seemed to love me as much as I loved her, but she never had time to sit and talk with me alone.

There was a honking in front of the house.

"That's for me," Philip said, nodding his head toward the window as he grabbed his jacket off the back of the couch. "I'm sure Becky and Elizabeth will be along . . . oh, here they are now."

A taxi pulled up behind his friend's green sedan. Elizabeth never learned to drive and never wanted to. She said she simply had to make enough of a living to afford taxis.

Becky saw me and came running from the taxi, up the porch steps, and into the house, "Oh, Jean, wait till you see what I bought. Elizabeth said I needed some new clothes for school and I bought *everything*!"

We stayed up half the night so she could try on and show me everything she had gotten. Elizabeth made some popcorn for us at midnight. Then she went to bed before us, saying she had to get up early to see someone at her office. Sometime late in the night or early in the morning we fell exhausted into Becky's bed and went to sleep.

Out of my dreams the phone kept ringing, waking me slowly. It was ringing downstairs, far beyond the closed bedroom door. I opened my eyes ever so slightly to see Becky in deep sleep, undisturbed by the ringing. It was quite light, so I guessed it was probably midmorning. Philip either didn't come home last night or was even more sound asleep than we were. Elizabeth was long gone to her office. I debated dragging myself down to answer the phone, but opted to drift back to sleep as the ringing thankfully stopped.

Suddenly I jerked up in the bed. What time was it? I had to crawl over Becky to see.

"Oh, no! It's after noon!" I cried out loudly. "Oh, Becky, I told my mother I would be home in the morning. She may have gone down to Grandpa and Grandma's. That was probably her calling me this morning."

"Who was calling?" Becky was shaking the sleep from her head.

I pulled on my slacks as I raced through my explanation of the earlier call. "I'm sorry to run off and leave you like this, but I've got to get home right now. I'm in big trouble if Mom was going to Grandma's, especially if she didn't hear from me last night and I didn't come home this morning."

As soon as I was dressed, I dashed out of the house, down the alley, and between the garages again. Our white Studebaker was parked in front of the house. I felt a wave of relief. Mom hadn't gone. However, as I crossed the street, the panic began to rise again. I wanted to run behind the house to see if she had driven off in the Buick, but it was too late. Dad was standing in the front doorway.

"Jean," he said with deliberate quietness, "come into the house."

I needed to go to the bathroom. I had run without stopping, directly after jumping from Becky's bed. Now I was acutely aware of my need. My stomach was empty. Except for the few bites at supper and Elizabeth's popcorn, I hadn't eaten. Panic shot into the pit of my stomach. I knew I was going to be beaten and there wasn't anyone home to hear me scream.

I trod fearfully into the house and Dad closed the door behind me.

"Where were you last night? You didn't go to Becky's." He was grasping my shoulder, his grip tightening with each word.

"I did go to Becky's last night. They were out shopping until late. Please, Dad, I need to go to the bathroom."

"Your mother called there last night and left a message for you to call home. You weren't there and you never called. You told your mother you would be home this morning. She needed your help to get the kids ready to go down to Grandma's. You didn't come home, she didn't get your help, and she left without knowing where you were."

"They're all gone?" my voice betraying my panic.

"Yes. You and I are here alone and we are going to learn several lessons today, young lady." He was nearly dragging me toward the basement door.

"Wait, Daddy, please. I really have to go to the bathroom, please!"

He released his grip and I raced up the stairs. He came up behind me, two or three steps at a time. As I ran into the bathroom, he followed, catching the door I had shoved, keeping it from latching. He paced angrily in the hall, as I emptied my bladder and began to shake with fear.

As I crept out of the bathroom, he attached his hand to my shoulder again, shoving toward the stairs. We descended the stairs into the living room in silence. As we rounded the corner to head for the basement, I fought to turn to face him.

"Please, listen to me, Daddy! I really was at Becky's last night. She's home. Call her, or call Elizabeth at her office and she'll tell you. I'm sorry we overslept and I didn't get home this morning. I'll make it up. I'll wash dishes and clean and anything. Please don't spank me, Daddy! Please!" I began to cry.

"That's not all we have to *discuss*," he said, drawing out the last word. His eyes began to take on that frightening evil look again as he opened the stairway door and shoved me through it.

I nearly stumbled down the stairs into the basement and

he jerked me up and along by the arms, and on into the laundry room.

In the laundry room was one of the dining room chairs. He had been waiting for me and brought it down before I came home. I knew it was going to be a long day, alone in the basement with him.

It was Shadowman. His eyes burned through me. He had told me. He had warned me. But Jody never listened to me. I told her over and over not to go to that place. I told her, "He can hear you. I know he can. Don't go there. He can hear you."

Now I was here in the basement. He put the boards in the windows and turned on the light. He shut the heavy wood door. I stood there and waited for him. There was nothing I could do. He was going to kill me. He began to take off my clothes. He pulled my shirt over my head and knelt to pull my pants and panties down to my ankles.

He sat down in the chair, pulling me across his lap. I fought to stand.

"Bend over," he ordered and I bent over his lap.

"What did you tell them? I know you went over to that center. You tell me or I'll beat you to within an inch of your life!" With that he began to spank my bottom with his hand.

"I didn't tell them anything," I tried to explain through my tears. "I just talked about school and my friends and stuff like that."

"Well, you won't again. You understand that? You won't ever go back there, do you hear me?" He was yelling into my ear, all the while hitting me. "I'll teach you to go telling people about me. You'll learn this lesson. You'll remember next time!"

I knew there was more to this lesson. Underneath me, I could feel his penis getting harder, pressing up into my stomach.

He stopped hitting me, slid his hand between my legs and

slipped his fingers inside, pressing me open with two of them. His hands were huge and his fingers hurt.

"Oh, no!" I cried, "Don't!"

He pulled his fingers out and spanked me several times more. Then he pushed me off his lap and onto the floor and unzipped his pants, pulling them open far enough to stick his huge penis out in front of me. He had no underwear on.

He grabbed my hair and jerked my face up to his penis.

"Suck it!" he screamed at me.

I tried to push away from him, but he grabbed my hands and holding them both with one hand, grabbed my hair again and jerked my head back up onto his penis.

"*Suck it!*" he demanded, pushing it half down my throat.

I fought choking as I tried to suck. It seemed endless hours. I couldn't breath. He thrust it in and out of my throat so quickly that I could hardly get any air in between.

"Suck it, you dirty little girl," he said several times, as he pulled hard on my hair.

Then suddenly he pushed me away from him back onto the floor. He pulled his pants off and yanked mine over my ankles. He shoved me down onto the floor, his weight nearly crushing me. He pushed his penis into me so hard I thought my hips would crack on the cement floor beneath me. He held it hard within me.

"Say 'please,' " he demanded.

I cried but said nothing.

He pulled out and plunged back in again hard. "I said say '*please*'!"

From somewhere inside me steel resolve let me say "No."

Oh, God, please become my rock, I begged silently.

"You will say 'please,' " he said, repeating his press and rocking harder.

"No!" My fingers gathered lint from the floor around me and tightened into a fist.

He began to pump on me faster and harder, "Say it. Say it. Say *'please!'*"

I am never going to say it. God will hold me. No matter how much he hurts me. I am never going to say please.

"You will say *'please,'*" he spat through his teeth, as he drew away from me.

I screamed out and then reached into my rooms. The red and blue walls of my rooms were soft and I fell through them into the colors. I could go to the colors. There he couldn't reach me.

He grabbed my shoulders and rolled me over onto my stomach.

God! He's ripping me in half! His penis was pounding into my bottom. The pain was too much. I tried to say please, but all I could hear was someone screaming. I couldn't move my mouth; I couldn't breathe. My stomach hurt, my head was screaming. Stop! Stop! Stop, please stop! My rooms. Where are my rooms? The colors. Where are they? My hand began to feel their softness when suddenly he was done. I didn't think I could go on.

Please let me die now, God.

He drew away from me and got up.

"Oh, shit!" he gasped at me. I looked up to see a terrible fear crossing over his face.

I tried to roll back over, but the pain was so great, I could hardly move at all. Blood was running between my legs. He'd killed me and he knew he had killed me.

"Here, hold this towel on your bottom and go clean yourself up."

My head was spinning. I didn't think I could get up.

"Go!" he ordered.

I grabbed the towel and pressed it against my sore bottom. How it hurt to touch. I couldn't stand up. I crawled over to the stairs and worked my way up as quickly as the pain would let me. Blood was dripping all over the stairs, but I couldn't stop to clean it.

Please don't let anyone see me, I thought, as I crossed the living room and struggled up the next stairs.

I crawled along the wall so I wouldn't get any blood on the hallway carpet. I managed to get into the bathroom, but before I could get to the toilet, I began to vomit. There wasn't much in my stomach, but I kept feeling that I had to throw up something more. Still on my hands and knees, I got some toilet tissue and tried to wipe up the blood and vomit from the bathroom floor.

I pulled myself up to start the bathwater running. Getting into the tub was terribly painful, but the warm water began to feel good. My head was still spinning. The room faded dark and light and dark again.

Suddenly he came in. I hadn't heard his approach. The water was beginning to have a lot of blood in it.

"Are you okay?" he asked, that look of fear in his eyes yet.

My eyes wouldn't close. I wanted them to, but they wouldn't. My mouth said "Yes, I'm okay," but I don't know how the words came out.

He had handfuls of paper towels. "You made a bloody mess of the floor and stairs. I've almost got it cleaned up. I told you to hold a towel on it."

"Yes," I answered him, but maybe only in my mind.

I learned my lessons well. Jody would not go back and I *would* say please. . . .

I moved my leg. It made me so cold. I opened my eyes. I was sitting in cold water. Why? I didn't remember. When did I run it?

The unlit bathroom was nearly black. Outside the window, through the oaks, the sky was darkening. The hallway light glowed dimly on the bathroom wall through the door, slightly ajar.

As I struggled out of the cold water and pulled the plug, I began to shiver violently. My bottom throbbed with pain at every movement. My whole body ached. I turned on the light and winced as it glared into my eyes.

I had to get into some hot water, but the bath was still draining slowly. The water was a strange orange color, almost like the iron water at summer camp. To warm myself, I ran hot water in the sink, and I soaked my wrists under the running water. The bathtub was still draining, so I gave up and went to my bedroom to find some clothes. I felt weak and shaky. I pulled a pair of slacks out of the box in my closet, and panties and a shirt from my bureau and began dressing quickly. Pulling on the panties and slacks was hard. Dad must have really given me some beating. I found a sweater in the corner on the floor and put it on. I knew there were no clean socks in my drawer; I hadn't brought up the laundry yet.

The laundry room. Why did he use the laundry room to beat us? Where was he, anyway?

I walked quietly into the hall and peered into his dark bedroom to check the time. He wasn't in there. Eight-thirty. What happened to the whole afternoon and evening?

Let's see. I came home from Becky's after noontime. Dad took me to the basement and beat me. Sometime after that I took a bath and fell asleep in it. Strange. I felt dizzy. Why couldn't I remember anything? My head ached with the thought and each movement.

I went slowly downstairs; every step seemed an effort. Only the light next to Dad's chair was on, but he was not there. Since I could see the Studebaker out front, he must have been in the basement. I felt starved. I put plain lunch meat on bread and ate my sandwich hungrily. Dad must have eaten without me. I decided to go straight to bed. I felt sick.

I'm going to sleep now. Please, God, don't let Shadow-man come get me again tonight. Please let me sleep, JD begged.

He was shaking me. My eyes squinted open in the morning light. I was still in my slacks, half-covered with my bedspread.

"Get up, Jean. Get up, it's time to get ready for church."

I looked up at his face. He was smiling.

"Come on, now. We only have about a half hour to get dressed or we'll be late."

I jumped up. Even though I still ached severely, I had to hurry. I loved to go to church with my Daddy.

"Oh, Jack!" I sobbed, wiping the tears from my cheek with one hand and fumbling for a tissue with the other. "How could anyone do that to me? I didn't know. I couldn't know. What am I going to do?"

"Accept what you remember, what JD remembers."

"How can I? This was my father. I loved him." I felt a wave of renewed pain and anger. The tears gathered in my eyes again as I slowly raised my head. Jack shook his head slightly, but waited silently for me to answer my own outcry.

"No wonder I've been crazy. No wonder I've suffered hemorrhoids all my life. Why didn't I bleed to death then and let him try to explain it?" The anger was beginning to rage up in my head. No, I couldn't say that; JD had endured the ordeal. "I'm sorry, JD. I didn't really mean it. I guess I understand now why she couldn't talk to anyone for so long. Somehow he found out I'd been seeing that counselor. I guess the ironic part of all this is that I didn't even know what he had been doing. So I couldn't tell anyone in the first place. Jack, what am I going to do?"

"Survive. That's what JD was there for, so you could survive."

"I'm not going to be able to handle much more of this. What else can there be?"

"I don't know, but remember, JD's been living with it for all these years. You'll have to accept her memories as what happened to you. It did happen to you."

Me. This happened to me. Accept that this happened to me. I tried not to shake my head.

"Will I ever be well?"

"Yup, I think you're well on your way." Jack was reaching for his appointment book. I was grateful today that my time with him was ending.

SIXTEEN

OVER THE YEARS, I'D BEEN READING A LOT OF BOOKS ON healing. Many of them had related problems that the survivors of sexual abuse had experienced after the memories of abuse surfaced. I hadn't had any difficulties with my sexual relationship with Don. I decided that it was probably due to two factors: Don had been working through the abuse memories with me, and secondly, it was probably JD who was experiencing the problem. I thought about how she couldn't stand to be undressed or in bed with Don, even though he kept reminding her that she was married to him.

Don wanted a child of his own. I wondered how JD would react to a pregnancy? Even though I had had my fallopian tubes fused, I was sure that I could reverse the procedure and give him one. I knew that reconnections were more successful than ever and I pictured Don with a blond son on his shoulder, my son.

We checked all over the country for the best doctor to do the job, one with a high rate of successful pregnancy after reconnection. We found one right here in Seattle at the University Hospital. Many tests, and six and a half hours of microsurgery later, I was repaired.

Don and I were to wait before trying to conceive. The doctor suggested three months to give the reconnection, as well as the wide hip-to-hip-incision, time to heal. However, toward the end of March, my second month of recovery, my job took me off to California for a week of training. It had been nearly two years since our first date. This was the first time Don and I had been apart for more than two days in all that time. We missed each other. When I returned, Don and I got wrapped in each other and carried away by our emotions and physical desire.

A couple of weeks later, Don said, "We only have to wait about two more weeks, before we can start trying to make a baby."

I smiled, and said, "Too late. Just like us, your child was too impatient to wait." I could feel my body making changes already.

In the months that followed, the doctor ordered an ultrasound scan and amniocentesis, a test of amniotic fluid around the unborn child. The test would primarily screen for Down syndrome, a form of retardation, much more common in babies with mothers in their late thirties and forties. A week after the test, we received the news that our little one was healthy and a boy.

Toward the end of December, I went into labor, but was sent home from the hospital after not sustaining it. Don and I tried in vain to convince the doctor that our baby was due, that we knew exactly the day he was conceived. For the next few weeks, I had many trips to the hospital, but could not sustain labor. I was certain my age prevented the normal delivery.

Finally, in the third week of January, the doctor brought me into the hospital and induced hard labor. Knowing what the doctor refused to accept, that the baby was a month overdue, Don and I worried about the baby's health. How had he survived the weeks of contractions?

Our doctor went off duty and his associate took over. He put a monitor on the baby.

"He's in distress," Dr. Black said to the nurses. "Prepare for a C-section." Then he said, more calmly to me, "We have to deliver him immediately. You'll have to push him out in the next three minutes or we'll have to take him surgically. He's running out of oxygen."

I grabbed the rails and pushed with all my abdomen muscles.

"Good. Good," said the doctor. "He's coming. I've got his head and one hand. We're going to pull now."

Out came a very large, deep blue baby. As soon as his chest was free, he took in a gasping breath and let out a scream. The nurse took him from the doctor and moved him onto a cushioned table, warmed by overhead heat lamps. The nurses cleaned out his mouth and nose and put him on oxygen. In a few minutes, as they worked with him, his color began to change and he turned a pinkish color. His collarbone had been broken by the swift delivery, so his left hand was taped to his chest to keep it from moving. The nurse wrapped the crying baby tightly in a blue baby blanket and handed him to Don.

As Don carried his newborn son over to me, I took their picture. There were tears of joy running down his cheeks and mine. Our son was born, alive and well.

For the next three days I visited our little Jason in the hospital nursery. He didn't look so little there, though. They had "stuffed" our ten-pound boy into an incubator to keep him warm until his blood sugar could be brought up. With one arm taped to his body and the other taped to a board to keep an IV in his hand feeding him glucose, he couldn't even rub his nose if it itched.

His incubator was next to another holding a tiny, premature girl weighing slightly over two pounds. She was dressed in a doll nightgown a little too big for a Barbie. Jason looked almost grown compared to her.

While I was still in the hospital, Don drew out JD to hold Jason.

"This is our baby, your baby and my baby. Do you know that, JD?"

I hugged the baby boy. This was my baby too. I had Don and now I had Jason. I cried.

Don's father came to the hospital two days after Jason's birth to hold his only grandson. Jason's grandfather was dying of cancer, but he had hung on to see the boy. In the hospital nursery, I took a picture of the three generations together—Grandpa, Daddy Don, and Jason. It was the only picture I ever got of the three of them together.

After three days, the hospital put Jason into a normal baby bed and that afternoon we took him home. His arm was taped for a couple more weeks, but his collarbone healed and soon he was moving as if nothing had ever happened to him.

Jason was not the only one who suffered in his rapid delivery. I needed some reconstructive surgery to repair many of the torn muscles, but I put it off; I didn't want to be incapacitated until Jason was older.

It was early September of the next year, when Don took Jason and me to the Western Washington Fair in Puyallup. Red and orange zinnias and bright yellow marigolds lined the grassy areas between the buildings housing the livestock, craft, hobby, and farming displays. The air was summer warm, but a breeze was blowing the promise of colder days to come.

Jason was too young to appreciate most of the exhibitions, but he loved the train rides and was fascinated with all the animals. We wandered the fair without a plan, stopping to see the chain-saw wood carvings of dwarfs and eagles, again to hear a choir singing in one of the halls, and again to let Jason pet a sheep being sheared in the aisle of a farm building.

After we had lunch at one of the smoky barbecue-chicken pits, we strolled by a display of an old-fashioned farmhouse. All at once JD grabbed control and rushed away from Don and Jason.

"Wait!" Don called. He pushed Jason's stroller over quickly to where I had paused, trembling with fear. My fingers hurt and I grasped the left digits with my right hand.

"JD?" Don asked, bending his head to peer into my face. "Yes?"

"Come on," Don said gently, taking my hand in his and pushing the stroller with the other. "Let's get away from everybody. I need to talk with you."

We walked silently to stand by a large flower bed planted in a spiral design of colored flowers, surrounded by chain-link fencing. Don gave Jason a bottle from the diaper bag that he eagerly accepted and settled down to drink.

Don put his arm around my waist. "JD? Can you talk to me here?"

"Yes," I said. With my head bent down, I looked up through my bangs at Don. He looked concerned and loving as he always did whenever he talked with me.

"What was it there that frightened you? What did you see?"

I bit my lip. I didn't want to talk about it. I didn't want to think about it.

"JD, I want to help you. Can't you tell me what scared you in that display?"

I leaned against the fence, curling my fingers around the wires. My hands ached and the wire felt cool against the throbbing fingers.

"Please tell me, JD. I want to help you. I love you."

"Um," I said, not knowing how to tell him. "It's Shadow-man."

"Shadowman? What about him?"

I didn't know how to tell him. The pain in my left hand was becoming fierce.

"Look. Shadowman isn't here. He can't ever hurt you again. Whatever you saw over there reminded you of something with Shadowman, but whatever it was, he can't ever hurt you again. You know that. I'm here with you. I won't let him hurt you again." He waited for some answer, but I still couldn't talk.

"JD," he asked finally, "can I talk to Jean?"

"Oh!" I exclaimed as I regained control from JD and withdrew my tightened fingers from the fence. "I understand what was so scary."

"What?" Don asked.

I shook my head as I answered, "The wringer washer."

"Oh, no. What about it?"

I sighed and looked down at my left hand. "No wonder I've had trouble with circulation in my fingers. Shadowman pushed my hand into the old wringer washer in the laundry room."

"Why would he do that?" Don said, disgusted.

"I don't know. It has something to do with eliciting my agreement to never tell anyone about what was going on in the basement, but I can't get a clear picture. All I know for sure is that my fingers got mashed in that old wringer."

"I need to help JD get past this. Let me talk to her again."

"Okay." JD, come on back.

I bit my lip and started to grasp my fingers again, but Don took my hand in his and rubbed the fingers. "Your hand is okay, JD," he said. "That happened a long time ago. It's healed now. I want you to do something for me."

"What?"

"I want you to come back and look at the display. You need to see there's nothing there that can harm you now."

I nodded and went with him as he pushed Jason's stroller slowly back to the farmhouse.

We stood in front of the glass-enclosed room, but I avoided looking at it by staring down at Jason. His eyelids were heavy as he slumped back in the stroller, sucking the last of his bottle. Soon he would be asleep.

"JD, please look at this room," Don pleaded.

I wanted to do whatever Don wanted me to do, but I was frightened. Don stood beside me and wrapped his arm around my waist, turning me slightly toward the window. Slowly I looked up at the room.

In one corner was an old black wood-burning stove and a cast-iron sink with a hand pump. Next was a long, dark wooden table with benches, similar to picnic-table benches, and a tall sideboard containing stacks of heavy plates, and large blue-and-white bowls. A fake fireplace had been positioned in the center of the room. Before the fireplace were two straight-back chairs and a weather-beaten wooden rocker. Finally, in the far corner was the old wringer washer with a couple of galvanized washtubs and a rickety wicker basket.

I winced as my eye passed over the washer. Don gave me a quick squeeze as he felt my reaction.

"Now, go back and look at it. It can't harm you. There's nothing here that can hurt you now."

Slowly I drew my sight back to the washer and its horrible wringers. I leaned into the warmth of Don's side as I looked at it. It was just a thing, sitting there in a display window. Shadowman was not here and could not hurt me again. I was with Don. I would always be with Don. Tears welled up in my eyes as I hugged him.

"You okay?"

"Yeah. I'm okay now. I'm sorry."

"There's nothing to be sorry about, JD. You went through some terrible pain. It's understandable that you can't bear to remember it." Don drew back to look into my face. "But it's over now. You're grown-up and married and safe from Shadowman. And I love you."

"And I love you."

As I hugged Don, Jean took control.

I looked around to see if anyone had witnessed our little drama, but everyone seemed to be going somewhere on their own agenda. I was still uncomfortable when Don spoke to JD in public. Nevertheless, I loved Don and I was amazed at his ability to draw out and comfort JD. Because JD was with me, and aware of what I was doing so much of the time, I would have to deal more and more with this kind of reaction. Someday, somehow, we would face the last of it and she and I would be totally together. I was certain of that.

In November, Don had to make a week-long trip out of town. It had been a long time since he and I had been separated for even a day, but it helped to solve one mystery for me.

I sat staring at another expensive vacuum cleaner. I barely remember the salesman showing me how it was so powerful, it could pick up a standard bowling ball. The contract for its purchase lay on the end table. I picked it up and looked closely at the signature. The name was mine, but the cursive letters were so carefully drawn, my "J" looked like a bow tie.

"All right, JD. I know this is your doing. Why the hell do you keep buying vacuum cleaners?" I wondered how much trouble I would have getting our old canister vac returned.

JD was reluctant, but slowly the memory became known

to me. She *had* to have an expensive vacuum. Nothing we ever had picked up baby powder.

It was the summer after Ailene was born. I was eleven and Luke would be four in August. Mom had taken Ailene to bed for a nap, leaving me to watch Luke. Everyone else had gone out for the day. Summer was when I read all the mystery novels I could find in the library, so I took Luke out on the screened porch. I stretched out in the porch swing to read one while he played with a couple of toy trucks.

I must have been engrossed for a long time, totally forgetting my charge, but he was busy.

Suddenly I heard Mom shout, "Luke, what are you doing? Jean Darby, where are you? Get up here right now."

I jumped up and started to run into the house, but stopped cold at the doorway. Before me was a winter scene. Luke had taken Ailene's baby powder and sprinkled the entire downstairs—not just the floor and the table and each of the chairs, but under the couch cushions, on each of the books, over the sheet music in the piano bench, everywhere. He had been thorough. He had pulled each drawer in the kitchen and powdered the silverware and the utensils. He had opened each cupboard door and powdered the pans and the mixing bowls. He had even opened the refrigerator and powdered the food. Then he had gone upstairs where Mom discovered him coating the upstairs hall.

When I saw what had happened, I whipped out our old upright vacuum and tried to sweep up the talc. Some of what it picked up from the floor and the carpet blew right back into the air. There was no way to vacuum the bookshelves or the cupboards. Baby powder was next to impossible to sweep or wipe up. I tried wet towels and everything I could, but there was no way to get it all. Furthermore, I didn't find all the places Luke had put the powder. As I began to realize that my father would soon be home to punish both the helpless boy and me, I went into a panic.

Over the years, we'd laughed about Luke's actions. He had so diligently carried out the work, never imagining the consequences. However, JD's memory of the incident was not funny. After my father beat the little boy, he came after me. I had no way to protect my baby brother and certainly no way to help myself. And it didn't end there.

It became an ongoing live nightmare. I remembered weeks after the incident, being in my bedroom and freezing in place when I heard my father scream "Baby powder!" when he discovered it in yet another place. I peed my pants as I heard him bolting up the stairs three at a time to slap me to the floor again for not cleaning it up.

But that was then. Now I lived with Don. There was no one to beat the living daylights out of me and I didn't have to fear for my younger siblings.

"What's going to convince you that you don't need another vacuum?" I asked JD. "How can I assure you that we're safe and we don't need more than we have?"

After a couple of phone calls and a short trip to Federal Way, I had returned the expensive machine and retrieved our old one. When Don came back, I related the whole incident.

"I tell you, Don, I can't persuade JD that there is no way to go back in time and clean up all that baby powder. I'm at a loss."

"I know what to do, Jean." Don pulled the vacuum into the kitchen and brought some talcum powder from the bathroom. "Let me talk to JD."

I knew Don was mad at me. I clasped my hands and looked at the floor past them.

Don knew at once. He moved close in front of me, "Can I have a hug?"

As I hugged him, he assured me that he wasn't angry.

"I only want to help," he said. "Look, I'm going to sprinkle a bunch of Jason's powder on the carpet. I want you to use our vacuum here to sweep it up."

He dumped a lot of powder on the floor and handed me the hose attached to the vacuum. I turned on the vacuum and pushed the power head over the talc. It took it up. All of it. This vacuum would clean up baby powder.

Don reached over and shut off the vacuum. Pushing it aside, he wrapped his arm around me.

"See? It picks up baby powder, doesn't it?"

I bit my lower lip and answered, "Yeah, it works good."

"But, you know, you can't go back. What happened, happened a long time ago. I wish there was something I could do to change it, some way to make it not happen, but I can't. I can't any more than you can go back and clean up all that baby powder. I'm sorry. But you're here now. No one is going to hurt you for the mess anymore. I love you. You're safe."

I fought back my tears as I hugged him, and I told Jean I wouldn't buy any new vacuums.

Maybe I wouldn't get more vacuums, but there were other painful memories for JD to impart.

One day I studied the picture in the corner of Jack's office, but envisioned the three-story drop from the window behind me. A slight shiver ran through me.

"Sure you don't want any tea or anything?" Jack asked. As I shook my head, he sat down. "So what's been happening?"

"I've always been terrified of heights. Until a week ago, I couldn't make sense of it." I paused and sighed. Jack waited.

"Sometimes I think I can't take another instance of JD's dumping on me. I know every time she does, I get another clue to my life, but I want this all to end. Maybe I have to know everything JD knows, but I still can't handle it." I thought, why does this have to be so hard? I don't want to be me. Well, I don't want to be JD. Sorry JD, but you do know what I'm talking about.

"What did JD tell you?"

"To understand it, I have to tell you something about my grandmother, his stepmother."

"Your father's?"

"Yes. I think his relationship with her was key to what happened to me with this particular incident. In a way I think he tried to gain her respect all his life, and out of that desire, he feared her. JD somehow summoned up the strength to threaten to expose his behavior to Grandma Sarah and suddenly he had to find a way to prevent that from happening."

Jack tilted his head slightly the way he did when he was listening closely.

"Grandma Sarah told me very little about herself," I continued. "I know they were so terribly poor when she was growing up, she and her two sisters had only one pair of black patent leather shoes that the three of them had to share. She was quite young when she married my grandfather.

"My dad was eleven when his own mother died—drowned after having a heart attack while she was swimming. When Grandpa married Sarah, Dad was about fourteen, and he had a hard time accepting a stepmother. Sarah said that because she was so young herself, she had never been able to get close to Dad, but she was very close to Dad's sister."

"Your aunt is younger than your father?"

"Yes, about three years. She seemed to need a mother more than Dad, and Sarah filled the need. Although . . ."

I thought back to the last time I saw Grandma Sarah alive. I was on vacation and pregnant with my third child.

Grandma was lying on a daybed in the living room. She was losing her fight with shingles and her weight had dropped to less than eighty pounds. Her long, bony fingers played lovingly over a blue-flowered platter.

"Your father gave this to me," she said, tears welling up in her eyes. "I want Fred to have it back. I don't know if I will ever see him again in this world."

I stared at the platter. It was thick china. I'd seen something like it in the local thrift store, though not quite as large. A lump began to form in my throat.

"It was nearly a year after I married your grandfather," she continued. "I had tried to be a mother to the boy, but he wouldn't have it. He loved his mother so much, he couldn't bear her death, even three years later. I knew that, but I never knew what to do about it." She stopped and rubbed the rim of the oval meat platter.

"I thought he hated me." A tear ran down her fleshless cheek. She seemed not to notice. "Anyway, on Mother's Day, just after his fifteenth birthday, he gave me this. I don't know where he had it hidden away, but I can still picture him, walking down the road, a tall, thin, handsome boy, carrying this platter like it was gold. It really is, you know." Another tear dripped from her chin. "I want you to give it back to him."

"But Grandma," I protested, fighting back my own tears, "don't you want to keep it?"

"I've kept it all these years. Now I want him to have it back. I won't need it any longer, and I don't want it to be lost after I die."

"Now, Grandma, don't talk that way. You're going to get better."

Please, God, let her get better. Don't take her now. I want my little girls to know her too.

"No." She had decided that this was the end. "Please, take it to Fred."

The lump in my throat blocked any words I may have offered. I bent to take the platter from her outstretched hand. Her strength would not let her lift the heavy dish up to me.

I sat back in my chair and sighed as my last picture of her faded and Jack's office returned.

"You loved your grandmother very much?" Jack asked.

"I hardly knew her at all as I was growing up, but I remember her as being loving and giving. I don't know why, but she was closest to JD and I'm now gaining her memories of Grandma Sarah. Of course I have some very early Jean memories of her, but they sort of end with the episode with Dad in the railroad station."

"The railroad station?"

"You remember, where Dad left me alone when I was four?"

"Yes, of course. Your father frightened you as a punishment. That makes sense then—JD wanted to protect you from any more of that kind of terror. What about this latest JD memory?"

"Well . . ." I stared at the rug, tracing along from chair leg to chair leg, running along the desk, around the base of the wastebasket, and beyond to the corner of the room.

It isn't that hard to explain; just tell him, JD pushed me.

Hmm, why don't you come tell him yourself? She disappeared.

I began again, with a bit more irritation. "Okay. It was before Tina was born, so I was eleven or twelve. Grandma Sarah was ill then, but not incapacitated. My father decided to drive down to North Carolina to visit his dad and Sarah. He took Mark, Luke, and me with him. I remember the trip going down, but once there, it was JD who had control."

"Even around your dad?" Jack looked up suddenly.

"Yes, I think it was to be near Grandma Sarah. JD mostly avoided him. I don't think Dad was comfortable being around Sarah, but JD loved to be close to her, so . . ." I caught a snapshot of Dad driving away in the car with Grandpa and the boys, as I stood in the kitchen with Grandma. Then as I began to relate it to Jack, JD's memory engulfed my mind. . . .

As we were finishing up lunch, Shadowman said to me suddenly, "We've been here for several days, and the boys and I have been out riding with Grandpa. How about you and I taking a drive this afternoon?"

He stretched, his long arms nearly reaching both ends of the table. Then he pushed his chair back from the table and waved for me to go with him. "The boys can help Grandma clean up, can't you, guys?" He flashed an angry glance at Mark and Luke to punctuate his directions.

"Come on, Jean." He motioned to me to hurry, nodding his head toward the door. Something in his rush frightened me. I didn't want to go. I didn't want to be alone with him.

"But I want to walk over to the cemetery this afternoon," I protested.

"You can go when we get back if it's not too late, or tomorrow. Come on." He had made his way around the table and gripped my shoulder. "Maybe we can go up to Mount Mitchell."

"I want to go too," little Luke chirped.

"No!" Shadowman said with firmness.

As we reached the door, I looked over my shoulder at my grandmother. Grandpa sat with his back to us, still enjoying his lunch.

"'Bye, Jean. 'Bye, Fred," Grandma called. "Don't be too late. I'll have supper on about six."

I had to get away from him. I didn't want to go with him. He opened the car door.

"Come on. Get in." He shoved me toward the seat. I got in and shut the door. As he rounded the car and opened his door, I sent my unspoken plea back at the house. *Oh, Grandma, don't let him take me away!* She waved lightly in response. It was as if I were being swept to sea on a riptide as she stood on the shore, mistaking my outcry for joy, waving "Have a good time!"

The Blue Ridge Parkway was only a few miles from the house. All the way there and on up to Mount Mitchell, Shadowman talked, but I knew nothing he said meant anything. He was taking me away alone because he wanted to hurt me. I knew he was going to hurt me. Where could I go? Even with my grandma I couldn't be safe.

I looked out the window as the autumn mountains flew past. I rolled down the window and let the incoming breeze numb my face. As the road climbed higher, a green pickup truck went past from the other direction, pulling a long, boxy travel trailer. Why couldn't I jump out and go away with them?

We pulled off the parkway and drove into a parking lot. He parked down at the end, away from a trail that led up to the top. There were no other cars.

"Come here," he said in his warmest voice, pulling me up close to him and wrapping his right arm around me. "We haven't had any time together since we left home." He clasped my left hand, put it down on his lap, and rubbed it on his pants.

"Oh, that's nice. Here, why don't you make it feel really good?" he said, letting go of my hand, long enough to unzip his pants, but quickly grabbing it again to thrust it through the opening. As he wrapped my fingers around his penis, he slid his other hand from around me, and up my leg, pushing up my dress.

In the split instant when he released my hand and other shoulder, I jumped away from him, opened the door, and leapt out. I yelled through the open window as I slammed the door, "I'm gonna tell Grandma what you do to me! She won't let you do these things to me! She won't let you hurt me!"

Shadowman sat there stunned, his hand in his lap covering the open pants.

I fled to the trail and didn't turn back until I was well up the path toward the top of the mountain. As I gasped for air, I looked down over the otherwise deserted lot. I could see him standing outside his car door, looking over the roof at me. Even from my distance I could see how angry I had made him.

Dear God, what had I done? He was going to kill me. Now I really had to get away. I rubbed my face with my fingers. My knees felt weak and my hands and shoulders began to shake. I turned and ran farther up the path. I didn't know where I was going to go. There had to be another way away from there. There had to be, even if I had to climb all night.

The path leveled out for a short stretch and I ran among the rocks and brush. Then it began to rise again and my legs felt heavy. I slowed, then stopped to rest, leaning against a boulder. Let me breathe, I thought. I coughed. Oh, my sides ached.

Looking back, I could see the path for a distance, but not down to the parking lot. I took in a deep breath and let it out slowly. I didn't think he'd been following me. Maybe he was just waiting for me to come back down. I was never going back to that parking lot. I'd find some other way to go back to Grandma's.

I looked out across the Blue Ridge. From here, I could see mountain after mountain, fading into dimmer shades of purple, until they were lost in the afternoon haze. Birch trees mixed yellow and orange leaves among the pines on the hills below me. I slumped down slightly to relax a moment. The wind had begun to blow harder. I hadn't braided my long hair or pulled it back in a ponytail, and it began to fly in my face. I pushed it back and took in a huge breath of the wind.

Suddenly I heard the sound of shifting gravel. Oh, no, he was coming after me!

I jumped and ran up the path, but I had barely made another hundred feet when he was there. How could he come so fast?

He grabbed my left arm from behind and swung me around, nearly knocking me to the ground.

"Where do you think you're going?" he demanded. "There's no way off this mountain. Come on, I'll show you." He dragged me. It wasn't far to the top.

The path ended at one large chunk of rock and we stood on the highest point in North Carolina. He was wrong; there were several paths running off, but maybe they all ran back to the parking lot; they were on the same side.

Beyond the rock was a drop of several hundred feet, broken only by a few jutting rocks and clinging scrub pines. Far below there were the same kind of rocks and brush that I had passed coming up, but the mountain swept down very steep slopes.

"Look down there," Shadowman shouted at me, pushing me before him.

I knew I was going to be there soon; he didn't have to tell me. My knees were collapsing; only his tight grip kept me standing.

Please, God, help me. Please come and take me away from here. Don't let him throw me off this mountain.

Suddenly he jerked me right to the edge.

"When you hit the first rocks, your arm will fly off over there!" He pointed off to the right, "and the next time you hit, your head will pop off and roll away, over there." He pointed off to the left. Then drawing out each word, he seethed, "Your blood will splash all over the mountainside, and if any little bit of you gets down to the bottom, they'll have to pick up the pieces with toilet paper."

"No. Please don't push me off. Please!"

"You're going to tell your grandmother all about it, are you?" he yelled at me, his eyes nearly stretching out of their sockets. I just knew he was going to kill me then.

"No, please," I begged, with as quiet a voice as I could through my chattering teeth.

Suddenly he jerked me past the edge and nearly fell forward himself. He braced himself against the rock, hanging on to my arm.

I was dangling like a rag doll over my imminent death. Small stones cascaded over the edge as I made a futile effort to dig in the toes of my shoes and grab the earth. I watched as the stones were falling forever, down and down. There was nothing for me to hold. The wind whipped my hair in my eyes as I looked down into the emptiness—dropping far below my feet—as I hung there only by his grip on my arm.

Help me, God.

"You're not telling anyone anything. Do you hear me? Or you'll be in hell before you're finished saying a word. I can hear you, don't ever forget that. Wherever you are, I can hear you. Do you hear me?" He was still yelling, but I was beginning not to hear him.

No. No. I'm going to die now. God, please take me with you. Don't let me go to hell.

I felt light-headed. My arm was coming out of its socket. I could hear a terrible pounding in my head. It sounded like a marching band drumming closer and closer. I wondered how they got them up here. I wondered how long it would be before the first rocks tore me apart. Blackness was coming around me. I wondered vaguely how it got to be night so soon.

It seemed like a terrible, black night on the mountain. I couldn't see anything, but I could still hear the wind whipping around my face. I had a terrible taste in my mouth. The loud drums were still pounding. My legs and arms seemed to be jumping on their own accord.

"Stop it! Stop it!" Suddenly Shadowman's voice was yelling at me again, close in the darkness.

His hand grabbed my chin and shook my head. I squinted open my eyes to see him squatting next to me. The sun glanced off his shoulder as he bent forward and the sunbeam blinded me for a second. The ground felt hard under me.

To my surprise I wasn't dead. I turned my head and spit vomit from my mouth. The jumping stopped, but I was still shaking.

"Get up. Hurry," he urged, pulling me up by the right arm. My left arm was throbbing. "Hurry, there's someone coming."

I couldn't stand. My legs wouldn't hold me.

Shadowman gathered me quickly in his arms and started down a different path. As we rounded a curve in the path, I looked back and saw two boys running right up to the edge.

"Come on, Mom. Come on, Dad!" They were yelling. "You should see it from up here! It goes way down!"

I laid my head against Shadowman's shirt and the black took me away again.

I opened my eyes and looked up at Jack. I shook my head and smiled a sort of half smile.

Jack said nothing, but looked shocked by my experience.

"Whenever I get close to the edge of a cliff or at the top of a building, I always picture myself falling and breaking into all those bloody pieces he described. I just never knew why the pictures were so vivid."

"And how old did you say you were when that happened?" Jack asked, appalled.

"Let's see, about eleven or twelve."

"It's a wonder he didn't actually drop you."

"I probably didn't weigh a hundred pounds soaking wet, and he did brace himself."

"My God, though! It was so dangerous!" Jack shook his head and shuddered.

"I think that might have been the last time he sexually abused me, except once when I was fourteen. That last time, he came into my bedroom when I was home alone and raped me, all the time telling me how I was going to hell. But before that, I think JD must have scared him badly enough by threatening to tell Grandma Sarah that all he could do was threaten in return." I sighed. "And that event, of course, terrified me of heights for the rest of my life."

Suddenly I had another thought. "Jack, why is it whenever I find myself in any high place, the first thought that comes to mind is to jump? I don't want to jump and I'm terrified, but that's what immediately comes to mind."

"Because that's the fastest way to get away from the situation. It's not that you want to be hurt. You just want to remove yourself from the fearful place."

Sometimes Jack's logic amazed me. Maybe now I could stop being afraid that I might jump.

"I don't know how I am ever going to get past this. I remember how ill I got when someone told me about a woman who jumped or was pushed out a window up in the John Hancock Building in Chicago. I pictured the same horrible, gory scene Shadowman had described would happen to me."

"No doubt." Jack pursed his lips and shook his head slightly.

I rolled my shoulders to relax a bit and wished I had accepted Jack's offer for tea. I had a bad taste in my mouth again.

SEVENTEEN

NEARLY FIVE YEARS AFTER JASON'S BIRTH, I HAD DECIDED TO use my reconstruction surgery as an excuse to take the summer off from work. It was more than an excuse; the complications were still tiring me easily. I had also wanted extra time to be with Jason before he started kindergarten. Somehow the summer was racing by, and I had been caught up in getting a fence installed, a garden terrace built, and so many other projects, that I just hadn't given him the attention and the time I had thought I could. Then Don and I took the trailer up to Discovery Bay one weekend. We had such fun that I decided to take Jason up there for a week.

For one glorious week Jason and I played. We walked on the beach holding hands and collecting shells in plastic bags. There wasn't much of a variety on the clam beds, but each one was a treasure. We climbed up into the woods and got all scratched by the underbrush. We read stories and drew pictures. Jason penciled little mazes and laughed uncontrollably as I took all the wrong paths. We dug and steamed clams or barbecued hamburgers on the little grill outside the camper. We loved each other.

I had picked the Fourth of July week to go away with Jason. It meant that Don could take off a day from work and join us for a four-day weekend. Moreover, it was the week my parents came to visit in Seattle. I wanted to avoid Dad for the present. I didn't know how to deal with him. With all that JD had dumped on me, I wasn't sure I could maintain the nonentity relationship that had served me in the past. I had sent him a birthday card and even a noncommittal Father's Day card, but to contend with his physical presence would be difficult.

However, there were plans for the folks in my absence. Between Sandra, Ailene, and Tina, they had room to stay, and activities to entertain them. When Dad flew back to Chicago, Mom and Sandra went down to a church conference in Portland. I made plans to see Mom when she and Sandra got back. After my week of fun with Jason, I decided to take Mom and Jason back to Discovery Bay for at least part of another week.

Sandra and Mom came back from the conference early Saturday. Considering how much I had left to do, Sandra took Mom for a round trip over Snoqualmie Pass to drop her son off at summer camp. I had time to finish packing the car by the time they got back. I came out on the porch to meet them as they pulled into the drive. Sandra bounded out of the car and up the steps before Mom could barely open her door.

"Jean!" Sandra cried softly, trying to catch her breath halfway up the porch steps. "You won't believe what Mom asked me on the way back. She wanted to know if there had been any sexual abuse in our family when we were little!"

"What?" I couldn't believe it. I didn't want to believe it. I shot a shocked glance over my left shoulder. Mom was making her way slowly up the walk, purposely lagging as if to give Sandra time to explain. "What did you tell her?"

"I almost ran off the side of the road," Sandra said with a

nervous laugh. "I couldn't believe she would ask, just out of the blue like that."

"So what did you tell her?" I asked through clenched teeth.

Mom rounded the corner and started up the steps. Sandra paused and waited for her to get within earshot.

"I told her there had been and you would tell her all about it." Was there was a mischievous smile behind those apologetic eyes? She couldn't wait for my response.

Suddenly I felt that Sandra had really wanted Mom to know. She had left little traps all over the place for her, like leaving her copy of *Courage to Heal* on her coffee table.

I felt betrayed. I wasn't ready to confront anyone yet. I wanted to get through this myself first. Worse, I didn't want to bring on all the pain I knew this would bring Mom. Maybe I would just deny the whole thing and leave Sandra's honesty up in the air. Maybe I would mock my mother's own words about me: "She exaggerates everything."

I smiled an obviously forced smile at my mother.

"Well," Mom began slowly, matching my uncomfortable smile. "I sort of dragged the cat out of the bag. You want to tell me about it?"

"Hell, no. But Sandra didn't leave me much of a choice, did she?" I drew in a breath; it came out a sigh.

Mom struggled with the smile a bit more. She nailed me. "Were you girls abused or not?"

"Yes, but I'm not sure I want to tell you all about it, as Sandra puts it."

I had to turn slightly to get Sandra into view. She had backed slowly away as though she had passed on a sticky baton and wanted nothing more to do with it.

"Thanks a lot, Sandra. Drop a bombshell on my doorstep and then run off, knowing I'm trapped with it for the rest of the week." Adrenaline was surging up; I wasn't sure whether I was angry or just excited. Hadn't I wanted Mom to know, too? Didn't I want her support? Would she believe me? Would she support me? Or would she hate me?

Mom came to her defense. "Hey, I'm the one who asked." She thought it over quickly, then added slowly, "Although, it was somewhat obvious when Sandra went off to a sexual abuse seminar when I wanted her to come to an evangelism workshop. It wasn't like I hadn't had clues."

"I can see we're going to have four days of fun in the sun." What was I going to do? What was I going to tell her? "Let's move your stuff out of Sandra's car and into the Subaru." There wasn't much I could do about it now. I had my chance to deny and I didn't.

After we moved the luggage, I slipped back into the house for the draft chapters of my book and my letter file. Jack had encouraged me to organize some of the information in my letters into a book, filling in the discussions. I didn't know how much I was going to tell Mom, but I needed my documentation, my security blanket to the past.

On the way to Discovery Bay, I put a tape on for Jason, who sat in the backseat. It would cover up the quiet yet lively conversation Mom and I were bound to have.

"Why did you ask Sandra?"

"As I said, there've been a lot of clues lately. I think Sandra wanted me to know except she didn't want to tell me."

"So what exactly did Sandra say?" I was feeling very anxious.

"She said you remembered most of what had happened to you. She is still struggling to remember anything, although she's sure she was sexually abused as well. She thought maybe all you girls had been. What do you think?"

"I don't know, Mom. I have some strong suspicions about Sandra and Tina. I have no idea about Ailene. All I know about for sure is me. I've been working on a book about it, and about my healing process." I floundered with what I would tell her and what I could hold back. I didn't want to hurt her. I loved her. What was this going to do to our relationship? Would she defend Dad? Would she believe me?

"Can I read it?"

"Not now. Maybe never. I don't know. I'll share some of it with you. There's parts I can't show you now. Some I can." What the hell was I going to do? Why did I tell her about the book? Maybe Sandra told her anyway. I did tell her last year I was writing, but not the subject.

"You know, Mom, I have been unwell all my life."

"I know you've had some problems. I just didn't know what they were."

"I've been in the hospital four times in my life with this crap. It doesn't go away on its own. It's only been in the past ten years, working with Jack, that I've even had a clue of what's been happening to me. I believed all my life I was crazy. I sometimes wish I still could."

"What does Jack think is wrong with you anyway?"

"Multiple personality, Mom. There were three of us in this head. Now there's only two—me and the abused child."

It came too easy. It was anger. I fought it back. She was the one who was going to get hurt this time. I didn't really want to hurt her. She was the one married to the man who abused her child. Was she going to believe that? Did I care?

Yes, yes! I cared desperately. What was I going to do if she didn't believe me? Who was I going to be? I'd be worse than the man without a country. I'd be the woman without a family. An outcast. They'd all whisper behind my back, repeating the comment my mother had once made: "She's the one with the exaggerated memories. Listen to what she's saying now." Who was I, if my mother denied me? Who would believe me? She was there, back there, somewhere in my childhood. Somehow she didn't know what was happening. Would she accept it now?

All the way up we talked about the multiples. I wasn't

sure how to explain without getting into detail, but I managed.

Playtime with Daddy caused the Jody personality to emerge from Jean when I was maybe three—guilt, guilt, guilt. Something we couldn't tell Mommy about, a naughty secret fun of Jean's with Dad.

"Where was I all this time?" Mom kept asking.

I didn't have an answer. Where was she?

"Mom, I know you can remember the differences between Jean and Jody if you think about it. Sandra could. Think about the obedient Jean and the independent Jody."

"I can certainly picture different behaviors in you as a child, but I wouldn't know if they were different personalities. I would have to think that little girl standing in the hallway with her fists on her hips defying your father would have to be Jody."

Mom turned to look at the Tacoma Dome as we passed, and asked, "That's not the Kingdome, is it? No, it's too small. Have I been here before?" She seemed so distracted and unaffected by our conversation.

"I think so, Mom. At least you had to pass it to go down to Olympia." My tension seemed to be overwhelming and she was asking about the roadside sights. Was it a ploy to keep her emotions in check? Or had she already discounted what Sandra and I had told her?

"Yes, I've seen it, but I don't know if I've been in it. Well, where were we?"

"We were talking about seeing the differences between Jean and Jody, Mom. I think you can identify Jody even as an adult. Think about Ailene's wedding."

She stared out the front window for a few moments. "Sure," she said, recollecting the day. "You and Hank and the girls came in late the night before. I remember Ailene saying everything would be okay, now that Jean was there. We used to call you the organizer. And it must have been

Jody I remember at breakfast. Your dad and Hank got into a big fight over your girls or something. Suddenly you came running in and told them both to shut up. I'd never seen you handle Hank that directly. I guess I'd seen you talk back to your dad, but Hank? Never."

"Yeah," I laughed. "I told Hank that it was Ailene's wedding day and I was not going to let him, or Dad, ruin it for her. If he couldn't act like a civil human being, he should get the hell out and leave us in peace."

"It sure did the trick," Mom said, smiling. "For the rest of the day and night, I had never seen him so cooperative. So that was Jody, eh?"

"That was Jody. But now I can say it was me, since Jean and Jody are one and the same. I didn't remember that I had chewed out Dad and Hank until I got the combined memory recently."

"So, you're doing better now?"

"I wouldn't say better. When the real abusive action began, it caused the abused child personality we call JD to appear. I'm dealing with that now."

"What happened? What's the real abusive action?"

I couldn't tell her.

"When did this happen? How old were you?"

"Eight. Nine. I'm not sure, Mom."

Oh, Mom, I thought. *I didn't want to dissect this with you, especially with no help.* Somehow I had pictured that I would be sitting in Jack's office with her when this all came out, not alone in the wilderness for four days. Worse, I had Jason with us, and I didn't want him to hear what was bound to be an emotionally painful debate.

Jason's tape ended. We were crossing over the Narrows Bridge.

"Look, Grandma," Jason called excitedly, "the boats look like toys way down in the water!"

It was a relief to drop the subject and enjoy the scenery.

• • •

For three stress-filled days and nights we discussed my
childhood and adult problems, trying to entertain Jason and
make sure he didn't hear what was going on. We cried until
two in the morning and woke each other again as the sun
rose at five or six o'clock. Mom pressed me for details, but
I didn't want her to have that pain. She didn't want to believe. She wanted to find holes in everything I told her. Was
I eight when this began? No, it was earlier. Didn't I just con-
tradict myself? Was I eleven? No, that was another time, another incident. Wasn't I beginning to trip over my facts? I
nearly went crazy trying not to give her details, but trying to
make her believe that I was sexually abused from my earliest memories. Sleep deprivation and depression were beginning to take their toll on my mind.

"Your father isn't like that," Mom explained. "I know he
lost his temper and I couldn't control him. I know he got violent when he was angry, but then he got over it. I just can't
imagine him doing anything like that. I'm sure he thinks he
was a good father to his children."

I struggled with my feelings for my father and with her reactions. How could I convince her? I carefully selected
some of my letters to Jack and let her read them.

She responded in tears, "I've always known there was
something wrong with you. I remember when that lady from
the children's center called and wanted me to come talk with
her. I've felt guilty all these years that I didn't go. But then
you stopped seeing her and I just let it pass. I knew you had
problems. I didn't know how to help you. There were so
many kids. . . ."

"I know, Mom. Besides the kids, much of what happened
to me occurred during the period you were driving down
and taking care of Grandma."

The thought of her own mother during that time must
have triggered her own childhood experiences. She sat for a

while, staring out the camper window across the shimmering blue bay before she told me, "I had one incident myself when I was about twelve. It was with my best friend's father. He didn't really do anything, but he tried."

She sat a little longer without speaking. I could see in her face that the memory was still painful even these fifty-some years later. Finally she decided to share it.

"Sharon and I were best friends. We went to school together and walked home together. We went to church together. We slept over at each other's houses at least once a week, usually Friday nights. My parents knew them—well, of course, they went to Dad's church.

"Anyway, one night I came over to her house and Sharon's mother had gone out for the evening. After we got ready to go to bed, her dad called us down for a good-night hug and kiss. He always hugged me as well as Sharon, but I never liked it. This particular evening, he told Sharon to go on up, that he wanted to talk to me, and I would go up in a minute.

"After Sharon went upstairs to her room, he pulled me onto his lap and started reaching up my nightgown. He was squeezing me tightly with one arm and feeling my underwear with his other hand. I managed to get away from him and run upstairs. I rushed in and got into bed with Sharon. I asked her to tuck the bedcovers around me tightly so we were lying on some of them. Sharon asked me why, and although I wouldn't tell her, she complied.

"Sharon's father came up and sat on the bed. He kept trying to poke around the edge of the blankets while he was talking to us. He asked, 'How have you kids got these covers?' and Sharon asked him, 'What are you trying to do, Dad?' She kept watching him closely and he never did get his hand under the covers, and finally left.

"The next morning I went home and never went back. I stopped playing with Sharon, who didn't understand why.

She called and called. Finally her mother called asking if I would come over, but I wouldn't go."

"Did you ever tell your mom?"

"Well, not directly, but she did find out. My sister, who was grown and married by then, came over to talk to me about it. Mom and Dad didn't understand why I had dropped Sharon so quickly. Since I wouldn't give them an answer, I think they called my sister to help check it out. I told her and she told the folks. Apparently Dad visited with Sharon's dad, because they suddenly stopped coming to his church, too. But I still got the willies every time I saw him anywhere."

"Did they ever talk to you about it?"

"No. My sister did, and she made me promise to tell her if anything like that happened again, but it never did. It took me a long time to get over that. Sharon's dad smoked cigars and for months, maybe years, afterward, even the smell of a cigar would make me physically ill."

In a small corner of my heart, I was both sad and elated by her experience. It gave me a tiny common ground where she might relate to my pain.

Carefully, I approached it. "You see, Mom, how hard it was for you to recover from that. You can imagine why I had to wall off part of my mind to protect me, to separate what happened with my own father."

Tears leapt into her eyes again. Resting her head on her hands, she looked down at the table and shook her head.

We talked through the night and into the early morning.

She read some more of the letters and part of the book. I wouldn't let her read the scenes of sexual abuse, but she picked up on comments in the letters and pressed for more details. She continued to pick apart my generalities of abuse and questioned how Dad could have done anything like that. It went on for hours into the next night after Jason was sleeping.

Finally, too exhausted to hide my anger, I practically screamed at her, "Okay, Mom. I didn't want to give you specifics, but I can give you specifics! He raped me! He sodomized me! He tortured me! He beat me! He terrorized me!" I broke into tears and dropped my head on my hands to sob. I had begun to feel like the accused in an integration lockup.

"Rape?" she asked in horror. It was obvious that she had tuned out after that first word. "Wouldn't that be terribly painful for a child? I mean, your father wasn't . . . wasn't exactly . . . small."

"Yes, Mom," I answered, trying to calm my internal rage. I really didn't want to get into a discussion of the specific aspects of the abuse with her. I simply wanted her to accept the reality of the sexual abuse and my problems in healing.

"No, no, it can't be true." She put her head down on the table, her hands crossed in her hair, and cried.

Once again, my emotions went into a tailspin. Did she mean it couldn't be true? Was I lying? Did she mean she didn't want it to be true? I didn't want it to be true. I hadn't wanted to hurt her. Why had I been so blunt? Damn it! This wasn't my fault. Why did I have to feel so guilty?

Finally, we crawled into bed and slept a short while, until Jason woke us.

Later that day it began to hit her that she was going to face Dad soon; her vacation was almost over and she would be flying home. What was she going to do? How could she face him? What would she say?

Finally I ran off to a local pay phone and called Jack. He agreed to meet with us. Mom didn't want to go, but I persisted.

"I know what he thinks of me," she insisted. "I don't need him to tell me."

"No, you don't, Mom," I retorted. "We're not going there for Jack's opinion of you anyway. I think you need some help on how to handle this with Dad. That's what we want from Jack. I could care less what he thinks of you personally."

The day of the appointment was hot and sunny. I had arranged for Erin to meet us and watch Jason during Jack's meeting. Jason loved the drive to Bainbridge and the ferry ride to Seattle. He also adored his sister Erin; he couldn't wait to see her.

Mom was not so enthused. In Jack's office, she was very defensive, "You must think I'm a terrible mother."

"No," Jack assured her. "All of your girls speak highly of you. They're caring people with high ideals, and they had to get them from someone."

"But with all this?"

"Mom," I interrupted. "You were not responsible for Dad's behavior. I'm sorry that you couldn't control him back then, but you couldn't."

"I know, but I could have done something." She looked around the office as though she had misplaced a valuable. Her breath became short, as in panic. "I remember when Matt stole some money. I agreed that he should be punished and it was really the first time that I let your father spank him. Then I was sorry because he was so hard on him. I don't think he realized how badly he was hurting Matt. I had to stop him."

She glanced around quickly again and shook her head to displace the memory. I wondered how old Matthew had been at the time. She took a breath and sighed.

"I know your father has always had a quick temper and he overreacts. But then, he gets over it and he forgets it. He's always been that way. I guess that's why I have such a problem with what Jean's been telling me."

"You don't believe her?" Jack asked quietly.

"Oh, no, I didn't mean that," she said quickly. "I do believe something happened. I just don't know what. I know

Fred loved his kids. I just can't imagine him doing . . . well, I wonder if Jean's memories are all that clear."

Jack quickly rebutted, "I have no doubt about that. Her father, your husband, did everything Jean remembers. One of the factors in multiple personality disorder is that since the child's mind cannot deal with what is happening, it seals off and holds those memories intact. So when the adult personality has to handle them, they're there with all the action, pain, terror, feelings, smells, tastes, everything. The adult Jean, or now Jean/Jody, has had to deal with JD's recollections and they are vivid and painful."

Mom looked horrified. Since we had arrived at Jack's office, she had not looked directly at me. I wondered if she couldn't bear to see me anymore. I felt guilty and dirty. I began to fight for my own strength. I was not responsible for what she was going through. I was the victim. I was not the predator. I was beginning to feel sad and betrayed. If she couldn't accept what happened to me, how would she accept me?

"Look, Betty," Jack broke the moment's silence, "we're not going to resolve your feelings or Jean's problems in the next few minutes. But you need to accept what Jean is telling you and you need to decide how it is going to affect your relationship with your husband. Are you going to be able to sit down and talk to him about this?"

Mom laughed nervously.

"Sure, sure," she said with a forced smile. "He and I say something meaningful to each other at least three times a year."

Jack looked very serious as he asked her, "I need to know why you stay with someone, if you have meaningful communication only three times a year?"

Mom became defensive, almost hostile. "He's my companion. He's very good to me. I go home and he's always there, waiting for me."

She shifted in her chair and continued, "He's very solici-
tous of my time and affection. For instance, he grows toma-
toes and makes up spaghetti sauce. He'll have a big pot of it
cooking for me when I come home from working in Mark's
shop all day. We like to travel together and watch TV or play
cards. He's good company."

"But he wasn't always." I risked the comment.

Mom shot a painful look at me and turned back to Jack.
"I know Fred wasn't always faithful, but I've done some terrible things too. I remember coming home late one night and
he was waiting up for me. He had supper cooked and the
table set. He wouldn't eat until I got there. I asked him why
he did that and he said he was afraid I wasn't coming back."

She looked down at her hands as she fingered her wedding bands.

"What are you going to say to him?" Jack asked.

Mom sighed deeply. She rubbed the diamonds on her ring
with her right thumb.

"I don't know," she said. "I wish I did. I don't think I can
ask him outright. I've been struggling so hard myself, I
don't know how I could handle the answer."

"The answer will be no," Jack said with conviction.

Mom looked up at him suddenly. "How can you say
that?"

Jack leaned forward toward her and stated slowly, "He
denied his actions to himself as soon as he did them. He had
to. He couldn't live with that knowledge. If you put him on
a lie detector today, it would read that he was telling the
truth. He would believe that he did no wrong."

"Well, I don't know about that," Mom said. "I think he
has such low self-esteem as it is. He may remember some of
it. I don't know."

"So what are you going to do?" Jack asked again.

"I don't know. I can't stay here forever. I have to go
home."

"Why?" Jack pressed.

Mom shook her head and sat up in her chair. "Because my life is back there—my friends, the rest of my family, my home. What do you think I should do, leave him?"

Jack smiled. "That would be up to you to decide. You need to determine how you want to live your life and how you're going to deal with your husband."

I jumped in. "Mom, I'm not asking you to leave Dad." I was sure that Jack was advising Mom to think about her options, but I was also certain that she believed Jack had just told her to leave Dad. "I simply don't want you to go back there unprepared. I wish we could meet with Sandra, Ailene, and Tina and talk it over. I wish we had invited them to be here with us today."

"Maybe that's what I should do. However, I have a ticket back for tomorrow and I really need to go. I have to take off again next Friday for the church conference on disabilities; I have to wash and repack my clothes." Mom looked anxiously at me as she reviewed her responsibilities.

"Mom, change your plane flight. Stay over this weekend and let's get together, the five of us women. I don't know what we can do, but I think it would be good for us to get together. Wouldn't you agree, Jack?"

He did.

As we left Jack's office, Mom was relieved, but she said she never wanted to meet with him again. We arranged another flight for Tuesday. We called my sisters and set up a Sunday meeting. Then Mom and I picked up Jason and headed back to Discovery Bay. On the ferry ride back to Bainbridge, we talked softly as Jason watched for whales off the front of the upper deck. The wind and waves nearly drowned out our voices.

Mom tried to focus her emotions.

"I remember another time when I was faced with a case of sexual abuse," she said. "I was working with a paraplegic girl of about twenty years old, named Lori. She was also mentally handicapped. I became good friends with her mother. I liked her mother a great deal and I was proud of how she had dealt with bringing up this child, basically on her own. The girl's father, and it was her real father, had never accepted that this girl was his. I guess he couldn't stand to think he had a retarded child."

I nodded slowly.

Mom noted, "There are lots of people like him—people who have been looking forward to having a child and then are faced with a handicapped one. They reject and abandon them. They can't deal with it. They feel somehow they have failed; they haven't brought a perfect little person into the world. So, they decide somehow that child isn't theirs, even when, as in this man's case, they live with the child day after day, year after year."

"So what happened?"

"Well, one day Lori asked to talk to me. She told me that her father was touching her and hugging her. I knew the man. I couldn't believe he was doing anything improper. Still, I wasn't sure. Lori wasn't the kind of girl to make up anything and she was frightened."

Pausing, she looked into my eyes, as if to question her judgment in bringing the whole incident up.

"So, what did you do about it, Mom?"

She sighed and turned to look out across the water. I thought she must have been sorry she told me anything.

She sounded defensive as she said, "Well, I probably did the wrong thing, but I did what I thought was best at the time. I talked to Lori's mother and said the girl was afraid of her father and I didn't think it was a good idea for her to be left alone with him."

"That doesn't sound so bad."

"But that wasn't the end of it. One night Lori's mother called me. She said Lori was screaming hysterically and wanted me to come and talk to her. I rushed over to their house. Only Lori and her mother were there; her father had gone to a ball game in Chicago. Once we got Lori calmed down, I spoke with Lori alone. Apparently the father had left for the game and Lori's mother went out for the evening. After the mother left, the father came back, raped Lori, and left again."

"Oh, Mom!"

"Yes. I didn't know what to do. I couldn't bring myself to tell Lori's mother what had happened. I just couldn't do that. It would destroy their marriage and that wouldn't help Lori. So I moved Lori out of their house to a halfway house down in Aurora."

"No, Mom. You couldn't. How could you? You punished Lori for what her father did and let him go free." I was shocked and horrified by her actions.

"It isn't like that. If I had called the police and had him hauled off to jail, I would have destroyed the whole family. If I told her outright, Lori's mother would have had to choose between her child or her husband. You don't know how hard it would have been on them. Women couldn't go out and support themselves and their family then as they do today. Lori's mother wasn't an educated woman. She hadn't ever worked outside her home."

So that was it. She had placed her empathy with the mother, not the abused child. Poor Lori. I wanted to cry for her. I could hardly bear to think of this young woman who had coped with her mental and physical disabilities, only to be raped and then punished for being there to be raped. There wasn't anything more I could say.

I wondered if Mom would make the same choice for me.

EIGHTEEN

Sunday mom and her four daughters gathered around a table on Sandra's patio. Before we started our discussion, we joined hands in prayer.

"Our dear Father, bless us in our meeting today. Strengthen us in our love for one another. Bring us closer through understanding, acceptance, and forgiveness. We ask in the name of Your son, Jesus. Amen."

The tension around us was nearly visible. We looked back and forth at each other silently for a moment.

Finally I spoke. "I guess I should start since I'm the one who called this meeting, although Sandra . . ." I paused and looked at Sandra out of the corner of my eye. She smiled slightly, but looked away and said nothing.

"Well, actually I wanted us to get together," Mom said. "I need to know what to do. I have to go home to your father and I want to know what you think I should do. I can't just pretend I don't know anything." She tried to sound confident, but her voice was edgy.

Everyone nodded in agreement, but Mom held the floor. "And I know what Jack thinks I should do—leave him—but

I . . . I can't do that either." She seemed pained and sad, but I wondered if she was worried more about herself and her relationship with Dad than her children.

"Well, Jack's wrong," Sandra said. "We don't think you should leave Dad. We only need you to understand where we're coming from. We need your help."

I said, "I don't think Jack said he wanted you to leave Dad; he wanted you to look at your options."

Mom shot back rapidly, "Oh, yes, he did. He made that very clear to me."

I sensed that her anger with Jack was equally divided with me for having taken her there in the first place. I felt betrayed again—what else could I have done? Had she believed me at all before Jack verified what I had told her? "But, you know, Mom, Jack's not a Christian. He doesn't understand what the final goal is, or at least he doesn't seem to think it's a priority. That final goal for me has to be forgiveness. I won't be at peace with myself or God until I get to the point of forgiving Dad."

Ailene said, "Boy, I can understand that. Anger and revenge, the old eye-for-an-eye attitude, is so destructive." Ailene seemed the most uncomfortable of all of us. She didn't believe she had been sexually abused and was struggling to accept what Sandra and I had told her. Still, she wanted to be active in her support of both Mom and her sisters. She shifted in her chair often, as her emotions must have been shifting.

"However," I added, "even given that goal, I can't jump directly to forgiveness when I don't even know all that has happened. That's what Jack really meant—in order to forgive, I have to be able to live through my pain and anger and work through the grief first." I looked at Mom; she avoided eye contact with me. It tore me. I loved her and I didn't want to bring her such anguish.

"Exactly," said Sandra slowly. I wasn't sure she had seen

or comprehended Mom's evasion. "I don't even know much of what's happened to me. So much of my childhood memory has been blocked. Every once in a while, I get little bits and pieces and even that makes me physically ill."

Tina had been sitting very still in her chair, turning her head only slightly to look at whoever was speaking. She must have sensed it was time for her to make a statement. She said, "I can't say anything happened to me, other than Dad was always yelling at me."

"I don't know. Jack thinks your lack of trust may be due to childhood sexual abuse," Sandra pointed out. I knew Sandra was worried about Tina. Jack had mentioned that Tina's reactions were very similar to JD's when questions of childhood were raised.

"Didn't you fly back to Chicago to check with our niece?" I asked Tina.

"What?" Mom responded in shock. She sat forward in her chair.

"Oh," Tina answered, "I, uh, did fly back to Chicago after the four of us sisters talked a while back. I remembered what Matt's wife had said about her oldest daughter several years ago and it worried me."

"What did she say?" Mom asked.

"She, uh, told me her fourteen-year-old daughter complained that Dad tried to fondle her breasts. I told her at the time she must have been mistaken. Whew! Dad wouldn't do anything like that. I said maybe he was just trying to give her a hug or something."

"Well, Matt's stepdaughter was always precocious," Mom said. "She always wore really tight clothes and lots of makeup."

"Mom!" I was shocked. "There is no way a precocious child of fourteen is inviting someone to mishandle them. That's like saying some women invite rape by wearing short skirts!"

"Anyway," Tina persisted, not wanting to get sidetracked into a social debate, "I went to speak to Luke's daughter about good and bad touching. I was always her favorite auntie and I thought she would tell me if Dad had tried anything with her. I didn't ask her specifically about anybody, only about the touching. She said nothing had happened and she promised she would tell me if it ever did."

Mom bit her lips and looked worried. Her voice revealed a forced calm as she asked quietly, "Did you tell Luke and his wife why you were there?"

"No, Ma," Tina answered. "I said I was passing through on business, which was sort of the truth. I did have to go down to Denver; I just took the long way, through Chicago."

Mom was visibly relieved. It worried me. Was she going to try to fly away from us back to her safe haven, among the family who did not confront or offend her?

Ailene said, "I don't think I was sexually abused. But I never felt like I was worth anything. I never had anything and no one ever showed me how to take care of myself. One very painful memory I have is from second grade. I couldn't find any socks to wear and you had to have socks at school. I remember all morning I tried to hide my feet so my teacher wouldn't see. We had to wear dresses so I couldn't cover my ankles with pants. I wrapped my legs around the legs of my chair. Try as I did to hide the fact I didn't have any socks, the teacher found out and said something to me in front of the whole class. I was so embarrassed."

Tears collected in Ailene's eyes, as she continued, "I never knew what to do with my nails or my hair. All through high school I wore my hair tied up in a bun. Once a boy at school even asked me why I always wore it that way. How could I tell him I didn't know what else to do?

"And clothes. I never had any clothes. I went all through high school wearing Mark's old T-shirts." With that, Ailene began to sob. I felt sorry for her. Mom had at least taught me to be a little more self-sufficient; in high school, I made many of my own clothes.

"We all had hand-me-downs," Sandra added. "I remember when Mom's friend Wendell bought me three new dresses at one time. I would have been overjoyed to have one new dress, but three? It was unheard of."

"It was Earl, the old guy next door, that bought me a lot of my clothes," said Tina, "although it really made Dad mad. He didn't like Earl giving me anything. Once Earl gave me a sack of plums and Dad took them back over and told Earl that he would provide his kids food."

Mom put her hand over her mouth and closed her eyes for a second, wincing with the pain of her now-grown children.

I felt we had sidetracked to a less painful subject, one that Mom could relate to. However, my emotions were back with the subject of child abuse, so I had a difficult time generating as much sympathy for the current discussion as I might have under different circumstances.

Then Mom looked around the table and said, "I know I didn't do well keeping you kids dressed. First, we didn't have any money, and then there wasn't enough to go around. I guess I greased the squeaky wheel first. Sandra and Tina were more vocal about their needs, so they got more. Jean and you, Ailene, never pressed me for much of anything, so you didn't get anything. I'm sorry I didn't handle things better.

"As far as doing your nails or hair," Mom continued, "remember, I grew up with parents who belonged to a church that didn't believe in makeup, or even colored clothes when I was a young girl. I couldn't teach you because no one ever taught me."

"It wasn't just the squeaky wheel, part of what happened was due to family dynamics," I said. I wanted to lead us back into the main topic somehow. "When I was little, Dad was running around and Mom was home and dependent, with new babies on the way every two and a half or three years."

"Yes," Mom agreed. She wet her lips, swallowed hard, and we could see she was preparing to disclose something painful. "When I was pregnant with Ailene, your father was seeing a beautiful, you might even say glamorous, woman. She was involved with the city government and instrumental in getting Eisenhower to tour our town before the election. Once she had a half-page picture in the local newspaper. I kept that paper. I lined the bottom of my lingerie drawer with it. Then every time I got out a pair of panties or nylons, I would see her. It reminded me what I was up against, who was my competition." She paused, looked off into the trees, and then said as if to defend herself for not leaving an unfaithful husband, "I knew your father could leave and have anyone he wanted. It wasn't that way with me. I had six, and then seven kids. I couldn't leave." She laid her hands open in her lap in a display of despair. We waited for her.

"I had the feeling that your father dropped me off at the hospital to deliver you, Ailene, and then ran off to see his girlfriend. I was usually closest to my new babies, but I felt rejected when you were born and had a hard time bonding. I got a job in the evening and your dad took care of you a lot more than he did any other of his babies. You had to grow up faster and with a lot less closeness than any of the other kids."

"Oh, I don't know about that," I said with irritation. "Remember, none of us had you exclusively except Matt, and not even him for long. I was born when he was barely a year and a half old." I didn't feel any less neglected than Ailene must have. I remembered my terrible loneliness that had driven me to the children's home to find anyone with a sympathetic ear.

"I know. I know. I've always had a lot of guilt about you

kids," Mom admitted. She shook her head, pinched up her eyebrows, and studied the labeling on her pop can as though it held some valuable advice.

Sandra said, "Yeah, but with Ailene, Mom had all but deserted. Then when Tina was born, she was really close to her new baby."

"That's true," Mom said. "When we moved to Chicago I was a lot more independent than ever before. I used to take Tina with me a lot and leave the rest of the kids with your father. Of course, Matt and Jean were married by then and Mark was away at school."

"Boy, do I remember that," I said. "Mark stayed with me two summers between his college years, because he couldn't stand to go back home. He didn't want to live with Dad again."

Good, I thought. Maybe now we will talk about abuse and Dad and why we were meeting here in the first place. I felt frustrated. I was beginning to be angry with Mom. She seemed so quickly to take the blame for neglect, lack of necessities, anything, as long as we avoided discussing Dad. However, I couldn't lead the discussion into the right direction. We continued discussing our collective unhappy childhood for several hours.

Finally I couldn't stand it. "Getting back to Dad, though," I said firmly, "I think one of the most upsetting things for me, is that once I started remembering some of his violent actions, Tina came back and said, 'Mom says you always exaggerate everything!' That still hurts. Even now, I can't believe you would say that about me. It's become a little less painful since my sisters started remembering things that happened to them."

Ailene said, "It took me a long while to recall how hurt and humiliated I was when Dad slapped me in front of Allen, and I was eighteen at the time. But, I guess, one of my most clear memories is when Dad kicked the cat."

"He was always kicking the animals," Mom said with disgust. Then to Sandra, she said, "Remember the day of Jean's wedding? Your father kicked your dog and the dog went howling up under your bed. I yelled at Fred and we all went running up to try to get the dog out from under it and ended up knocking down the whole bed. Everyone was screaming as we pulled the mattress and springs off the dog. I thought Fred had killed the animal, but the dog was okay."

"But, Mom, that's not what I'm talking about," Ailene insisted. "It's that Dad denied it *immediately*. Once he came stomping into the dining room where I was sitting, mad about something, and he kicked the cat. The cat hit the wall a couple feet up and went screeching around the corner out of the room. I was in shock and said to Dad, 'You kicked the cat.' He whipped around and yelled at me, '*I did not kick the cat!*' Well, I thought, it's time for me to leave now. I might be the next one who *doesn't* get kicked." Ailene cowered down in her chair. "As I was going, I was thinking, 'He did not kick the cat. The cat just jumped sideways onto his shoe, leapt up the wall a couple of feet to bash his head, slid down, and went yowling from the room. Nope. Nope. He did not kick the cat.' "

We all laughed and shook our heads. There was a long pause as though no one wanted to leave the humorous moment, even though it was so pathetic.

"I guess the thing for me was that Dad's violence was so unpredictable." I needed to continue; we were getting closer to the subject. "I remember once when I was about seven or eight. I came in from playing jump rope. When I got upstairs, Mark—who was what? uh, maybe four and a half?—grabbed the rope and we started fighting. Just then Dad came home and bounded up the stairs. He grabbed me and started whacking me for fighting with Mark. Then you, Mom, who had been sewing in your bedroom, called out, 'Jean had the rope first.' And Dad simply pushed me aside and started whacking Mark. I ran out of the house, first because I was hurt and scared, and second because I couldn't stand to see him beat Mark."

"That's just it!" Sandra's anger was rising quickly and she sat up abruptly. "The operative word here is *unpredictable*. Don't you see, Ma? It wasn't that violence occurred every day; maybe it did, maybe it didn't. The point is that we lived in fear of it every day of our lives. You can't grow up in that environment and feel secure."

"Especially," I added, drawing out the word, "when really terrible things were going on in the basement."

Mom tensed up. She was backpedaling mentally. I was anxious and hurt that she had so successfully avoided this all evening. I knew she was sorry I'd brought the subject of sexual abuse back up.

Mom voiced her concern that perhaps Dad had been molested by his own father when he was young. Jack had told her that it was possible—that most sexual abusers were themselves sexually abused. I wondered if she was looking more for an excuse than a cause for Dad's behavior.

"Your grandfather used to paw me whenever we went to visit. We'd arrive and he would meet us at the door. Grandpa would kiss me on the mouth and hug me and squeeze me, as though I had married him instead of your father. I told Fred to get his father in line and tell him to keep his hands off of me. I don't know if he ever said anything, but if he did, it didn't have any effect. After Matt was born, I thought maybe if I carried the baby in, he'd leave me alone. That was a mistake. The only difference was that I didn't have my hands free to defend myself. From then on, I made Fred carry the baby."

I thought about Grandpa. He had no patience with children and he kissed everyone on the mouth, but that didn't make him a sexual abuser. He'd always been okay to me. I wondered how my brothers felt about Grandpa.

"Well, girls," Mom asked finally, "what do you think I should do?"

"I think you should go home and do whatever you feel is right," I answered.

Everyone agreed. If she wanted to confront Dad with her knowledge, she should and could do it. If she didn't, that would be up to her.

"I'm definitely going to ask Fred whether or not his dad ever abused him, but I'll have to decide how I'll handle your situation when I get there. I'm not sure yet what I'm going to do. Maybe it will depend on what your father tells me about Grandpa."

After everyone else had left, Sandra made one last angry comment to me. "So she's going to decide how to handle *our situation*? She doesn't believe a damn thing we said. You know, she'll go back to Chicago and we'll never hear about this again unless you or I bring it up."

I cried all the way home. *Oh, Mom, why did we even do this? I think Sandra's right. You don't believe us. If you had never known anything about our sexual abuse, my sisters and I could have been supportive of each other, and we could still have a relationship with you.*

Now things would be worse than before, whether or not she ever confronted Dad. Would she hate and avoid me? Or would she come through with the love and support I so desperately needed?

The next morning Mom flew home and we all awaited her decision.

It was nearly two months after Mom flew home that I talked to her. She wouldn't telephone me and I was afraid to call her. Although I had maintained written correspondence with a number of people over the years, since I had been working with Jack, I had reduced my communication with my parents to monthly phone calls. Now there was silence.

Finally I could bear it no longer and risked getting my father on the telephone.

"Hello," Mom answered.

"Hi, Mom." I was relieved. "How's it going?"

"Jean, I'm glad you called." She sounded happy to hear from me, but there was a strained edge to her voice. "I've been meaning to call you, but with the trip and Mark's new shop . . . Did I tell you I've been working down at Mark's print shop? I've learned how to print multicolored pages and bind and drill holes, all sorts of useful tasks."

"Mom," I interrupted her, "I talked to Tina. She said you called and told her you had confronted Dad about all this. I need to know what he said."

"Oh," she said quietly, her disappointment audible. She paused. "I couldn't go home with him from the airport not knowing. As soon as we got in the car and headed away from O'Hare, I asked him if he had sexually molested any of his children. He was very sad to hear about it. He said he never did anything like that. I think he believes he was a good father to all you kids. I don't think his self-esteem could be any lower. He's very depressed about the whole thing."

Poor Dad.

Why did I feel so depressed? Didn't Jack say his answer would be no? He probably only remembers the good times he had with his kids. He can't possibly recall all the fear and violence that were part of our daily lives.

"What did you tell him?" I felt anxious.

"I basically told him everything you girls told me."

"You told him that I remembered being sexually abused?"

"Yes. I said the other girls didn't remember specifics, other than his anger. You know, he's very dejected about all of this. He really tried to be a good father. He was always a good provider. I also asked him about his father, and he said his father never touched him either."

Either? She had accepted his denial. I felt even more depressed. I also resented that her remark about the provider was undoubtedly aimed at my many difficult financial years with Hank.

"Yes, I know," I admitted sadly. "He did a lot of things with his kids and for his kids. I'm sorry he's depressed, but I have to deal with my healing right now."

"Aren't you and Don going to Florida soon?" She changed the subject abruptly. I let her.

"Yes, a week from next Friday. As a matter of fact, I'm going over our packing list now. We have to pull Jason out of school for two days, but I don't think it'll matter much for kindergarten."

We chatted for a while and said our good-byes without another mention of the abuse. That was that. She had decided to shove it all aside and feel sorry for Dad. It angered me that she had probably gone back to thinking how it was only in my mind, and maybe didn't happen at all. I doubted if she would ever call me again. The last thought saddened me. Maybe I'd lost both parents.

The year passed and the next summer came. During that time I continued to work with JD, both with Jack and with Don. I had called Mom at Christmas and again at Easter only to exchange holiday greetings. Other than that, there was no word from my mother.

In a way, it was better. If I dealt with my conflicting feelings about my parents, I would have had a harder time working with JD. This way, I could direct my emotional energy into my own healing. JD and I became closer. Each of us was more aware of the other even more of the time. Then we were together much more frequently. JD even helped me document some of the sexual abuse. I realized that she and I were becoming one, just as Jean/Jody had become, as I was able to draw upon her creative and artistic abilities.

Jack was convinced that the element still keeping JD and me apart was my refusal to deal with the anger toward my parents. I couldn't convince him otherwise. Somehow I felt that if I emotionally treated them as gone from my life forever, JD and I could resolve our differences.

Don came with me to several of Jack's sessions. At one Jack asked him, "How do you feel about all of this? You don't seem to be angry even with Jean's father."

"Personally," Don answered slowly and deliberately, "I'd like to greet him with a two-by-four. The man's a monster, but my number-one priority is to help Jean get better. I don't want to hurt her recovery."

"You don't think she should press charges?" Jack asked.

"Yes! Yes, I think she should. I'd like to see the man in jail. He needs to be. But again, Jean's sisters are in various stages of recovery and I wouldn't want to mess up their healing either with the trauma of going through a trial. However, I have a real concern that no one else gets hurt. I know Matt's stepdaughter said Jean's father had tried to fondle her. If I thought there was *any* chance that that man was abusing someone else, or even had the opportunity, I'd insist on charging him right now. I don't think that kind of person outgrows their sick behavior."

Jack nodded agreement.

Although Don had said similar things to me, I watched him closely as he spoke with Jack. I realized the depth of Don's anger and concern. I hadn't considered having my father arrested for what he had done to me and my sisters, but it was obvious that both of them had. The possibility of charges and a trial frightened me, but the possibility that the abuse continued with yet another young girl scared me more. I prayed that no one else was within my father's grasp. I prayed that I wouldn't be required to press charges.

In the summer, Mom and Dad flew out to visit again. I wouldn't have even known they were coming if Tina hadn't called a couple weeks before they arrived to let me know. I arranged a day off to take them to the waterfront. I needed to test my own mettle facing the man I had accused. But somehow I didn't expect it to be much of a challenge. I seriously doubted if either parent would bring up the subject. JD began to retreat as soon as she knew I would be seeing them again. It troubled me to lose the ground we'd worked so hard to gain.

I didn't see the folks the first week they were in Seattle, but early Sunday morning, Sandra telephoned.

"They're downstairs watching a movie with my son right now. I came up to my room so they wouldn't hear me. I just had to call you," Sandra exclaimed.

"What's the matter?" I asked.

"The folks and I were having breakfast and reading the newspaper. I came across an article about that eleven-year-old in Tacoma that was being sexually abused. You know what I'm talking about?"

"I think so. You mean the girl whose mother was offering her to men for sexual favors. I heard something about it on the radio." It made me sick to think about it, poor child.

"Well, you'll never guess what Dad said about it." She couldn't wait for me to ask what. She enunciated deliberately and with clear disgust, "He said, quote, 'If the girl enjoyed it, it wasn't abuse.' Unquote. Can you believe that?"

I caught a quick breath. It made sense. He believed children were physically and emotionally able to comprehend and enjoy sex. *Oh, God, why was he that way?*

"Jean?" Sandra was impatient for my reaction.

I drew in a full breath and began slowly. "It's consistent. You see that, don't you? I can't imagine why he would say it aloud." I sighed and shook my head. "But it's consistent. How else could he justify what he did?"

"I can't believe he would say it though." Sandra's shock was clear.

"Does Mom know you're calling me?" Suddenly I had a greater need to know Mom's reaction.

"No." Sandra sensed my need. "But when Dad said that, she set her coffee cup down and said 'Fred!'—like she was shocked too."

"That's all? And what did Dad say?"

"Nothing. He just shrugged his shoulders and sort of laughed. He ignored it and looked through the comics, but he believed it. I'm sure of that. But, Jean, I still can't believe he actually came out and said that about an eleven-year-old child—my son's age and our niece's age."

"But Sandra, it doesn't matter to him. The age doesn't mean anything. It could have been an eight-year-old or a three-year-old. He doesn't understand that children can't deal with sex. Don't you see? To him a child is just a little adult. Dad always expected the kids to think and act like adults. It didn't matter if it was handling a cup of milk in a high chair or any other activity, including sex. I'm so glad he said it where Mom could hear. Maybe now she'll understand what I was trying to tell her."

When I hung up the phone, I stared at it in total disgust. Hurt began to swell up in my head until tears squeezed out my eyes. I had been three when Dad played sex games in bed with me, and JD and I had been eight when he started sexual violence in the basement.

He didn't care then and he doesn't care now.

Later that Sunday evening, three of the four daughters met again with Mom. Dad stayed at Tina's house alone, filling out some of the hundreds of entries for sweepstakes that he spent his days entering since his retirement. Tina went out somewhere else for the evening. She wouldn't take part in the meeting, saying it was too emotionally draining for her. She said she supported her sisters in their recovery, but she knew it would be painful for Mom and she didn't want to deal with it again.

Sandra had written her feelings into a letter to Mom and had held on to it. She wasn't sure it was something she would ever have shown her. She said she hadn't edited it, but simply dumped out her feelings as they came. She called it her "mind dump," showing how angry she was that Mom had been so unsupportive of our pain. Sandra felt that Mom had basically ignored the situation and gone on living as though no confrontation had ever taken place.

I had wavered with my feelings over the past year. I had been angry, but most of the time I had tried to rationalize Mom's reactions. I couldn't help feeling that Mom was incapable of dealing with what had happened, just as she had been unable to control Dad's violence in the past.

Sandra gave a copy of her letter to each of her sisters to read. Should she show it to Mom?

I read Sandra's missive carefully. Much of what Sandra had written applied to me as well. Ailene would have to decide for herself. My vote was to let Mom read it. She should know how her silence had wounded us.

Ailene thought the letter was too punitive for her own needs, but agreed that Sandra should do whatever she thought best.

So as we gathered in Sandra's living room, Sandra gave Mom the letter. She went off by herself to read it.

Dear Ma,

Since talking to you on Thursday, I have been thinking a lot about what you said. I have a few thoughts to offer you and would like your reaction to same.

You sound like you are wallowing around trying to understand what really happened so many years ago, and unwilling to deny either your daughters or your husband their credibility. You are hurting your daughters through your apparent inability to believe them, and yet you can't bring yourself to accept the "truth" for what it is. You also cannot categorically deny your daughters' accusations, because you have never known them to lie to you, either. And why would they anyway? You are caught in trying to look at the details of the accusations and finding inconsistencies and illogical elements that give strength to your disbelief.

Everyone out here has much sympathy and love for you and your reactions to the terrible news. We were all hit as hard—No! harder!—with the same "news" when we first started to remember and believe! It is not fun! Nor will it go away with time and ignoring. Can you even try to imagine the horror, pain, and disbelief that first hit each of us as we had to admit that *our father* was a child molester—physical, verbal, and sexual abuser? Yes, dear mother, we *do* feel your pain and disbelief as you try to deal with the similar situation of having a husband accused of such a thing! And yes, there will be anger on all sides as we work through how this could ever have happened and what we need to do next. But remember also that we love you and hope you can bring yourself to deal with this and *help us*. Make up for some of the times you *couldn't* help us.

At this point in all your daughters' lives (I think I can speak for all of us on this) we are *not* after revenge or looking for your divorce or any major pain afflicted on Dad. We are looking for some understanding, sympathy, and help from *you* to help *us* understand what really happened and how we can grow together and be closer. How you mesh that with your relationship with Dad is not really my concern right now. I wish him no

ill. I wish him only to acknowledge his part if he can,
or at least *STAY OUT OF IT!* If he is able to confuse
you and keep you from accepting the truth, then
maybe you would be better to leave him. If you can
accept what happened and help us, while staying with
him, far be it from *me* to suggest otherwise. I am not
interested in telling you what to do with your life. I
understand loneliness and do not wish it on you or
anyone else. But please don't let him get in your way
of finally seeing reality and doing good by helping
your daughters!

Sandra

Mom came back in tears. "I don't know what I can do to
help you," she sobbed. "I haven't been ignoring you. I've
been very busy this year. You know I confronted your father.
There's little I can do about his memory of the past. I can't
fix what's happened."

We spent several hours talking again about the good and
bad times of our lives. Mom cried a lot, but we kept trying
to assure her that we did understand how hard her life had
been with Dad. Also, if she didn't know what was happening, she couldn't have done anything about it.

Although we tried to stem Mom's tide of tears, I could tell
Sandra was getting angrier as the evening passed. Sandra
had been closer to Mom as we were growing up, and she
wanted to feel her support now, but it was an impossible
dream. I wanted to hug Sandra and make up for the mother
that was not there for her any more than she had been for
me.

As I watched the increasing pain, I wanted to escape; I
wanted to be someone else. I began to feel somehow this
was my fault, but how could I have denied JD?

In a quiet moment during the evening, when Sandra had

left to make popcorn, and Ailene and Mom went to the bathrooms, I tried to draw out JD and get her feelings on this situation. JD was hard to find, but I learned why she didn't care. She was not angry at my mother. When she had been alone with Shadowman, she had cried out to God, the source of her strength and the only support she had ever known. Most injured children would have cried out for their mother.

There was no mother for JD.

I thought about having a mother. My mother had been close and loving for my first three years of life. Then she became Mark's mother for two and a half years, until she became Sandra's mother, and on down the line. She loved and doted upon her infants, but beyond those first few years she could make no emotional investment. Her children became supportive of her life instead of the other way around. She might give them time, making Halloween costumes or typing term papers into the night, but the emotional support was not there. JD was right—she had no mother—she had come into existence at eight, an orphaned child.

When everyone returned, I had withdrawn emotionally from the battle; no discussion or tears seemed to penetrate my detachment. I no longer wanted to convince anyone of anything.

However, when Mom and Ailene left for the night, I remained to talk with Sandra a bit longer. She was terribly angry. She felt Mom had derailed our discussion into "a poor-me session" again, in spite of her letter. Once again she had turned her children into her support system. Once again she had refused the emotional investment.

"You know what infuriates me most," Sandra said. "It's Mom's comment, 'I believe you believe these things happened to you.' It's an open denial. Mom can't say, 'I believe these things happened to you.' She doesn't."

NINETEEN

The following day, I vacationed from work to take Mom and Dad to Seattle. It was a wonderful, sunny day along the waterfront, both in the weather and in our dispositions. I spent the whole day with them. I wanted to see how I could cope with the man I accused—and how he would react to me. I didn't really expect a fight, but rather some signs of wrath that I had disclosed his past to his wife. But that man never showed up—the man who came was the nonentity of my early dealings. I retained my detached feelings for both of them and pretended that we were just good friends on the outing. It worked for all of us.

I noticed a few small changes in their behavior, however. As we walked along the docks and took our boat ride around Puget Sound, my mother made sure she was always positioned between my father and me. Dad limped terribly and carried a cane to help with each step. He pointed out sea gulls, a seal, a heron, boxcars being loaded onto a freighter, and other sights, but for the entire day, neither parent mentioned anything personal about me or my family.

The man who had terrorized my childhood, who had always displayed such seething anger, was gone. In his place was an elderly, white-haired gentleman, who never showed any signs of aggression, but thanked me cordially for the day on the way back.

As I left them, a sense of sadness crept over me. I wasn't sure where it was coming from. Was I disappointed that he hadn't confronted me and had it out right there with Mom present? Or was it that I saw such a drastic change in the man? It was almost as though some wild animal had been captured and totally subdued, now that he was getting old and partially disabled. Maybe now *I* frightened *him*.

Later that week, I agreed to take them to the airport to catch their flight home.

When I arrived at Tina's house to pick them up, Dad had his suitcase in hand and was standing in the doorway, ready to go. I gave him my van keys and walked down the hallway to the bedrooms.

"Mom?" I called from the hallway, "Are you about ready?"

"No." Her snuffled answer came from one spare bedroom closet.

I went into the room. It was furnished with a mattress and pillows on the floor and a chest of drawers. Mom's suitcase lay open in one corner and her dress bag lay across the pillows.

Mom was crawling about on her hands and knees, pulling shoes out of the closet and checking them.

"These are Tina's," she sobbed. "I can't find my black open-toed shoes."

"What's the matter, Mom?" I asked, but I knew.

She sat up on her knees and looked at me. Her face was aged from the stress of the past days and this morning's tears. For the first time she looked her nearly seventy years of age. I wanted to hug her but thought better of it. If I did, I might weaken and deny JD. I had to be firm.

"I don't think I can ever come back here," she cried. She swiped her nose with a wet tissue, balled it up and threw it into the corner of the room. She crawled over the mattress and pulled another tissue from the box. Her words tore at my heart. I loved her, but I had to get well.

I took a deep breath to calm myself.

"Look, Mom, nobody wants you to be miserable. Would you rather punish us again and stay away? We're your daughters and we love you. We have to deal with our own healing."

She sobbed harder. "I didn't come out here to be beat up. I have to go home and live with your dad. There's no place out here I can take him anymore."

"Mom, you know that isn't true. My house is the only place that's difficult. Don just doesn't want to be around Dad. You can understand that. Don's had to deal with me and what I've been going through. But you and Dad can stay here or with Sandra or with Ailene. And Don doesn't care if you come over to the house; he simply doesn't want Dad to stay there."

What does she want anyway—that Don should forget the whole thing? Poor, sweet Don, he'd had to put up with so much and he'd been so good with JD and me. So who could blame him for not wanting to deal with Dad ever again?

"But it's so awkward coming over to your house when Don gets up and leaves whenever we arrive," Mom continued in anguish. "And now everyone knows and we can't be comfortable anywhere."

"Mom, you've been coming out here for years. Do you think the guys just found out at the same time you did? Of course not. Each of our husbands has had to deal with each of us all along. Nothing's changed, except your perception."

"Really?" Mom looked surprised. Hadn't she thought of

it before? Had she somehow expected that each of us had kept our conflicts with our memories and our relationship with Dad secret from our husbands?

"Yes, Mom, for years."

She put her head in her hands and wept.

"Mom. Stop it. Look, I'm sorry if you felt as if we beat you up Sunday night. That wasn't our intent. We only wanted your help, not to make you feel so bad." I felt frustrated. Sympathy was not working. I had to get her off the subject. I heard Dad come back into the house, but I was sure he wouldn't bother us.

"You need to stop thinking about this whole trip as a terrible experience." I tried to refocus her attention. "Didn't we have fun Monday?"

I knew she had been crying for hours and I wanted her to avoid thinking about it. The whole time, I struggled with my own internal conflict and guilt. I knew I wasn't responsible for her pain, but I felt so bad seeing her cry. I tried not to think about how much I wanted to deny JD and say that I lied about everything, anything to get her to stop crying. I knew I couldn't do that and live with myself. I asked JD to help me distance those feelings. *Be strong*, she told me.

Mom looked up suddenly and squeezed a pained smile on her pinched face. She blew her nose with her tissue and shook her head slightly as if to shake off the terrible sadness.

"Yes," she replied, "Monday we had a wonderful time. Your dad and I so enjoyed the boat ride around the harbor, especially sighting a seal and a bald eagle. And the aquarium, too. You know how your dad loves those kinds of things."

She paused and looked down at the shoes. For an instant I thought she would cry again.

"What is it you're looking for, Mom?"

"My black shoes. Tina has a bunch of shoes in this closet, but I thought I had put them in here too."

I stepped back into the hallway and called, "Dad?"

"What?" he answered. "What is it?"

"Keep packing," I said to Mom. "I'll be right back."

I went down to the living room. Dad was reading the newspaper on the couch. As I came into the room, he tossed it aside.

"What can I do to help?"

"Have you seen Mom's black, open-toed shoes? Will you try to find them? It's a good thing I came over early. We would never make it to the airport on time."

"Well, I tried to get us ready," he answered defensively, "but you know your mother. There's no hurrying her."

He showed no anger about the possibility of being late. In past times I had seen his fury, but his words and movements were passive. I wondered if he would always act that way around me now. I'm sure he didn't believe what I told Mom to be true. I knew he denied his abusive actions immediately. I wondered what he thought of me now. I felt a sense of pity for him, but JD was angry. I tried to keep her as far away from me as I could until I could get Mom and Dad on their plane.

Dad got up and began looking under the dining room table and chairs for the shoes.

As I headed back to the bedroom I wondered why it was all going so slowly. Did Mom want to stay here? Maybe she was afraid to leave with this business so unfinished. Maybe she actually felt that her going back with him meant she was deciding she didn't believe us.

Mom was busy packing her dress bag with blouses. Her face was again clouded and she threw another tissue into the corner as I entered.

"Come on, Mom." I needed to hurry her. "What else do you need to pack?"

"I'm almost done," she sobbed softly, "but I need to clean up before we leave."

She stopped and pulled the covers down on the mattress, but I stopped her from stripping the bed. "No, Mom," I said, kneeling and taking the spread from her hand. "We just need to get your bags and get to the airport. Tina will clean up. I'll come over and help her if she needs help."

"Will you?" Mom looked up. "I hate to leave her a mess after she was so good to let us stay here."

"Yes, yes. Come on. Is there anything else that needs to go into this suitcase?"

"I only need to check the bathroom." She grabbed the tissue wads off the floor in the corner as she rose. There must have been a couple dozen.

"I found your shoes," Dad called as he came down the hall.

I zipped up the dress bag and handed it to him, saying, "Thanks. Now put this in the car. We'll get the suitcase and get out of here."

On the way to the airport, Mom sat in the back of the van and attempted to rescue her face. Dad sat in the seat next to me. He pretended not to notice Mom's pain or recovery.

"Well, it certainly has been a nice trip to Seattle," he said earnestly, looking out as we descended to the freeway.

The sun was breaking through heavy white clouds above us, and though the valley before us was scattered with industrial buildings, the hillside beyond was green and inviting. The rain of last evening was drying, as were my mother's tears. I hoped her disposition would change with this sunshine as well.

By the time we arrived at the airport, I feared they would not be able to make the plane if we went in to check the baggage.

"Grab a porter on the walkway and check the bags here," I instructed Dad as I pulled up to the curb.

I stole a glance over my shoulder at Mom. She was applying a last film of powder to her face. The years were falling away from her as the sad, pinched look faded.

I parked in the unload lane and hopped down from my van seat. As I hurried to open the back, Dad came over from the porter stand.

"Our flight is at one-thirty, not twelve-thirty. I told you to check the tickets," he said to Mom. There was a little exasperation in his tone, but he seemed to check it as he saw me look up.

"I'm sorry, Fred," Mom said. "But if we have time, maybe we can grab a bite before we go."

"I know a wonderful little place just across from the airport where we can get lunch," I said. "Go ahead and check your bags here and we'll run over there."

"Can we get over, have lunch, and get back here in a little more than an hour?" Dad asked me with disbelief.

"I don't know, but we can try. We'll ask the waitress when we go in. They deal with airport traffic all the time. Worse comes to worst, we'll run back here and you can grab a sandwich before the plane."

The restaurant lived up to its reputation of quick service. The waitress brought us soup and salad immediately and we would have plenty of time to get back.

I watched Mom and Dad as they ate their lunch, making small talk about how crowded the airport had been and what a nice little restaurant this was. Neither Mom nor Dad was making eye contact with me. I now felt totally detached, almost as though I wasn't sitting at the same table. I wondered what they were actually thinking. I could guess.

I thought about the sweater Mom had picked out for her birthday present from me as we wandered the piers at Elliot Bay on Monday.

"Oh, Dad, you were supposed to pick out a birthday present too. We never did shop for it."

"Jean," Dad said, looking me straight in the eye for the

first time this trip, "with all you've done for us, if you never get me anything else, you will have done too much."

Was he being sarcastic? It sounded as though he sincerely meant it. I had bought him some expensive clothes. He had even worn the suit I bought for him to church this past Sunday, and was disappointed that I hadn't gone and seen him in it.

I felt guilty. I was playing a charade. I was giving presents to my father, but he was no longer that man. I felt betrayed that this man was wearing my gifts to my father. My mind was churning. He really was the same man. I simply wanted to believe somewhere there was another person, someone who wouldn't hurt his own child and block it out, someone who loved me as a father should love. It was that figment of my mind—the daddy of the princess—to whom I bought and gave presents.

We finished our lunch and I rushed them back to the airport. I forced myself out to hug them on the sidewalk. Dad looked surprised as I gave him his hug. I wouldn't let him see how I felt. I looked at the white hair. I might never see the old man again.

"Now run," I told them. "You have less than twenty minutes and you need to get out to the south satellite."

I watched them go through the sliding doors into the building and I ran back to the van. As I got into my seat, they turned and descended from view on the escalator.

I started the van, but because traffic was heavy, I waited for my turn to pull away. I felt sad and alone. I had loved my mother and father, but where had they gone? I fought back tears. I didn't want my eyes clouded when I needed to see to drive.

We had sat in silence. I knew what happened to me; JD had shared so much. Mom knew what I'd told her. Dad knew what Mom told him. Yet here we had been, together in silence. I didn't have the strength to break it. Was I intimidated by him, or was I still trying, as Mom was trying, to preserve the family unity?

I shook off the despair and tried to concentrate on what I was doing. I needed to get to work. I pulled into the break in the traffic.

It had been nearly a year since I'd seen my folks. Sandra and I had met and talked. As her early memories were beginning to unfold, her anger toward both Mom and Dad was increasing. She and I could not seem to agree on an appropriate reaction to either of them. We decided that this was okay, given our different situations.

"Don't tell Mom to call me and fill in my childhood with all our good times," Sandra requested. "I don't want to remember the good times when I'm dealing with my pain. It confuses the issues. She doesn't want to accept what we've said. She won't acknowledge our suffering. If she talks about it at all, it's always in the context of her pain."

"I don't know what to think, Sandra. I feel so disconnected from them both right now. I have to deal with JD. I can't spend my energy worrying about Mom's reactions."

A few days later as Don and I had cuddled up for the night, JD took control to talk to Don.

He squeezed my hand in recognition. "Are you with Jean most of the time now?"

"Yeah, most the time."

"What do you think is keeping you two apart now? What do you need to do to integrate with Jean completely?"

"I don't know for sure." I tried to think what was the matter with Jean. "I guess she's afraid to be angry."

"Afraid to be angry?"

"I don't think she knows what to do."

"Let me talk to her, okay?" He leaned on one elbow and watched as I gave Jean control.

•   •   •

"Jean, did you hear what JD was saying?"

"Yes, but I'm not sure what she means. I know she's not upset about Mom—she doesn't care about that—she just can't understand why I'm not mad at Dad."

"So, why aren't you?"

"I don't know, Don. I can't seem to get in touch with my feelings right now." I was feeling too tired to get into a lengthy discussion. It was late and Don had to get up early in the morning. "Let's get some sleep. We'll talk about it tomorrow, okay?"

Then it filtered down into a dream for me. I was in Jack's office and I was extremely angry. Someone must have tied my hands to the arms of the chair. I was jumping around the office, hopping the chair on its legs, and screaming irrationally. I could feel Jack's presence but I didn't see him in the dream.

When I woke up, it was in the middle of the night. I got up and went down to the living room at the other end of the house, so as not to wake anyone else. I began to think about anger.

I remembered an incident from the years I had been with Hank. I had called Jack one night when I had "let go." It had been mostly out of frustration with the catch-22 situation I was in with Hank—nothing I did was ever enough. Hank was so effective at setting up no-win predicaments. I had thrown some dishes and pans in the kitchen and it had frightened the girls. I had even picked up Melissa's shoe and thrown it at her. It hit her and I was sorry because I hadn't meant to. Finally, in fear of what I might do, I ran out of the house and drove to a phone booth to call Jack. I was scared of what I might do. I was out of control. His advice had been to stay gone long enough to get over it and go back home.

The operative phrase here was *out of control*. That was the problem. Of course, I was detached. I couldn't be screaming, raging angry. I'd be out of control, *like Dad*! I'd be destructive. I'd hurt someone . . . maybe even me. And, as I was processing this thought, I realized why I couldn't be angry. It wasn't only my fear of being angry with my parents, but also and perhaps primarily that I was so angry with JD, with me.

For an instant I could see a vision of throwing myself through a picture window or out some twelfth-floor window like one of my friends' sister had done when she was angry. But why?

Because, in spite of all the healing books I'd been reading, and all the talking Jack and I had done, I had never forgiven myself. I was furious because I allowed myself to be small and helpless, because I allowed myself to be victimized and never told anyone, because I hadn't really killed him when I wanted to and had the chance, and finally, because it had taken me so damn long to be angry.

Perhaps God was there with me as I sat in the living room. I looked up through my tears to see a grocery bag standing on the floor in the corner, partially hidden by a small box. The only thing I could read on the bag were the words "You can survive . . ."

Yes, Lord, I thought. I had survived.

I walked across the living room and I picked up the bag. The rest of it read "a major earthquake." I sighed. My life had been shaken up for a lot of years.

I sat in the rocker and tried to decide what I could do. How could I change? I had always needed to be calm. Sometimes I had been the only calm person, the eye of the hurricane that had been my family—whether I had been living with my parents or with Hank.

But that was over. I lived with Don now. Not that he didn't get irritated with me or make me upset sometimes; he simply didn't become the screaming, raging animal that I was afraid of becoming if I got angry. I couldn't be out of control. So what could I do with all this pent-up anger?

I decided to write to Jack. I didn't want to lose these thoughts. I knew I hadn't reacted appropriately yet. I'd been upset at the things I'd learned, but I couldn't or wouldn't let go. Jack would understand. I was talking about my courage as Jody to scream at Dad or Hank, and my inability to scream at Dad now that I knew what he'd done. I wanted Jack to know that I had recognized the base of my problem. Maybe I could finally close the loop and accept that JD was me.

In the morning, I let Don read my letter to Jack.

"People can get very angry and still take rational actions. They do it all the time. What you and your siblings grew up with was unreasonable behavior. It's no wonder you think anger is so fearsome."

Later I phoned Sandra. She was feeling very depressed. I read my letter to her.

"Wow, you must have been mad—'I didn't kill him when I had the chance,' you said?"

I shuddered. "No, Sandra. I didn't mean that literally. I couldn't kill anybody. Somehow I just wanted the violence to stop. But do you get the point?"

"Sure. You know, Jean, I have the same problem. I don't know what to do with anger either. I have that same fear that somehow when I get mad I'll become irrational."

"You know where that 'chance to kill him' came from, though? I went to the opera with Mom and Dad. We had seats in the upper balcony and the folks were sitting directly in front of me. At the intermission, Mom went out and Dad stood up, turned around, and started to talk to me. JD was there with me and she had the strongest urge to push him over the seats backward. But she didn't. I could feel it in my arms as she drew back from the impulse. I'm not sure it would have killed him, but he would have been hurt."

"If you had, no court in the land would have convicted

you. I'd be in there telling them what he did to us," Sandra assured me.

"But I didn't have to. I see it as a real success. It's the first time I can remember where I recognized my anger and controlled it completely. It's a good sign that JD and I are getting a lot closer."

She sighed. "I'd still like to see you get angry."

"I do have a way of releasing some anger, though. When I was first married to Hank," I told her, "I used to go down to the Goodwill store and buy some old dishes. The house had a stone wall in the basement. When Hank made me so mad or frustrated I didn't know what to do, I'd go down and throw those dishes against the wall. I can't begin to tell you what a release that was. All that wonderful noise and all I had to do was sweep up the mess afterward. And here's for coming home late, then complaining 'cause your supper was cold. Smash. Crash. Rattle. Rattle. And here's for not taking me to the laundry and then complaining because I've washed diapers in the bathtub. Smash. Crash. Rattle. Rattle. And here's for—"

"I get the picture." Sandra laughed. "Sounds like a wonderful outlet."

"Well, you want to do that?"

"What do you mean?"

"How about this? I'll pick up some dishes at a second-hand store and we'll go out in the woods on your property and smash them."

"Yes! Yes! Let's do it. I feel better just thinking about it."

"Okay. I'll get some and see you Tuesday."

Together, somehow, we would all heal.

TWENTY

DON, JASON, AND I WERE OFF TO FLORIDA FOR NEARLY three weeks of fantastic vacation fun. I had packed us up on the last night to fly home in the morning and climbed into bed exhausted. Jason was already sound asleep.

As I drifted off to sleep, Don whispered, "You feel so good and Jason's asleep. Let's take advantage of the moment."

As Don caressed me awake, JD leapt from my presence. In that one short instance, I caught a passing emotion from JD. I knew it well—it had separated Jean and Jody for so long: guilt. Don's touch felt wonderful. Even JD had been enjoying it until her feelings of guilt began to surface. However, in this case there was no reason to feel guilty. I responded to Don, but I warned JD, *You and I are going to talk to Jack about this. This is too important.*

"JD, I can see you're very upset," Jack said. "Do you want to tell me about it?"

Slowly I shook my head no, but said softly, "I don't want to tell you, but Jean said she would tell you if I didn't."

He waited while I twisted the strap on Jean's purse tightly around my finger and gathered my courage. I pulled on the strap and it slid off my finger again.

"Don is mad at her, because I spend so much time playing games, I don't let her get her work done. She wanted to call you the first day we came home from Florida, because she said it was too important, but I wouldn't let her."

I sat on the edge of the couch. Every muscle was tense. I took a big breath before I started again, "I had a dream. It was while we were on vacation. In my dream, Don was mad at me. He took me into the yard and out into a garden. It wasn't like my house. There were lots of trees and bushes. Everything was dead and dark brown and black. Don was mad at me because I didn't take care of the garden and it had all died. All of a sudden, I was with Hank instead of Don. He told me that Don didn't love me anymore and that I would have to stay with him. He put a belt around my neck and pulled it through the buckle. If I didn't come with him, he could pull on the belt and it would choke me. He pulled me into bed next to him. Then I woke up and I was next to Don. I moved very close to him and hugged him."

I was getting very nervous. I didn't want to tell him what happened. I won't tell him. I'm going away.

"JD needs to talk with you," I said, as she forced me into control. I pushed the purse aside and sat back slightly. "What happened was too important. I know. I've been through the same feelings."

He ignored me and spoke directly to JD. "You have something more to tell me, JD. Won't you please come talk to me?"

Reluctantly I came back. I didn't want to tell him; I didn't want him to know I was bad. I grabbed the purse and clung to it, sliding forward to the edge of the couch.

"JD, I'm glad you came back. You know you can talk to me."

"I know," I said, but I fought with what to say. "I had to leave after I hugged Don. He started to touch me. I—"

I shuddered and stared at the rug.

"It reminded me . . ." I started to cry. "I'm not a bad person, not really."

Out of the corner of my eye, I saw Jack shake his head.

I thought of Shadowman again, touching me, saying, "Doesn't that feel good?" Even though I knew that what followed was horrible, for that one moment, it had felt good.

"I hate him! I hate him!" I cried, burying my head in my hands. "Some things he did made me feel good and then he told me how bad I was. He told me I was going to hell. I didn't want to be there. I didn't want him to touch me."

"JD, you feel bad because you liked some of the touching?"

I nodded.

"You didn't want to be touched?"

I shook my head and wiped my nose with my finger. He got up and handed me a box of tissues. I took one and then turned to stare at the rug.

"Do you think I'm bad?" I asked him. Oh, please don't think I'm bad, I begged him silently. If he thinks I'm bad, where will I go? I started to cry as he didn't answer immediately. I looked up at him. Jack was shaking his head, his mouth open to answer.

"No, JD, I don't think you're bad. When I see how bad you're hurting, I want to give you a hug. JD, people have feelings they can't control. If someone twists your wrist, I know that it hurts. If you poke a needle into your finger, I know the poke hurts. You can't help that from happening. Sometimes when someone touches parts of our bodies in certain ways, it feels good. You can't help that any more than if someone twists your arm behind your back and it hurts. It's the way bodies are. We can't control how they feel. It's not your fault."

I felt confused. Was this something I couldn't control? Was it really not my fault?

"Like breathing?" I asked.

"Yes, like breathing."

I took a deep breath and let it out slowly. I could control my breathing, but I couldn't stop it altogether. If I held my breath so long that I passed out, my body would breathe again without my thinking about it.

"I can't stop breathing unless I'm dead."

"That's right."

I tried to think. I was too excited. Maybe I wasn't bad. I couldn't help that some of it had felt good.

"I didn't want to be there," I said again. "I didn't want him to touch me."

"No, you didn't, did you?"

"No, he made me stay there. He did those things to me and told me how bad I was. He was bad. I hate him!" All at once I felt guilty. God doesn't want us to hate people. I started crying again. "No, that isn't right. I know it isn't, but I can't help it." I looked at the doctor and asked, "God doesn't think I'm bad because I hate Shadowman, does he?"

"No, I don't think God would blame you."

"I mean, I didn't do anything to him. I could have, but I didn't. He's a bad person and God will punish him sooner or later. I know God doesn't want me to hate him, but I can't help it."

"JD, God knows you're not a bad person. It's not like you had a choice. Could you say, 'Gee, Dad, I don't want to be here,' and then leave, or 'Gee, I have a choice, Dad, and no I don't want you to touch me?' "

I laughed, bit my lip, and shook my head.

"Well?"

"I'm not a bad person. He just made me feel like a bad person."

I stared at the doctor's footstool. It all made sense. I hadn't wanted Shadowman to touch me, but he did anyway. And he knew I couldn't help how I felt, but he still told me I was bad. *He* was the bad person. I had now figured it out. I laughed.

"It's like a game," I said, "and I just won. I won, because Shadowman thought he knew all the right things to do to make me feel bad, but I found out it was a trick."

Suddenly I felt sleepy. I hadn't slept well for lots of nights, ever since the nightmare.

"I'm so tired."

"I'll bet you are," Jack said. "I feel like celebrating and you probably want to sleep."

I nodded. "But I'm very excited too. I won two games. First I didn't hurt him when I could have, and now I figured out how he tricked me."

"JD, now can I give you a hug?"

I nodded, and he dropped down on his knees in front of me and hugged me as I sat on the couch. I hugged him back. He had helped me find Shadowman's trick.

When he sat back in his chair, I said, "Jean was right, wasn't she? It was important."

"Yeah," he said. "She's pretty smart. You two should work together more."

I smiled and then another thought made me frown again.

"I feel a little guilty about something else."

"Oh, what's that?"

I looked out the window and studied the bend of a dead branch on a tree on the hillside, wondering how I really felt.

"I guess I don't mean so guilty as I mean I feel sort of sad. When I was eleven, Jean got real sick and had to go to the hospital. When we came back, he didn't do anything more to us. He took Sandra."

Jack shook his head. "You feel guilty about that—that you couldn't protect her?"

"No, I couldn't protect her any more than I could protect me. I feel guilty because I was glad it wasn't me . . . but I didn't want it to be anyone else either."

"No, you didn't. You haven't done anything to feel guilty. It's time to go. Can I talk to Jean for a minute?"

I let Jean have control again.

"Same time, next week?"

"Sure. I told you this was important. I had felt so guilty about my playtime with Daddy when I was only three years old, it had forced Jody to become real. When I caught JD's emotion, just in that one split second, I recognized it. I think this might even help our relationship with Don. Do you think so?"

"Maybe," he said, giving me a good-bye hug as I left.

In the following months, both Sandra's and my healing processes changed drastically.

Sandra was seeing her therapist on a regular basis and dealing with the frightening childhood memories that were starting to surface for her.

It was nearly suppertime one day when the phone rang. Don was working in the room when I answered, "Hello?"

"Hi, are you busy?" There was something urgent in Sandra's voice. "I need to talk to you, but . . . but . . . it would be better if I could meet you somewhere."

"Well, I was about to start supper, but I guess I could run out if you need me."

Don frowned questioningly and I shrugged my shoulders and gave him my I-don't-know-what-the-matter-is look.

"This is ridiculous. I'm in one of my panic moods. I needed to tell you that I remembered some of the same stuff that happened to you. When I saw my therapist today, I told him about remembering Dad threatening to kill me if I told. I can't remember all the details like how old I was, but I was young enough for him to easily pick me up and threaten to throw me over the edge of something—I think it was into some water. Jean, was there a water treatment plant down by the river close to our old house on Webster, one with a high tower or tank?"

"Not that I know of. Maybe what you remember happened after you guys moved to Illinois. Seems like there was one along the river near that house, but I don't know for sure. Maybe you should ask Mark."

Don whispered, "What's up?"

I lowered the phone and whispered back, "She remembers."

Don replied with a solemn, "Now there are two."

"Was that Don?" Sandra asked.

"Yes." There was a long silence from Sandra. Finally I asked, "You okay?"

"Yeah, I think so. It hit me funny, I mean, scary."

"Why? You know I share everything with Don."

"No, I don't mean Don's knowing—it's anyone's knowing. When Don said, 'Now there are two,' it means that Dad can't hide behind his old excuse that it's all your craziness. It means he has to deal with both of us. Suddenly I don't feel safe anymore."

"Dad's not going to do anything. He wouldn't make a move if we all came out saying this is what he did to us. He's not going to do anything that would jeopardize his relationship with Mom. He'll continue to say he didn't do anything to us and leave the sorting game to Mom. Since she can't handle it, nothing will come of it."

"I know. I know. Still, it's like I've *told*. Now part of me fears he'll come kill me."

"I'm sorry, Sandra. I know what you mean. I went through some of the same fear for a long time. I didn't see anyone in the family, hardly talked to anyone for a couple of years. I couldn't have coped with the denial and the lines drawn if the truth was told. I didn't even go to the hospital to see Ailene's baby when she was born, because I was in such deep fear and stress. Of course it was a little easier for me than for you. Everyone else was living a couple thousand miles away then."

Later I called my brother Mark. He knew I had been writing, and during the conversation he asked me about the book.

"You know what this book is about?" I asked him.

"Well, actually I do. I talked to Sandra and she said you were writing about our abusive childhood."

"It's a little more than that." I carefully explained, starting out with my healing and slowly backing into the sexual abuse. Mark and I had been close. He had lived with me between his college years to avoid Dad, so it wasn't too difficult for him to comprehend how much worse it had been for his sisters.

"Does everyone out there know about this?" Mark asked.

"Yes, the four of us sisters are supporting each other, but Mom and Dad know too."

"Really? They never said anything about it."

"But, Mark, what would they say? I'm sure Mom will throw a fit when she finds out that I've told you. She'd like to keep our little secrets out here in the Northwest. She doesn't want anything to disrupt her safety zone there."

"Well, I sure won't tell her I know anything. Does Matthew know? or Luke?"

"No, I'm going to call Matthew, but I don't think I'll have any problem with his believing me. You know that Dad tried to fondle Matthew's stepdaughter?"

"Yeah, I remember Matthew mentioned that years ago. Jean, I believe you. I put up with a lot of crap from that guy too. I remember getting pounded on and the milk-bottle-over-the-head bit. You didn't think I'd doubt you?"

"No, I didn't mean to imply that. I've had such a struggle with Mom. I understand where she's coming from—she has to live with him, but she has all but ignored me since she was out here. If she didn't call to thank me for her birthday and Mother's Day presents, I wouldn't have heard from her this year."

"Don't you call her?"

"Once in a while. It's so hard, though. She sounds pained to hear me. I don't know what I'm going to do. I love her, but I have to work through this, and Sandra has to too. The whole subject of abuse is like an elephant in our midst."

"What are you guys going to do when the folks move out to the Northwest? They're talking about retiring out there. How are you going to handle things when they're living so close?"

"Honestly, Mark, I don't think I'll have a problem. I think Mom and Dad might have a problem with being around me, but not because I'll be causing it. This isn't my fault and I'm not going to be blamed for their discomfort. I simply won't bring it up and we can pretend there isn't an elephant walking around the house when they're out here. If Mom wants to discuss it, fine, we'll discuss it; if not, then the subject won't be discussed. If the elephant steps on their toes, it'll be their own fault for bringing it up."

In the next few months, Mom and Dad came out to visit and put a down payment on a residence in a large Northwest retirement community. Sandra took a trip while they were here; she couldn't deal with either of them. Mom and Dad had been encouraged by all their children over the years to sell their home and move into a living situation where they would have a closer community of friends and medical support if they needed it. However, now the folks would be here, close by, for the rest of their lives. How would that affect us?

After the folks flew home, Sandra called me. "I was surprised when Mom said they were going home to sell their house and move out here. I thought Dad wanted to retire to Florida."

"Can you blame him? With all that's been going on with us, I can't imagine that he wants to move out and be our neighbor."

I could hear Sandra's shudder in her breath. Then she laughed. "Mom must have made him come here. Hey, maybe we could get Mom to come out here and Dad to retire to Florida anyway."

"I doubt that."

We joked about it, but as the months passed and the house sold, Sandra became more and more unable to cope. She gave away her business leads, stopped functioning on her job. She withdrew to her home office to play computer games or ran off to her best friend's house on the Kitsap Peninsula to work jigsaw puzzles. And in fear, she began to scheme how to move away.

One day, Sandra called me. "Hi. It's me, but I'm off to Alaska."

"What?" There was something wrong in the breezy attitude she conveyed.

"Yeah. Ben and I found a little fishing lodge up there and we're gonna go check it out."

"To buy?"

"Yes, to buy. It's what Ben's always wanted to do. He's excited about it."

"Wait a minute, Sandra. You just built your dream house looking right over at Mount Rainier, and now you're going to run off to Alaska?"

"It won't be all the time, only during the summer."

"So you're going to keep your house?"

"No, we won't be able to afford it. We'll have to sell it to buy the lodge, then rent some place for the fall and winter, but hey, we haven't even seen it yet."

"Sandra, tell me what's going on with you."

There was a silence as though she had stepped back from me, as if I had shaken her momentarily. When she spoke, a sense of solemn dread wound through my phone cord.

"Jean, I have to get away from here. I can't even feel safe in this house. Last night I had the worst dream. In it, I was home by myself and Dad came to visit me. When I answered the door, I said I was just preparing to leave, so I couldn't invite him in. Then I shut the door and he walked away around the corner of the garage. I started to go back to the office when I saw him from the kitchen window. He was walking slowly back to my door carrying a gun. I woke up and hugged Ben. I was so frightened."

"Sandra, you know that's a dream."

"Of course, but it's not only that. Even if I try to tell myself it's illogical, I'm scared. My mind keeps playing the same recording of Dad, 'You tell anyone and you're dead.' His threats were so effective! I don't want to be here alone anymore. I want to get away from here, as far away as I can. I can't function. I can't think.'"

"I know. I know."

"This is something Ben's wanted to do for years. He was surprised that I was so willing to look into going back to Alaska, but I was very happy when we lived there before. Somehow I feel if I can put enough distance between me and Dad, I'll be okay. When I rent a house here, I don't want you or anyone else to tell Mom where I'm living."

"You know I wouldn't."

"Yes, but I'm getting so paranoid. I know whatever I say to Mom goes directly to Dad."

Shortly before the folks moved out into the retirement community, Sandra and Ben bought the lodge in Alaska and moved into a rental house. Within another month, they were on their way to Anchorage and points beyond. I felt an overwhelming sense of loss. It was not only that I had lost contact with my sister, but my partner in healing—we needed each other.

One day Mom called me. She was upset that Sandra had avoided her and now moved away without so much as a good-bye.

"Mom, Sandra has to deal with her healing in her own way."

"I simply don't understand it. I can believe something happened to you, but I won't believe Sandra was sexually abused. I don't believe it. I can't believe it."

I was too shocked to answer. I knew Sandra hadn't told her anything specific, but why wouldn't she believe if one of us was abused that others were? Because she still couldn't believe *anything* had happened to me. My defenses rose with the hair on the back of my neck. I bit my tongue. Mom was busy trying to pack. I didn't want to argue with her and add to the stress.

Suddenly she said to my father, who obviously was in the same room, "Fred, what are you doing? With all the stuff that needs to be sorted out, you're soaking stamps off envelopes?"

I couldn't hear his answer, but Mom nearly screamed at him, "What stuff? Try the hundred or so boxes you have lined up the hallway wall. That's all your stuff—sort it or throw it out."

Then she was back to me. "I don't know how we're going to get out of here, Jean. I can't get that man to help at all. What can he be thinking? Are we going to have less to move because he's soaked his stamp collection off their envelopes?"

"If I was there, Mom, I'd dump the whole mess, water

and all, into a box, tape it up, and ship it out, so he wouldn't have it to waste time with."

"He'd find something else to fiddle with. I should box him up and send him out there."

I shook my head.

"Anyway, I talked to Mark the other day. He still doesn't think we should move out there with you girls accusing your father. You know, he said he didn't remember your dad being violent. He said that milk bottle thing was an isolated incident."

I sucked in my breath and clenched my teeth. I'm not going to fight with her. Why is she saying this nonsense to me? Mark would have never said such a thing. Maybe she wanted to *believe* he had said it, but I knew he hadn't. I excused myself and got off the phone.

Later I dumped on Don. "An isolated incident? She thinks that's an isolated incident? And she can't believe anything happened to Sandra? How dare she say those things to me?"

"Calm down. Don't yell at me. Did you yell at her?"

"No, I didn't. I didn't know what to do. Tina said Mom has such high blood pressure, she was taking tranquilizers so she can get moved. I didn't want to make it worse. She thinks the milk bottle was the isolated incident? What does she call the rest? Dad's pounding Luke when he broke Dad's precious HO–gauge train station? Or his knocking Mark over backward for mouthing back at him? Or slapping Sandra into the wall because he didn't like her answer and she tried to run away from him? Or— Which is the isolated incident?"

"Nevertheless, she's the one who's pulling the crap. You ought to tell her."

I sighed and dropped my head into my hands. "I'll write her a letter."

I did write the letter, but I couldn't send it. Instead, I took it to Jack, who nodded slightly as he read it.

•   •   •

Dear Mom,

Our conversation the other night made me so angry,
I couldn't comment to you at all. I cannot believe you
would say the things you have said to me and about
me. You are so insensitive to all of this that you are
making the whole process worse. As a result, I have
decided that I will no longer share any of our experiences or remembrances, nor will I discuss any of our
previous discussions with you or with Dad. You
choose to attempt to draw lines and say you cannot believe we were sexually abused and we are hurt and angered by your attitude. If I am going to maintain any
sort of relationship with you, I simply have to stop discussing any of this with you. That way we can maintain a civil, although not open or honest, relationship.
It will be sort of like the one I maintain with Dad—he
knows I know but he won't acknowledge it either, so
I just ignore the whole subject with him. So that's how
it will be with you from now on.

As for Sandra, she is where I was almost thirteen
years ago. At that time, I couldn't share any of my hurt
and bewilderment as memories began to unravel for
me. I was fortunate. I successfully avoided poor Ailene enough to not tell her anything, and everyone else
was far enough away that no one knew I was struggling with the horrible realities of my abusive memories. Whether or not Sandra was sexually abused is
certainly not for you to decide, but will come from her
own memory and may never be shared with you.
However, at this point in her healing process, as it was
with mine, she needs the distance/hibernation/isola-
tion/*safety*—whatever, to allow herself to remember

and to deal with what she does remember. She has not shared much with me, and I will not press her for fear of doing more damage to her poor soul, drowning as it were in her own fear and pain.

Let me present you with another case. Whether you EVER accept that I was abused, whether or not Sandra was abused or you EVER accept that she was, you had better stop forcing the issue with ALL your daughters. The more you press, the more damage you do. It may not have occurred to you in your deep state of denial that Sandra and I may not be the only ones. However, let me assure you that if you press Tina into denial, you may drive many more years into her healing process as well. *So don't do that!*

Give us all a break and when you come out here: let it lie where it is for all of us. When we included you in the group of the four of us, we had hoped for your understanding, acceptance, and support. It has become increasingly obvious that you are incapable of that, so step back and let us heal on our own.

Jean

"I don't think I've ever heard you so angry."

"See, Jack, I was angry with my mother. You keep thinking that my inability to resolve my differences with JD is because I haven't been angry with her. I don't think that's the problem. I recognized Mom was incapable of dealing with this long ago. If Sandra hadn't told her, I would have never shared anything with her."

"Are you going to send this to her?"

"I don't know. Not yet, in any case. She has to finish getting moved first. I don't know if I'll ever show her that. It's pretty caustic. I *will* tell her the points I tried to make in it, though."

"What does JD think about all of this?"

"JD doesn't accept my mom as her mom. She says she didn't have a mom or a dad; she only had God."

"Don't you think she should be angry about not having parents?"

"Jack, I've been angry about the neglect and abuse. Right now I'm trying to find out what separates JD from me and resolve that and I don't think the anger is what is keeping us apart. JD believes that God wants her to forgive Dad for what he did to her. I don't think I could ever do that."

"There are certainly things that are beyond us. I don't think you need to forgive him to recover, but . . ."

In the next couple weeks, I arranged a meeting with my pastor. I explained how JD and I were together so much of the time, but the final integration that had occurred with Jean and Jody hadn't happened for JD and me. I wanted him to understand what I felt were our differences. JD's special relationship with God meant everything to her. She was trying to find a way to forgive Dad for what he had done, but felt there was so much to forgive that she couldn't. I didn't think I could either and furthermore, I didn't feel the need. Yet, I felt guilty over my unwillingness.

"What do you want to happen, Jean?" the pastor asked me.

"I'd like to be at peace. I don't think there are any more conflicts to discover or deal with. JD has shared everything with me and I have come to grips with it. The situation with my mother will never change. My father will continue to deny any wrongdoing. Don thinks Dad will have to be repentant if my relationship to my father is going to change, but neither Don nor I foresee that ever happening. What I really want is to feel at peace with God, but if that means forgiving my father, I don't think I can succeed. I wish I knew how I could change." I fought back tears of guilt. There wasn't a way to resolve this last conflict.

"Jean, you're always going to be human. No one would blame you for not forgiving someone who was so abusive to you. You need to let God take care of it. It's sufficient that you want to forgive him, that you're willing to try, even if you're not able to do it. God will handle it."

On the way home, I thought over what had been said.

"It makes sense, doesn't it?" I asked JD. "We're not perfect. We both love God; we both want to do the right thing. The pastor and Jack both said there were some things that were beyond us. God will take care of those things."

A new sense of joy filled me. I didn't have to try any longer. It was sufficient that I was willing. I let go of my guilt.

My senses soaked in the sunshine on the rolling urban hills and fragrant sweet peas in disheveled jumbles along the roadside. Life seemed somehow fuller, freer, more worth living than it ever had before. I seemed to be newly aware of everything beautiful around me.

Suddenly I thought, *I'm* driving.

Of course, I'm driving.

I shivered with excitement.

It was JD! We were together at last . . . as one.

EPILOGUE

I'VE BEEN ON THIS JOURNEY ALL MY LIFE. FOR THE PAST FIFteen years I've been working with Jack and it's become a trip toward mental health instead of insanity. Jean, Jody, and JD have come together. I have finished silencing the voices in my head. No more screams, no more hidden pictures, no more missing time, and no more strange relationships haunt my life.

My father and I have not spoken of the abuse directly. He and I face each other without acknowledging any change in our relationship. I deal with him as a nonperson, someone with whom I have no past. Still, there is a small shift in his attitude. He brings and sends me anything he can find from my childhood—poems I wrote, drawings I made, papers I did for school. What can he be thinking? He never acted in anger toward me nor anyone else about my accusations through Mom. Is it because he does recall something? Is it because he wonders if he did these things, but somehow cannot remember? Or is it because, whether or not he recalls it, he is simply trying to preserve his marriage and keep his family intact?

In the more than three years since the initial confrontation with my mother, she has not accepted my suffering. At first she avoided me and the pain I must have brought her. After she moved nearby, we've enjoyed each other's company whenever we could be together, but anytime we've spoken about abuse, she has turned the sorrow toward herself or openly denied the reality of the problem she and I have with our relationship. Since I confronted her with her own statements and the anger it generated in me, we have not communicated on the subject again. Somehow she seems to think if she ignores the issues, they will all go away and her family status will not be affected.

My sisters have each changed through our experience together. While we are closer in many ways, the confrontation that so wounded our mother has caused us to avoid the subject when the four of us meet together.

Sandra is still fighting to regain more of her memories of childhood, as frightening as they may be. She seems more angry at our mother's attitude than the memories of abuse, but it will take some time for her to overcome her fears. She gets better all the time. Her "abused child" has been described as an elective mute, who communicates with Sandra more by way of physical symptoms than verbalized thoughts. Sandra says she envies the relationship I had with JD, but wouldn't care to exchange. She characterizes her life as living with a frightened child, always holding her hand and going everywhere with her, limiting her ability to interact in family situations or even with strangers. Still, recognizing and dealing with this child is making Sandra healthier and happier as she gets stronger and assures the child that she is safe.

Ailene has grown so much in her self-esteem and confidence. Once she realized that she had been programmed to feel useless and insignificant, she could rise above it and begin to reprogram to believe in her own self-worth. She believes that somehow she escaped the sexual abuse, but still has to deal with the long-lasting effects of fear and emotional abuse.

Tina has retreated from examining her childhood. She told me that she believed in and was supportive of everything that I had said and that Sandra was finding, but she was not yet ready to deal with her own problems.

Mark and Luke and their families in the Chicago area seem to ignore the drama and trauma that has and is taking place here in the Northwest. Distance is a great disadvantage. At a time when my sisters and I would welcome their support, we understand the difficulties of communication when we are so far apart.

However, Matthew is very sympathetic. Sandra and I met with him for an afternoon when he came to Seattle. Sandra told him that Mom had called our abuse "isolated incidents of violence."

"Bullshit! Isolated incidents?" Matthew said. "If they were isolated, it's because she isolated herself from them. Why, I was thirty years old before I stopped flinching when Dad came near." Although Matt's stepdaughter had accused our father, Matthew had not contemplated that Dad had sexually abused his own sisters while we were young. Matt said he was not surprised, however, and he accepted our memories unquestioningly.

If there's one lesson I've learned, it's that I've gained incredible strength in healing, in becoming a whole person. I've realized that to get here took great faith—faith in God, faith in myself, and faith in other people to support me.

The healing is not over, but I'm happy. For this period in my life, however stressful, has become increasingly better. I have it all, more blessings from God than I could ever imagine. Now I have a husband who loves and respects me. I have three grown daughters—who, although they are struggling with their own problems, generated from such difficult childhood parenting, are developing into intelligent, caring individuals—and a wonderful, healthy young son. I'm blessed also with friends and extended family, a nice home, a good job, physical health, and the vigor that comes from being whole.

This morning I offered my prayer: "Thank You, Lord, for Your healing power and the support of my family, my friends, and my doctor. Thank You for my life and all Your blessings. Be with all those who suffer and bring to them the strength that You have provided to me throughout my life. Amen."

AFTERWORD

J EAN AND I HAVE DIFFERENT PERSPECTIVES OF SOME OF THE things that occurred in therapy. This should not be at all surprising, even if Jean was not multiple. We all live according to our own perceptions and everyone sees things slightly differently. To my eyes, initially Jean seemed to present as a fairly straightforward case of depressive disorder. She had a fairly extensive psychiatric history, including hospitalizations. In the first year as therapy progressed, things just weren't falling into place. In fact, the more I knew Jean, the less things made sense. Her dreams were so disjointed that very little fit with the history she presented. Yet it was obvious that she was being sincere and working hard to try to help herself. At some point, Jean and I both became frustrated with the lack of progress. There was a nine-to-twelve–month hiatus in the therapy before we resumed. When Jean returned to my office, for reasons still inexplicable to me, she introduced herself as Jody. The confusion ended in a flash. The dreams were the productions of more than one part: The stories told were those of memories of more than one part. Then began the long and arduous task of meeting and working with whomever was present at a given session.

There have also been humorous aspects in working with Jean and her family. After I spent most of one session with Jody, I forgot that Jean had to make a presentation at work shortly after our appointment. Jody's personality alone successfully carried her through the meeting, since she knew nothing about computers, whereas Jean is an expert in the field. At our next session, I was requested not to make that mistake again, and that I have Jean leave the office at the end of the session if she has to return to work.

Jean's present husband has been as supportive a person in the healing process as could be hoped for. Involving family members is fraught with difficulties. There is some controversy about a spouse dealing with individual alters by name rather than dealing with all as a single-entity name, Jean in this case. However, Jean involved her husband and he ran with the ball, facilitating her healing with almost no feedback from me. After being raised in a terribly abusive household, Jean's first—and second, since she remarried him—husband was also abusive. Her current and last husband, Don, has totally removed her from the abuse cycle.

Working with Jean's youngest daughter, Melissa, allowed me to "see" Jean's behavior as a mother. At times she was the fun-loving mother, at other times a morose, rejecting mother. At yet other times, her daughters couldn't understand why their mother was huddled in the clothes closet in the fetal position. Learning about their mother's problems when they were teenagers and young adults did help the children understand their mother and their own childhood better. When they understood that their mother was a multiple, they retrospectively recalled the closet incident and other such scenes as humorous, because their confusion was now resolved.

JACK M. REITER, M.D., P.S.

QUESTIONS FOR DON CLINE, HUSBAND OF MPD PATIENT

As the husband of an MPD patient, I've often been asked these five questions. I hope answering these questions adds insight for you about *Silencing the Voices*.

Was I nervous about marrying a multiple?

Yes, I was nervous about marrying her. I loved Jean. I saw her not as a crazy person, but as a very stable, sane woman who had been traumatized. I knew both Jean (the merged Jean and Jody) and JD, and felt I could deal with them. My biggest concern was that there might be another personality that had not yet presented herself. I didn't want to find myself married to a stranger, or worse yet, married to only part of a person. I carried this concern for about two years.

I've become convinced that Jean split into only as many personalities as necessary to handle the horror that was dealt to her as a child, and that this was a sign of the stability and sanity that I've seen in her all along.

What was it like being married to a multiple?

When Jean and JD were still split, it was like being married to two people at the same time. Many times Jean was mad at me when JD wasn't and one time JD was mad when Jean wasn't. Sometimes they shared memories and sometimes they didn't.

How hard was it to tell the personalities apart?

It was surprisingly easy. The combined Jean/Jody had many of the outgoing mannerisms of Jody. JD was very reserved. So, to me, it was a difference in the mannerisms.

JD tried many times to fool me, pretending to be Jean. She said that she never succeeded. I don't mean that I always knew instantly. But I usually figured it out in a few seconds. The only time that I know that I have been fooled was a time that Jean became very concerned and withdrawn about something she was thinking about. She looked like JD trying to act like Jean. I realized my mistake as soon as Jean spoke.

What was the most unsettling thing that happened?

I did have a very unsettling incident. I got to know the merged Jean/Jody as Jean. I worked very hard to bring out the injured child, JD, and got to know her. So, to me, Jean was a person with two personalities.

At one point, the Jean I knew split back into the two personalities of Jean and Jody. The traits I knew as Jean's were separated, some carried by Jean and some by Jody. This was more unsettling to me than dealing with my abusive father-in-law.

What was the hardest thing you've been through?

To explain this, I want you to use your imagination. Apparently, the way to healing for a person with MPD is for each personality to accept the existence and memories of the other personalities. However, when a person has abusive memories that are, in effect, repressed in another personality, those memories stay clear and vivid—so vivid that you see what you saw then, smell what you smelled then, and feel the pain and emotion you felt then. In effect, you experience the experience again.

Now, imagine that you are a woman with MPD and you want to get better. So, what you have to look forward to tonight is becoming an eight-year-old child again, and being raped and tortured. Now imagine you are the spouse of the person. You can't take away any of the pain. All you can do is hold her. It's an incredibly helpless feeling.

JD's Song

I was alone and I lost my way,
And I didn't know who I should be,
And it wasn't clear when I looked in the mirror
That I knew, even now, who I am.

I was alone and I prayed to God,
And He came just to hold my hand,
And the only place that I saw in His face
Was the lost, lost child had come home.